BERTRAM MILLS CIRCUS: ITS STORY

Bertram Mills Circus: its story
by Cyril Bertram Mills

 Hutchinson of London

Hutchinson & Co (Publishers) Ltd
178–202 Great Portland Street, London W1

London Melbourne Sydney
Auckland Bombay Toronto
Johannesburg New York

First published 1967
© *Cyril B. Mills 1967*

*This book has been set in Baskerville, printed in Great Britain
on Antique Wove paper by Anchor Press, and
bound by Wm. Brendon, both of Tiptree, Essex*

*To all those dedicated people who made
Bertram Mills Circus possible, and to
Mimi, whose help has contributed so much
to this book*

Contents

Illustrations

Foreword

To follow the story of Bertram Mills and the circus which bore his name, it may be helpful to know a little of the man who started it, for so much of its growth and prosperity was based on the foundations which he laid, and these in turn were, in many ways, reflections of his personality.

At the age of forty-five he plunged into show business, of which he knew nothing, and the branch which he chose was nearly dead. His name was entirely unknown, yet within a decade it became almost a household word, for what he had started had, in the words of many people, become a British institution. Some said London would never be the same when there was no circus at Olympia and that time has now been reached.

He was a man of dynamic energy and great will-power, with an almost uncanny instinct of what was the right thing to do in any given set of circumstances. Board meetings and conferences had little attraction for him, as he knew what he wanted and usually how to get it done, but if he had a problem he consulted those who knew the subject and then took a decision quickly. If there were two ways of reaching an objective and little to choose between them it was reasonably certain that his way would prove right, if only because of the faith and determination with which he pursued it.

He was never prepared to accept second best or to side-step a difficulty and he did not like to be told something was impossible; the difference between that which was and was not possible was that the latter would require more perseverance and take longer. He gave us confidence in ourselves and overlooked our mistakes, assuming that they had taught us something and that we should not make the same ones again.

He had three loves—his family, his home and horses—and there was nothing he would not do for any of these; although his business and other activities involved long working hours he spent all his free time at home or somewhere among horses.

If he resented anything it was the wholesale and indiscriminate attacks made by some animal protection societies against everyone connected with circuses. He knew that animals could be and were being trained without cruelty in circuses and elsewhere and he did everything he could to demonstrate the truth of this, but at the same time he was the first to agree that if there were black sheep in the circus fold they should be rooted out and prosecuted and it was in a large measure due to his untiring efforts that the Performing Animals (Regulation) Act was passed in 1925.

There can be little more for which a young man can hope than to be able to step into a ready-made business and that my brother Bernard and I were able to do, but there are snags when the business has belonged to a man of outstanding personality and one who was loved by everyone. It is true that Bernard and I had taken most of the responsibility for running the circus during the last few years of my father's life, but the guiding light and the good councillor was always there.

When he died suddenly in his sixty-fourth year it had never occurred to anyone that this could happen so soon and that we should have to step out of the shadows and 'be' Bertram Mills and try to fill the space he had occupied. His standards had been so high there could be no question of improving upon them and we felt we should do well if we managed to maintain them, but I could never escape a suspicion that everything we did would be compared with what had been done before; when we made mistakes I imagined somebody would whisper, 'That would never have happened if Bertram Mills had been alive.' In fact, his friends and business associates were kind to us beyond words; that we were able to carry on was due to this and the fact that we had a wonderful staff. Everyone felt that Bertram Mills had started something which had to go on and it was for Bernard and me to see it did.

I have endeavoured to resist the temptation to repeat some of the stories of the publicity-stunt type which have made headlines and to stick to the truth. If there are untruths or exaggerations they have crept in unconsciously, for I wanted this to be a record of what really happened.

This, therefore, although it contains a sprinkling of personal reminiscences, is not an autobiography but an attempt to tell the story of Bertram Mills and the circus that bore his name, as I knew it, during his life and later. It is a story of trials and triumphs with sad and happy moments; it is perhaps one in which too few of those who contributed to its making are mentioned for there were so many of them—dedicated men and women upon whose loyalty we could rely through thick and thin.

It has been a labour of love and an attempt to pay tribute to a wonderful father and an equally wonderful mother without whose patience and support so much would have been impossible.

CYRIL BERTRAM MILLS

Chapter One
How it all began
The Great International
Circus

'I've just signed an agreement to run a circus at Olympia next winter.'

We stared at each other and there was silence, for we realised from the way in which the announcement had been made that it was no joke. When at last the tension was broken by my mother she said: 'Daddy, you have not very much money, but I am afraid you will lose it quickly.'

It was a February evening in 1920 and Mother, Bernard and I were dining at home with Father, and whereas we knew that he, who had been demobilised a little earlier, was considering his future, we had naturally assumed he was thinking in terms of the sort of thing he had done before the war—building carriages, coaches and motor-car bodies and importing American cars. What we had forgotten was an evening a few weeks earlier when we had been the guests of the directors of Olympia, at a time when there had been a circus there.

My father had always had a great love for horses, and that two of his best friends were directors of Olympia stemmed from the fact that the International Horse Show had always been held there. There was, therefore, nothing unusual in the fact that we had been their guests at the circus and had had supper with them after the show. Nor was there anything unusual when my father, on being asked what he thought of the circus, said we had all enjoyed it very much. But that answer was not accepted and when pressed he said: 'If I couldn't do better I'd eat my hat.'

A few days later Reginald Heaton, the managing director, told him Olympia would be free the following winter, that they wanted a tenant badly and that as they thought he had ability as an organiser they wanted him to consider the possibility of running a circus.

It sounds absurd to suggest that a man who had never had anything to do with show business should even consider embarking on such a venture, but the suggestion gave rise to thoughts, which in turn produced an idea which he did not mention to his friends at Olympia and of which we only learned a little later. At the New York Horse Show he had once met John Ringling, the then head of the world-famous Ringling, Barnum and Bailey Circus, and in the short time that had elapsed he had, by the exchange of cables, arranged for Ringling to bring his circus to London. So Olympia was to have the biggest circus in the world and it was to be presented by an unheard-of man named Bertram Mills.

Britain's shipping losses during the war had been enormous and he had stipulated that Ringling should procure ships to bring the show over. All went well until June, when Ringling cabled to say he was unable to arrange shipping space and must therefore ask for cancellation of the contract. Very sportingly he added, 'Let me know what I owe you.' Father's reply was typical of him and like many of his later actions. All he said after thanking Ringling was: 'You owe me nothing, I will produce my own show.'

There would have been only one alternative—to go to his friends at Olympia and ask to be released from the tenancy agreement—but that would never do. He had started something and it, like everything else he ever touched, had to be seen through to the end whether it was bitter or sweet.

15

Most of the work already done had to be scrapped, for the three-ring Ringling Circus would have had ten thousand seats arranged as they were for the Horse Show and Royal Tournament, but the circus my father planned was to have one ring like European circuses and the architects had to find a way to build the seating so that it was circular, or nearly so.

My father made up his mind that where the programme was concerned he would take nobody's word—he would see every act himself—and with that objective he and I set off to see all the circuses in Europe. I, of course, was the guinea-pig and in taking me I feel sure he was assuming that what appealed to a youth of eighteen would probably appeal to others of the younger generation. As we travelled we made our own notes of what we liked and only at the end of the tour did we compare them. It was surprising how much they had in common, but to make sure we revisited all the shows where there were acts which one, or other, or both of us liked and when we returned to London the programme was nearly complete. The biggest surprise I had during that tour was that Father was known to so many circus owners, but the explanation was that before the war he had exhibited at most of the big horse shows on the Continent, and whenever there was a horse show it was usual for a circus to play the town at the same time, as horse lovers are always good circus customers, and on countless occasions Father had gone to the circus in the morning to watch the training of horses.

One of the biggest problems in 1920 was that Britain had not yet forgiven the Kaiser and nobody dared present a German act or even one with a German name. The first crunch came when we saw the Schumann horses in Copenhagen, for then, as now, they were by far the best in the world. The Schumann brothers were, and the present ones are, Danes and Swedes, but their name sounded German so they were out, and Father settled for the horses of Henning Orlando which we saw in the old circus building in Stockholm.

At the age at which I was then I failed completely to appreciate the magnitude of my father's task. The circus in this country was in a state of deep depression—even decay. Nobody realised that a performance produced entirely by the members of one or two families was not good enough; if there were those who would have liked to produce a big international programme they lacked the courage, or perhaps the financial resources.

At that time the circus was considered to be non-U and this was a state of affairs which my father hoped to correct, and believed he could, if he offered the best talent available and ran his circus as a business, rather than as the half-hearted effort of nomads.

The first season was scheduled to run just over five weeks and the seating capacity was much smaller than in recent years; but, even so, some three hundred and fifty thousand tickets had to be printed and to find the right staff to handle them in the primitive building which then served as a box office presented a problem, which had not been solved entirely when the show opened. The theatre ticket agents had allocations of tickets, but they could not be expected to recommend their regular customers to buy seats for a show that was to be produced by an 'unknown', until they had had a chance of seeing it. Advance booking was therefore minimal and did nothing to lessen anxieties.

Father had felt that where the administrative side of the business was concerned he wanted new people, as he was determined to do things better than they had been done on the village greens. Among the small team of executives one man was outstanding—J. Russell Pickering. He, a chartered accountant with his own business, had been a friend of Father's when they were in the army during the war and having decided he could have no better man, Father telephoned and said he was starting a circus, and wanted him to be its general manager. 'Pick', as he was known to everyone, took it as a joke, thanked him, said he was very busy and put the telephone down. Father rang again and said he was in earnest and wanted Pick to meet him as soon as possible for a discussion. How a chartered accountant was persuaded to have anything to do with a new circus with the business in the state in which it then was is anybody's guess, but he agreed and there began a business association which, coupled with sincere friendship, lasted until 1947 when Pick died. He had outlived his chief by nearly ten years. He was able to keep a fatherly eye on our interests during the second world war and was of inestimable help when we had the task of restarting the circus in 1946. His loyalty to 'the boys' had been just the same as it was to Father.

Father and all those about him were green in the techniques of the circus: when told the diameter of the ring should be thirteen metres they assumed, logically but incorrectly, that this was the diameter of the circle in which the performance is given. In fact it is the outside diameter of the ring fence, so the one for Olympia was made larger than it should have been; but those with horses were the only ones who spotted the mistake and as it was not a big one, and as the fence was so well made, it was used until it almost fell to pieces over thirty years later. Father never did things by halves and whether he built something or started doing business with a firm it was likely to last a very long time—many firms which supplied the circus in 1920 were still doing so in 1965. His policy of loyalty to those who served us well produced countless friends and no matter what the circus needed, or how short the time, we were never let down; in the whole history of the circus at Olympia we were never unready for an opening at the appointed time.

My first job with the circus began on a December evening in 1920. Having spent four and a half years at Harrow, I had just finished my first term reading engineering at Cambridge and George—an Old Etonian friend—and I had decided to try to make ourselves useful. When we asked for a job we were told the bill-posting campaign was not progressing well and someone said three of his 'fly-posters' had quit and suggested we should fill in for a day or two.

We agreed and wanted to start at once, but it was explained that fly-posting was not the 'done' thing; it was frowned upon by all forms of authority and had to be done by night by even the most experienced men. Our two objectives were, therefore, to find good sites and post bills unseen by the law. Asked to do the same thing in London now I should want danger money, but in those days it sounded like an exciting game of cops and robbers, so we set off in a car with brushes, paste and plenty of bills.

The result was pretty discreditable, for we had no mercy on anything; we stuck bills on His Majesty's letter boxes, on the road at busy crossings and one on the front door of a friend, although in this case we we were decent enough only to paste the corners of the bill so it could be removed easily. When we boasted of what we had done we were told Father would probably be prosecuted for defacing Crown property, and for the next few days we were given chores in which we could not get into mischief.

A few nights later I was watching a troupe of flying trapeze artistes make the most of an opportunity to practise after the workmen had knocked off and nearly everyone had gone home. Everything they did was what the publicity blurbs have called 'the poetry of motion in mid-air' and it looked so simple. What, for instance, could be easier than just swinging from one platform across to the other? I persuaded the head of the troupe to let me do just that.

The climb to the net was not too bad, but the departure platform was at the other end. We have all seen people walk and run across a safety net and nothing could look easier, but my attempt produced more laughs than a good clown *entrée* and, having fallen several times, I was reduced to the indignity of crawling most of the way on hands and knees. The journey up the second rope ladder with nobody to hold the bottom was more difficult, and I was positively scared every time I looked down. The platform was only about forty feet high, but the net, the only thing between me and death, looked no stronger than a spider's web.

After a few moments, during which I tried to persuade myself that everything was all right, I took the trapeze bar and made ready. I had to get it over quickly if nerves were not to get the better of me and the thought that I might have to turn back was not pleasant. It would have made a good story the next day if the eighteen-year-old son of the owner of London's big new circus was too scared to drop into a safety net.

So I let go, assuming I should swing neatly across and land

on the platform on the opposite side. Not a bit of it; I had no idea that all my movements had to be in time with the pendulum of which I was a part, and after three or four short swings I came to rest over the centre of the ring and hung there like a clumsy gorilla, unable to make the trapeze swing an inch.

The reply to my 'What do I do now?' gave me a shock. If I dropped feet first I should go through the net like a stone; I must raise my feet until they were above my head and then let go, so that I should land on a rounded back. It was a preposterous suggestion and I said I could not do it, but the answer was that I must, so I made a supreme effort and managed to raise my feet until they were a little above the level of my hips. They just would not go higher and fortunately my instructor realised this and yelled, 'Let go!' The drop was no more than eighteen feet, but it seemed to take ages, and when I landed in an unorthodox and undignified position I must have looked very stupid, but both the head of the troupe and I had had a lesson. By the time I reached the ground I had resolved I was not cut out to be a performer and ever since have resisted all temptations to try to be one.

The first circus was billed as 'The Great International Circus' and down in the bottom corner there appeared in very small type the words, 'Organised by Bertram W. Mills'. The opening took place on the 17th December 1920, but it had been preceded by something which was to have a profound effect not only at Olympia but in circuses all over Britain.

That going to the circus was 'not done' by a great many people was one of my father's gravest anxieties, for the cost of an expensive show would only be recovered if it attracted people who could afford the expensive seats. He believed the best way to reach these people was through the press and decided to give a luncheon for them before the opening—in fact he gave two : one for the gentlemen and the other for the ladies, which shows how things have changed in a lifetime. The purpose of the luncheons was to create an atmosphere of good fellowship with the critics before they saw the show—and it certainly did this, for the day after the opening the papers were a sight for tired eyes. One headline read : 'Best show in London for many years';

another, 'Great Circus Revival'; and the one in *The Times* said: 'The Big Circus—Enraptured Audience'. In those days people paid a great deal of attention to the opinions of the critics and the rush for tickets began. No newcomer could have hoped for a better reception, and only the man who had staked everything he had possessed could know how it felt to be relieved of part of the load of anxieties he had borne for months.

However, he was not willing to let things rest there, for he saw the possibility that opening lunches could serve two purposes; they could also be the means of attracting people who, at that time, thought any circus beneath their dignity. For the lunches that were to follow he sent out many invitations, but only to those he thought were the right people. If he met a peer or an M.P. at a party, or a leader of industry at a horse show, they were sure to be invited the following winter. His old friend the Earl of Lonsdale became Honorary President of the circus in 1922 and presided at the luncheons which, from then on, were attended by the Lord Mayor and Sheriffs and their ladies who were the guests of honour.

By 1927 there were 350-odd guests and the table plan contained the names of the Rt. Hon. and Mrs. Winston Churchill, Mr A. and Lady Diana Duff Cooper, Mr. Charles B. Cochran, Viscount and Viscountess Furness, the Rt. Hon. J. Ramsay MacDonald, the Earl and Countess of Orkney, Mr. Bracewell Smith, Mr. A. J. Munnings, Lady Eleanor Smith and the Rt. Hon. J. H. Thomas. So, even at this early stage, the luncheon had become an annual function of considerable importance.

Ten years later everything had grown beyond recognition. None of Olympia's restaurants had been able to contain it for several years and it occupied the whole ground floor of the National Hall. Two thousand square yards had to be enclosed with decorated partitions, carpeted and covered with a muslin ceiling—a colossal job when it was only to be used for a couple of hours. There was space for a cocktail reception area, but the guests could not be announced and received as they were in later years, for no host could shake hands with everyone in the time available.

There were 139 tables of eight and the top table seated 281

guests so that the total number was 1,391 and even that was
not a record, for there had been 1,493 guests the year before.
The 1937 table plan looked like a précis of *Who's Who* or
Burke's Peerage, for it contained the names of sixty-three members of the peerage, three bishops, seventy-six baronets and
knights, fourteen members of the Government and Opposition,
two D.B.E.s, one judge, one field marshal, one admiral, two
Dominion High Commissioners, the chairman of the London
County Council, all the aldermen of the City of London and
the masters of five City Livery Companies.

To these names were added those of the leaders of industry,
the arts and the press and it is not difficult to imagine the size
of the task of sending invitations (which could not be printed
until the Lord Mayor had been elected), getting in the replies
and then deciding where each guest should sit in order of pre-
cedence. Those things done, a table plan was printed so that
everyone knew where to sit and could look up the names of
those who sat at every table. It was to drop a brick to invite
Mr. and Mrs. X if a divorce was pending and a bigger one if
they were divorced already. There was no feather in our cap
if Mrs. Y was not invited with Mr. Y to whom she might only
have been married a few weeks—and to invite anyone who
had died was shocking. All this meant that someone had to
search *The Times* every day, for there were more bricks to be
dropped if anything in an Honours List or a Service promotion
was missed. All this I was spared, for Bernard was responsible
for all the arrangements and they gave him plenty of worries.
On one occasion the American and Soviet Ambassadors were
to sit almost next to each other, but on the day before the lunch
there was a clash between Washington and Moscow so some
quick switching had to be done on the table plan.

That such distinguished people attended showed how much
they esteemed their host, for he made no attempt to conceal the
fact that the *raison d'être* for the lunches was to publicise the
circus and demonstrate that Olympia at Christmas time was
a place where anyone could, and everyone should, go. Many
people said they looked forward to the lunches from year to
year, but the invitation list had to be revised annually so that

those who had held high, but temporary, offices could make room for their successors as it was impossible to stretch the capacity of the restaurant.

Back in 1920, however, the thought that a member of the Royal Family might go to the circus never occurred to anyone, and the sight of mink coats and dinner jackets at evening performances put everyone in an optimistic mood.

I did precious little to help during the first three seasons, for Cambridge provided me with plenty of homework during the Christmas vacations. Most of my time at Olympia was spent watching artistes and animals practising, but I also kept an eye on the fun fair where I saw one or two things I did not like.

The circus only occupied about a third of the building and to make good use of the rest there was always a fun fair. Space was let to people who operated rides, games and side shows, but if anything went wrong it would be Father's responsibility, though he knew as little of the fun fair business as he did of the circus. It is therefore not surprising that, in the early days, a couple of unscrupulous get-rich-quick types rented space for games which sounded, and appeared to be, straightforward, but which I soon learned had what was called a 'ready'. This is nothing less than a swindle the result of which is that you can't win. One man had a game called 'The Swinging Ball' which consisted of a ball hung on string over a cone-shaped pin; all you had to do was swing the ball away so that it missed the pin on the outward journey and knocked it over as it returned. He showed customers how easy it was and let them have two or three successful tries. They were then persuaded to pay for the next go and always lost, but I spotted the 'ready' very soon from a point at which I could not be seen. Whenever the customer had paid the man leaned on the table so that everything was off centre and this made a win impossible.

The problem was what to do as one is always on thin ice when accusing a man of fraud, so I approached another concessionaire thinking he ought to know about the game. He told me he and others were at a loss to understand why this game was allowed, as everything else Bertram Mills did was correct. They were all saying they could not get an honest living while one man was robbing the public. That was good enough; the man's stand was dismantled in his absence and he was refused admission.

The following year another rogue took space for a game called 'Cover the Spot'. A red circle had to be covered with circular metal discs and although the owner could always do it no member of the public could ever win, so we broke into the stand one night. At first everything appeared to be above board, but a careful examination of the metal discs showed that they had been shaved a little on two sides and were no longer circular. Fraud again and another man forfeited his rent and that put an end to troubles of this kind, for news spreads quickly among rogues.

During the first season nobody had much time to think of the future, but by early 1921 it was safe to say that if no money had been made none had been lost and without a moment's hesitation Father entered into an agreement with Olympia to carry on for one, two or three more seasons but at this point history reared its ugly head. Olympia, first opened in 1886, had had fourteen Christmas shows in thirty-four years and of these six had been circuses, but nobody had been successful enough with the first to risk another the following year. It looked as if London only wanted a circus about once every five years, yet here was a man who was confident enough to go on at the point at which others had turned back; and let it be remembered that the spending spree which, as the result of war gratuities, had made things easy the year before, had ended.

Determination to succeed or bust prevailed and the second Great International Circus opened in December 1921. The programme was a marked improvement on the first. My father had booked Rastelli, the greatest of all jugglers, and had taken me to the States where we saw all the big circuses and where he booked three high-priced acts on which he had to pay return transportation across the Atlantic.

By now the confidence of the ticket agents had been gained and they went all out to sell tickets; advance booking was good and by the time the critics' reviews had been published success seemed assured and indeed it was.

The 1922–3 programme was even better and really lived up to its 'Great International' title. Among those who appeared was Baptista Schrieber, the German High School rider, who was certainly the best at that time. She, who ran her own circus in Sweden after World War II, had appeared at Olympia in 1914, but her horse had died and a post-mortem examination had indicated poison. Lord Lonsdale had come to the rescue by starting a fund and presenting her with a beautiful horse called Menelik in the presence of Queen Alexandra and Princess Victoria. Coming back to Olympia was, therefore, something about which she had mixed feelings and that she did so was probably because she would meet Lord Lonsdale again and show him the trained Menelik.

In the meantime a far-reaching decision had been taken. Until the autumn of 1922 most people must have assumed the man behind the circus was some self-effacing tycoon, but someone had persuaded him that it was *his* circus that people flocked to see. He had remembered that a product without a trademark is like a mule—without pride of ancestry or hope of posterity—and decided that his trademark must be his name. Henceforward he would allow his name to appear on posters which would proclaim BERTRAM MILLS CIRCUS.

During the first few seasons there was always a thrill act as a free thrill act in the fun fair to attract people and ensure that circus patrons went there after the show. One year it was Nick Chefalo who rode a bicycle down a sloping ramp, jumped a thirty-foot space and landed. He was a daredevil type who paid little attention to his rigging, and although he did not come to a sticky end, he had an accident which put him in hospital for part of the season. Another year it was the Helkevists, who dived from some ghastly height into a small tank of water, but the best of these thrillers was one called 'Motors that pass in the air' and was performed by the Fearless Greggs.

These people had a ramp about sixty feet high, at the top of which were two cars. In the front one was a man and in the back one, and a little higher, a girl; the cars were released simultaneously and when the first reached the bottom it was diverted upwards and did a somersault, while the one with the girl jumped a twenty-foot gap and passed beneath so that it landed in front of the one with the man. The Greggs had been brought from the States at a huge salary and after the first performance my father went to tell them how pleased he was. For men to do this sort of thing was fairly normal, but his admiration for the girl was unbounded and he could not resist asking her whether she was not terrified every time she did it. Her answer was, 'I was terrified once and that was the first time I did it twenty minutes ago.' The girl who should have done it was taken ill, and the poor kid who had taken her place should have been speechless with fear as she watched the building of the rigging, but she had not shown the slightest sign of nervousness. I expect she knew that silence was the price she had to pay for her job, for she would certainly not have been allowed to work if the truth had been known to us.

Having acts of this kind served one purpose, but defeated another, and very soon concessionaires asked for them to be discontinued, for they caused people to stand around without spending money before the act and as soon as it was over there was a rush towards the exits. Thereafter there was nothing of this kind, which was a two-fold blessing, for the space could be let for other purposes and about £3,000 a year was saved in salaries. The 'thrill acts' became part of the circus and, as the roof of Olympia is over a hundred feet high, it was possible to present acts of a kind London had not seen for ages.

It was in the programme of the show which opened in December 1922 that a name, destined to become famous and part of the British Way of Life, appeared for the first time and it is possible that it was the first time it appeared in print anywhere. Billy Butlin had returned from Canada and booked two sites in the fun fair. I suspect he was very nearly 'skint' and have no idea how he produced the rent, which had to be paid in advance, but if he had to borrow nobody could have put a few pounds in safer hands, for as well as being a tremendously hard worker he had what was then a new idea. He gave love birds as prizes and made them easy to win, so that by the time the fair had been open a few minutes there were enough people carrying the birds in little cages to give him all the publicity he needed, and everyone was looking for his stand.

The following year he had three stands, but he had his eye on the big things like Dodgems where the real money was. One year I found a portable figure of eight railway in Germany and whilst it was large enough to give a good ride it could just be squeezed into Olympia. As far as I knew nothing like it had been seen in a building in this country and I had to offer generous terms to persuade the owner to bring it over, but it coined money.

In letting space in the fun fair I had come to realise there was one man who deserved all the encouragement he could be given and, of course, it was Butlin, and he was sure of a welcome when he came to ask if he could have space for a similar ride the following year. His ride was better and took even more money than its predecessor and by the time we came to our last pre-war season all the big rides in Olympia were his, but even this and some successful amusement parks had not satisfied him, for he had seen the possibilities of well-run holiday camps and taken the plunge.

Side-shows have little appeal now, but thirty years ago there was considerable interest in those containing giants, midgets, fat girls, sword swallowers, snake charmers and tattooed people but nobody wanted to see those suffering from physical deformities which made them objects of pity. However, we did have one or two oddities and one of these came our way in an unusual manner. We had advertised for a charwoman and one of the applicants interviewed by Miss Moore, my father's very prim and unsophisticated secretary, was a woman of exceptional appearance. Having pretended this woman was suitable, Miss Moore made the excuse that she must consult her boss and went to Father to announce that she had discovered the 'Ugliest Woman in the World' and thought she ought to be given a contract to appear in a side-show as just that. Father never lacked courage, but to make such a proposal to any woman required more than he could muster, but he could not help being intrigued, if only by the enormity of the proposition, and asked for things to be arranged so that he could see the woman without being seen by her. She was indeed ugly, but somehow not in a way that was repulsive; nor was she an object of pity. Handled properly the woman had possibilities, but Father would have none of it, although if Miss Moore had the nerve to make the suggestion she could do so.

I would give a lot to have been a fly on the wall during what followed, but all I know is what Miss Moore told us afterwards. Yes, she could have the job as charwoman, but would she be interested in another job if she could earn more? The opening gambit sounded as if she was about to be recruited for the oldest trade in the world, but it is unlikely that that thought occurred to the woman. Would she be willing to work in a fun fair? Would she be willing to work in a side-show? Would she . . . ? The mind boggles at the thought of how the $64,000 question was put, but it was, and again the answer was 'Yes'; the only question she asked was, 'How much would I earn?' and when the answer was, 'At least £20 and possibly £30 a week', she was as pleased with herself as if she had just been elected Miss World. She appeared at Olympia dressed up to the nines and crowds went to see her; Ringling heard about her and she went to the States at the sort of salary Cabinet Ministers were getting and when I last heard of her she had retired a wealthy woman, and was living in Florida.

In 1926 my father engaged Schaeffer's midgets, a troupe of about thirty perfectly formed miniature men and women who did a little act in the circus, but for whom he had a bigger plan. They were to be the big attraction in the fun fair and a Tiny Town was built for them. There were miniature houses, stables with small ponies and a one-quarter-scale hansom and four-in-hand coach, both of which cost far more to build than full-size ones. Even buckets to stand outside the stables, furniture, cutlery and china had to be made specially, for ordinary things were too large and those made for dolls' houses too small. The cost was fantastic and because the whole show was so large it had to occupy the gallery of Olympia, and that meant building a ramp from the ground floor to get people in and out quickly. The results fully justified all the effort, for many people went to Olympia just to see Tiny Town, but once there spent money on other things.

When Schaeffer returned to Olympia in 1955, bringing many of the same midgets, he showed us something we had not seen for a long time—seven £100 Bank of England notes which he said were part of the salaries Father had paid him in 1926. He had carried them all through the Hitler days, when to have been found with them could have resulted in the kind of punishment only the Nazis could inflict, and wondered whether they were of any value now. Our bank confirmed that the notes were genuine and the numbers they bore corresponded with those on notes issued to us against cheques for artistes' salaries in 1926, and on the strength of this they were exchanged and Schaeffer's visit to London was much more profitable than he had dared to hope it might be.

Chapter Two
My early days with the circus
Plans for expansion

By June 1923 I had taken a degree at Cambridge and started work as an engineer. After a few months in England I went to Baltimore to study oil refining and by 1924 was in an oil refinery in a mosquito- and snake-infested swamp outside Rangoon. One night an Indian said he had been bitten by a snake on both sides of his heel and somebody who professed to know about these things said if he was allowed to go into a coma he would not live, so he was kept awake all night with a cane. Next morning, at the place where he said it had happened, snake hunters found a broken coconut shell with two sharp blood-stained points.

I made one trip to Mandalay and up into the jungle in the Shan States near where the 'Giraffe Neck Women' live, but was unable to see them, as the last part of the journey would have been by mule through uncharted country. One night was spent in a Dak bungalow and I asked my house boy who had come with me from Rangoon why the unglazed window frames had strong iron bars like a wild animal cage: 'Many tigers here, master,' was his reply, but even if he was pulling my leg

I felt better for the fact that I was armed, and that he took great care to make sure all the doors were securely bolted before we retired for the night.

The next day we wandered in the jungle and again I was glad to be armed, for Burma was notorious for dacoits—bandits who will kill at the drop of a hat for a handful of rupees. As my boy and I walked through a gorge three most unpleasant-looking characters approached and my first thought was that if there were others behind our chances would not be good. Looking back I was relieved to see there was no one else, but my boy was terrified and assured me the men in front were dacoits, so I decided to take no chances and fired one shot in their direction but well above their heads. They turned tail and fled—dacoits, maybe, but perhaps just innocent locals going about their lawful business.

Rangoon was a beautiful city and it was always worth the journey there if only to see the huge black clouds of flying foxes going over the golden domes of the Schwedagon Pagoda just before sunset, but I had to spend most of my time at the re-finery, as the plant we were building had to be completed before the monsoon. Life there was either dull or, as on the two occa-sions when there were sizable explosions, dangerous. In one of these I was soaked in burning oil and only just managed to extinguish the flames by rolling in the dust before a well inten-tioned Burman arrived with a soda-acid fire extinguisher—the last thing I wanted!

If I have any regrets about the time I spent in the Far East they are due to my failure to find anyone who could show me the Indian rope trick. Neither in Ceylon nor Bermuda did I even find anyone who had seen it, though there were countless tales of friend of friends who had and some of these even claimed to have photographed it, but no photos were ever to be found. Some said it had been done before large audiences, but I can-not persuade myself to believe in mass hypnotism, even if in-dividuals under hypnosis have been made to believe they were seeing it. I am almost convinced that it is just another traveller's tale which, like Hitler's propaganda, gained credence by reason of the magnitude of the lie upon which it was based.

When I returned to England in 1925 the circus had played five seasons at Olympia. It had established itself in the hearts of Londoners and appeared to have a future, so my father offered me a job. To accept meant taking the gamble of going into something for which I had no training, and to which I might be totally unsuited, but my mind was made up in a matter of moments.

By the summer of 1923 Olympia had built its second exhibition building, the National Hall, and this caused Father a great deal of anxiety, for it adjoins the main road and partly hides the Grand Hall. Worse still was the possibility that some kind of competitive show might be staged there during the circus season. Father decided he must do two things. First he must secure perpetual advertising rights on the main road frontage of the new hall; secondly he must occupy it himself at least until he could make a new agreement with Olympia which would ensure there could be no competitive show in it. But occupy it with what? Dancing might be the answer and he converted the hall into what was believed to be the biggest dance hall in the world. Seven thousand square feet of parquet flooring had to be bought and laid and the whole interior was decorated elaborately so that it was unrecognisable as an exhibition hall. A big 'name' band was engaged and there was room for five thousand people.

The first night was full of problems, for, although most of those present were guests who had never been to a dance hall before, the doors were open to the public and it was obvious that a large percentage of London's undesirables had entered. Something had to be done, for no decent people would patronise a place if doing so meant rubbing shoulders with the male and female scum from the gutters of London—and it had to be done quickly. All those available and some extras borrowed from the circus were given a pocketful of half-crowns and told to put out anyone who looked undesirable and refund the price of admission. Those who did the job must have been very shrewd, for there was not a single complaint, but the next day there were notices at the entrance, which safeguarded the position in future.

When I joined the circus on a permanent basis the dance hall had proved there was a demand for this sort of thing—it was continued until 1928—but it could only be run for a few weeks each winter, as the hall was let at other times for exhibitions and the cost of converting it each winter took a heavy toll on the receipts; all these factors caused my father to cast his eye around for another venue.

The Royal Opera House, Covent Garden, was always closed in winter and although it sounded preposterous that this almost sacred building should become a dance hall my father's persuasiveness, coupled with the offer of good rent, was too much for the authorities, and they agreed to grant him a long winter tenancy each winter for a period of years.

Pick had taken over the management of the Olympia Dance Hall at the outset and, of course, it was he who was made general manager of Covent Garden. Success there was instantaneous, for with the long season and the comparatively low overheads it was possible for those who could only afford half a crown to dance to the best and most famous bands of the time. Those of Jack Howard, Debroy Somers, Jack Hylton and Herman Darewski had been reserved for the very rich in the past, but now almost anybody could enjoy them. It was there that I landed as assistant manager under Pick in my first job as a paid employee of Bertram Mills and there that I met a man who has been a close friend ever since and for whom I have unbounded admiration on account of the magnificent job he has done—Carl Heimann of Mecca.

The catering facilities at Covent Garden were not good at that time and what was then a comparatively small firm called Ye Mecca Ltd. had taken on the catering; Carl was their representative. Those were the days when the great charity balls were held there—nights when tails and white ties were *de rigueur*—and the catering problems were enormous; but Carl tackled them with the courage and determination which have carried him to the joint chairmanship of the gigantic organisation which he and Alan Fairley now control.

My stay at Covent Garden was short, for my name was to appear on the 1925–6 circus programme as that of assistant manager and it was at Olympia that I was to try to earn the salary I was being paid. Bernard had also joined Father a few months ago and as Pick, who was billed as manager, had to spend most of his time at Covent Garden and the Olympia Dance Hall it looked as if we brothers should have plenty to do.

Nobody was ever a better man to work for than Bertram Mills. He did not believe in overloading people with instructions and in practice this meant that, having been given a job, we were expected to use our heads and get on with it. He had plunged into a business of which he knew nothing and had learned the hard way and that was how he wanted us to learn. If we made mistakes, as we did often, we were not hauled over the coals, for he assumed we had learned the lesson and would not make the same mistake again. On the other hand he had little use for those who were not intelligent enough to learn by their own mistakes and repeated them.

For the 1925–6 programme he had booked Truzzi's horses. Truzzi, an Italian by parentage, had been in Russia at the time of the revolution and having remained there had forfeited his right to leave; by the time the contract was signed it was the result of almost endless negotiations and at least one under-cover meeting on the neutral ground of the League of Nations in Geneva. There, through intermediaries, an arrangement was made whereby a large sum had to be desposited with a Swiss bank as a guarantee that both Truzzi and the horses would return.

If that had been the whole of the Truzzi story it had provided enough worry for one act, but two weeks before the circus was due to open the real pinch came. Father had sent an experienced horseman to Leningrad to ensure that the arrangements he had made were carried out and that the horses were well cared for during the voyage. In mid-winter Russia is snow- and ice-bound and the shock was in the form of a cable saying the harbour was frozen and that they wanted £1,000 for an ice-breaker to make a way into the Baltic for the ship carrying the horses.

It was a lot of money, but an Olympia programme without horses was unthinkable, so it was paid at once. However, as

Leningrad is one of Russia's main arteries it looked as if somebody had been smart enough to see the possibility of putting
an English circus over a barrel and I have always assumed
that somebody made a big profit on the deal, especially as a
large convoy sailed out in the wake of the ship with the horses.

My job that winter was to bring Captain Alfred and his
seventy lions from the Nouveau Cirque in Paris where they
had worked in November. Once we knew there were fifteen
wagons, and their size and weight, it was easy to make arrangements for the journey, but not to carry them out. I went to
Paris, taking with me our veterinary surgeon, who was to be
responsible for the health of the animals during the journey,
and arranged for the wagons to be hauled from the circus to
the Gare Batignolles—a heaven-forsaken place, if ever there
was one. Each wagon had to be craned on to a truck and when
we thought we were ready to travel a railway man announced
that none of the vehicles would pass through the tunnels. '*Démontez les roues*,' he demanded, so every wagon had to be
jacked up and sixty wheels had to be removed; then the wagons
were lowered on to the trucks on their axles. This took a long
time, for the wheels had not been off for years and were rusted
on and we missed our scheduled departure time, only reaching
Dieppe an hour before the boat was due to sail. The wheels
had to be put on to get the wagons to the ship and then, because they had to travel between decks, they were too high and
again the wheels had to come off.

By the time we sailed, having missed two tides, I was heartily
sick of hearing people say '*Démontez les roues*', but not nearly
as sick as I felt during the five-hour crossing to Newhaven in a
gale. The ship was a cargo one and the passenger accommoda-
tion limited, so Sheather, the vet, and I shared a cabin. He had
the upper berth and I the lower and I nearly learned a sharp
lesson on the stupidities of the English language when he, feeling very ill, shouted 'Look out!' when he meant that I should
look in.

I felt so ill that it would not have mattered if the ship had
sunk and Sheather was in no condition to worry about how the
lions were feeling, so we were relieved on arrival to see there was

no sign of their being anything but good sailors. Of course, we had the business of the wheels again at Newhaven, for our tunnels are lower than those on the Continent. We could have unloaded at the station adjoining Olympia, but the chance of getting publicity by dragging the wagons a few miles across London was too good to miss, so the train went to Willow Walk where a big reception awaited us.

During the three previous weeks London had been plastered with bills which read, 'Look out, seventy are coming' and this had caused a good deal of speculation as nobody knew what the seventy were or where they were coming to. A week before our arrival the words 'to Olympia' were added so everyone began to wonder what a circus could use seventy of. Horses seemed to be the only answer, but a circus with seventy horses would have too many, and in this event the publicity stunt would backfire.

By the time we reached Willow Walk all the wagons bore huge posters reading, 'Seventy Lions going to Olympia', for the benefit of the photographer and reporters who awaited us. From there to Olympia was easy and on arrival we were met by inspectors from the Ministry of Agriculture who were there to see that quarantine regulations were observed; they counted the lions and went away satisfied, but they probably had a shock the next morning when they saw newspaper photos of the seventieth lion walking down the steps from an Imperial Airways aircraft at Croydon. Again the temptation to wring the last drop of publicity out of the occasion had been too much to resist.

Seventy lions made a good side-show, but although it was impossible to get them all into the circus ring at one time, Schneider (that was his real name) had forty with him and, standing with his back to the bars of the cage, threw chunks of meat to each animal in turn. It was surprising that this did not produce fights, but Schneider knew his animals, for he had bred them, and if one attempted to steal he threw it a piece of its own very quickly.

Some time later he started a circus of his own and toured in Italy, but he was a better trainer than business man and soon fell on bad days and went bankrupt. A book was written about his misfortunes, but I always felt the title *The Lions Starve in Naples* was a little harsh, for to me at least it conveyed the impression that they died of starvation whereas they were, in fact, sold to circuses and zoos.

By the time I became part of the circus a great many of the problems of the first year had been solved. The box office had been taken over in 1921 by Lieutenant-Colonel Gleeson, a retired army man, who also ran the box office of the Royal Tournament, of which the seating capacity was much greater than ours. During the first two seasons Jean Houcke had been equestrian director and producer of the show. He, father of the now famous wild animal trainer Gilbert and Nadia who presented some of our horses in recent years, was married to the daughter of Rancy, the owner of a big French circus, and was a useful man, for he could also contribute to some of the horse acts. By 1921, however, it had become possible to engage people with German-sounding names and, of course, the first contract signed was that with the Schumann brothers. Ernst was to present their horses as he did again during the 1922–3 season by which time Willy, his elder brother, had taken over as equestrian director and producer of the circus.

The regulations concerning the employment of aliens were not as strict as they are now; the musical director was Merle Evans, who was then and still is the M.D. of the Ringling, Barnum and Bailey Circus, and the fun-fair manager was Clyde Ingalls, who managed Ringling's side-shows. With these two and Willy Schumann we had three of the most experienced circus men alive.

Willy was a master of his craft for the Schumann Circus was always presented immaculately; he knew all the techniques of the circus from those of the horseman to those of the aerialist and was a man of great business ability. His first job was to produce a running order and decide how many minutes each act should be allowed but it was then that the headaches began. By the time the guy wires of the aerial act were fixed where the artiste wanted them they crossed the path of the horses in the act that followed, so either the aerialists or the horses had to be moved to another spot, or there must be some act between them so that the wires could be moved without holding up the show. Such a change could mean too many animal acts bunched together in one part of the programme and too many human acts in another. All the girl acts had to be spread evenly, as did the comedy ones, and there were strong acts which had to have important spots and perhaps a weak one we wanted to see the back of in the early stages.

The one thing which was intolerable was a slow-moving show like many of those on the Continent which were the sources of talent. Father wanted the best of everything and that meant skimming the cream from the world's summer circuses. In many of these the owners were willing to pay big salaries to one or two acts and complete the rest of the programme with very ordinary material, but to get their money's worth they expected the expensive acts to stay in the ring so long that they cost no more per minute than the cheap acts. This meant the good acts had to spin out time doing very ordinary and sometimes worthless work before getting down to the things for which they were engaged, and they became so accustomed to working like this that they often reached the point where they thought they had a right to occupy every ring for a certain length of time.

This sort of thing was not good enough for London and both Schumann and Bertram Mills earned reputations for being ruthless when cutting acts to get only the best out of them. Schumann had one advantage which was never to be mine, for if an artiste objected to a cut he could always plead he was carrying out the wishes of the Herr Direktor and had no choice in the matter. When, some years later, it was my turn to do this work I was the Herr Direktor and if there were objections I had to be firm on my own account; but in being firm I had little difficulty.

Circus artistes are the least temperamental of all—some may be slightly mental but few have tempers—and we are spared the jealousies which often exist in the theatre. The reason is fairly obvious, for in the theatre there are seldom more than two or three leading parts and it is on these that everyone with ambition casts a green eye. In a properly balanced circus programme everyone does that in which he or she is a specialist. Why, therefore, should there be jealousy on the part of a horse trainer towards an acrobat or a clown towards a glamour girl aerialist? Even so, we had problems with some of the performers in the early days. Those who had worked in a small circus with star billing had been big fish in a small pond, but on arrival at Olympia they discovered that, while they were still stars, they were but members of a constellation.

The build-up of the circus and fun fair, for which we allowed nine days so that the dress rehearsals could take place on the tenth, was always one of the jobs on which I was expected to keep an eye, but whenever possible I watched artistes fixing their rigging, and the rehearsals under the direction of Willy Schumann, for I had realised that if I was ever to be anything other than the 'josser' I was born these were things I should know how to do myself—things which I might have to do one day.

Willy Schumann continued as producer of the show until the 1932–3 season, by which time Bertram Mills Circus was proudly proclaiming its thirteenth circus in thirteen years, which indicated that nobody was superstitious. His name was on the 1933–4 programme but he did not arrive. In Berlin, where he had gone to see a circus, he had a stroke and his telegram, arriving as it did less than two weeks before the show was to open, caused great anxiety. Either Oscar or Ernst, his brothers, could have stepped into the breach, but they were engaged elsewhere, for by this time we had the Polish trainer Mroczkowski and our own horses, which even the Schumanns said could give them a run for their money. Father's first inclination was to cable Houcke, but I had no hesitation in disagreeing with this. Houcke, by then, was a good deal older and, having seen a lot of his work during my travels, I was doubtful whether he could live up to the standards or fit in with the procedures of recent years, and it was just then that I opened my big mouth and asked to be allowed to do the job—I had taken on a similar one with the tenting circus two years before and with the help of Archie Pearson, the ringmaster, had struggled through somehow. Father agreed and I was stuck with a job that was to be mine for the rest of my days with the circus.

There are those who, even if they do not think the work easy, believe there is plenty of time to do it, but highly paid artistes are not prepared to stand around for days on end while a producer gets things as he wants them. Our contract provided for their arrival four days before the opening so even if they arrived punctually we only had three days before the dress rehearsals, which were attended by press photographers and underprivileged children. Before the artistes arrived the ring boys had to have drawings showing where every prop had to be stored, so that it would be available at whichever ring entrance its owner used and so that its movement would not obstruct or be obstructed by that of horses or elephants in an adjoining act. The band had to rehearse the music and that provided by some artistes was so bad or unsuitable that the musical director had to sit up all night rearranging it or providing something else. All the props had to be placed in the ring again and again until every ring boy knew where everything had to be, and if there were movable guys for aerial acts they had to be marked with coloured tape showing where they belonged and how far pulley blocks had to be pulled to produce the right tension. There were times when I had as many as two hundred hanging and guy wires over one ring and if one was put in the wrong place it could cause a hold-up or an accident. One year, when there were so many, one of the staff called them Cyril's knitting and another said: 'All we need now is a pigeon act.' A couple of years later when there were just as many, we did.

When prop rehearsals ended every act went through its routine until the M.D. and the musicians knew all the cues and then we had to rehearse the parade, which meant getting fifty or sixty animals and as many humans into marching order; the fact that during the whole of the rehearsal period all instructions, whether written or verbal, had to be given in at least three languages did not help. One thing always beat me; in forty years I never managed to get a troupe of Arabs to march in step.

The seventieth lion arrives at Croydon Airport, December 1925. It is
thought to be the first occasion on which a fully grown wild animal was
transported by air

Bertram Mills driving the Old Times Coach

(*Above*) *Sir Winston and Lady Churchill at the Circus at Olympia*
(*Left*) *The Queen receives a bouquet from Percy Huxter*
(*Right*) *The Duke of Kent and Prince Michael in the Fun Fair with the author*

PREVIOUS PAGE *The 7,000-seat circus at Olympia*

Next came the cutting of superfluous tricks and sometimes the varying of whole routines and each night, when all else was done, the wild animal cage had to be built so that the animals could practise and get used to the building, but it had to come down again when the practice finished even if it was after midnight, for the horses and elephants had to be exercised from seven o'clock in the morning. If we averaged no more than sixteen hours a day in the ring we considered things to be normal.

It was hard and nerve-racking work during which it was only too easy to catch cold, but even when that happened we had to go on, for time was so short. When opening day came I hardly felt like getting into a morning coat to receive the guests at the luncheon and during the meal I was often anxious about how things would go during the afternoon, and it was difficult to be a good host to the wife of an ambassador sitting on one side and the Marchioness of Exeter on the other. Fortunately, I did not have this problem when I first took over Schumann's job for it was Father who sat among the ambassadors and peers and my seat was very much among the 'also rans'.

Chapter Three
The Carmo Circus
Coco arrives

Early in 1928 we were faced with one of the most important decisions we were ever to take. By the time Father, Bernard and I had worked together about three years it became evident there were too many cooks or, alternatively, there was too little for them to do. We were fully occupied for about four months each year, but at other times there was little or nothing for some, or all of us, to do and we felt we must find a new outlet for our activities.

Bernard and I liked the thought of running a tenting circus, but Father, who was then about fifty-four years of age, was not well disposed towards spending a large part of his life in a caravan. For some years he had been a member of the London County Council and he hated to miss a horse show anywhere. As a hobby he ran stage coaches; one, the Old Berkeley, ran from London to Brighton and back on alternate days in 1926, to Box Hill and back daily in 1927 and to Oxford and back on alternate days in 1928. Seven teams were used on the Brighton and Oxford runs and in the case of the latter a cock-horse ridden by a liveried rider was used up the hill from West Wycombe on the down run, and from Aston Rowant to Stokenchurch on the return journey.

The coaches were run as they were in olden days, as public transport, and anybody could travel on them; you could even book all the seats and have the vehicle for yourself and your friends to ride to Oxford for £10—an expensive hobby for the man who footed the bill, but it gave Father immense pleasure and he drove the coach himself whenever he had time.

During one of his coach trips to Brighton he bought Sherry's and started to run it as a small-scale version of the Covent Garden Dance Hall, but it proved a dud and he sold it very soon after. As if all these interests were not enough he was nursing a constituency as a prospective parliamentary candidate during the last few years of his life. Whenever there was a meet within hacking distance of his home he was out with hounds and on many occasions he went to the meet driving one of his coaches and a team of four.

His decision about the tenting circus was that he would finance it and keep a fatherly eye on it, but Bernard and I should run it, although he would give us all the help we needed during the early days. One more thing and on this he was most emphatic; we must maintain the standards we had established at Olympia even if we were up to our necks in mud. His passion for good order and cleanliness were well known to every member of the staff and one day, some years later, when one of the men of the clean-up gang saw him approaching on one of his unannounced visits he shouted to the others: 'Get busy, boys— here comes the old man—we'd better start polishing the grass.'

During that summer representatives of the Greyhound Racing Association told us they wanted to find something to occupy their stadia during periods when there was no racing and proposed that we and they should join forces and form a company to produce circuses. For us it would mean good, ready made sites for the tenting circus we were thinking about, but even a vague hint of our intentions would have produced a situation which we were most anxious to avoid. The real trouble began when it was proposed that Bertram Mills should throw his Olympia circus in as part of his contribution. The suggestion that he should hand over his good will and substantial profits to a new company until it established itself was totally unacceptable and in any event there were not nearly enough tracks to provide grounds for a thirty week tour.

The following winter there was a fourth circus in London—at the Empress Hall, Earls Court. It was called Bostock's Three Ring Circus and was produced by Gordon Bostock, a member of the Bostock and Woombwell family. Advertised as 'Britain's Biggest Circus Ever' the programme included animals from Strassburger and other German circuses, but although it was said it would run to the end of January I was there one Saturday evening, about the middle of the month, when a notice was posted saying it would close that night. It cannot have been a success, but when we saw its early advertisements which appeared some time before ours we were struck by the fact that the only thing claimed for it was its size, so we rushed off an order to our poster printers which read, 'And now for the Quality Show—Bertram Mills Circus at Olympia'. When these appeared we had given ourselves a name that was to stick forever—and one we had to live up to.

In the meantime the decision to start a tenting circus had been taken. It was to open in 1930 and I went to the Continent to study transportation, seating, tents and other equipment in the best shows there. I was soon convinced that the big, well run circuses in Germany were years ahead of those here and that this was the case was largely due to the German's passion for rules and regulations and his inborn willingness to accept discipline. The circuses of Sarrasani, Krone and Busch had all the appearances of being, and indeed were, well run business organisations.

Every seat had a passage in front of it, whereas in this country one had to climb to reach a seat and then the only place to put one's feet was the plank occupied by the rear end of the person in front. Here, emergency exits and fire precautions were things nobody thought about, but in Germany the safety of the public was a matter controlled by the authorities. In tents the Germans had everybody beaten, for they used steel king poles which made the tents much safer in gales and enabled them to be made far higher, so that aerial acts could work at a height where their work showed to advantage.

We came to the conclusion that if we were to produce a modern tenting circus of the kind we planned the best thing to do would be to copy the equipment of one of Germany's best circuses. Everything demanded the utmost secrecy, as we did not want anyone here to know our plans. A tent was ordered from Stromeyers in Konstanz; their price was high, but all German circus owners said they were the best tent-makers. The name of the customer was never to be revealed and during manufacture the tent was known as M.1 and it was built to metric measurements, as feet and inches would have suggested Britain as a possible destination.

By good luck we heard that a printer in Hamburg had taken a complete seating in satisfaction of a bad debt and this, which was in excellent condition, was to be bought at a reasonable price and was exactly the right size for our tent.

Everything went ahead quietly until one day in September a friend who knew our secret came and said he had something important to tell us, but he could only do so if we promised not to repeat what he said or act on it. Fred Martin was a publicity specialist and a dynamic circus fan; he had advised my father about publicity for some years and had brought our advertising campaigns, which had been amateurish in the early days, into line with the twentieth century. His other great love was magic; he knew all the top illusionists including the Great Carmo who, at that time, was running a small circus, his first, in Ireland. Carmo had made money in Ireland and the news Fred Martin brought was that he was planning a big circus for Britain.

As a circus fan Martin would have liked to see twenty big circuses, but as a business man he knew that even two competing against each other in the early and difficult days would be too many and, worse still, two of his friends would become competitors. His proposal was that we should join forces on a fifty-fifty basis, so that if the thing was a flop each would only bear half the cost. By this time our tent was due to be delivered in a few weeks and the seating had arrived, but we had nearly eighteen months in hand for the smaller items and for booking a programme. On the other hand, Carmo had put the cart before the horse and had booked a programme having wrongly assumed that he would be able to get what equipment he needed in a few weeks. Therefore, if he was to open in 1929 as planned, he would have to present the show in whatever tent and with such equipment as he could get quickly, and in this event his attempt to produce a big modern circus would almost certainly fail.

We did not want to be pushed into anything in a hurry, but Martin's proposal had certain merits and we met Carmo to try to work out the details of a workable arrangement. Our first request was to see a list of the acts booked and this produced a disappointment for, although it was far better than anything Britain had had for a long time, it did not measure up to the standards upon which we had decided to stand or fall. An easy and friendly compromise was reached; the show would be called the Great Carmo Circus. Even this had a snag, for if the show succeeded Carmo would have a good start on us when we produced the Bertram Mills Circus a year later. The Carmo Circus would be known to the public, but against that we should be able to advertise 'From Olympia, London' which would be valuable for we had had a great deal of publicity in the national press for many years.

It was decided to open the Carmo Circus early in May 1929, which meant the things we had intended to do that year had to be done while we were preparing for and running the circus at Olympia, but by early April we were ready and by the middle of the month everything was moved to Catford where the circus was to open.

We had engaged an experienced tentmaster, but for the rest the Mills organisation did not possess anyone who had erected anything more than a bell tent and none of Carmo's people could help, for the tent they had used in Ireland, compared with our giant, was as a tug-boat is to the *Queen Elizabeth*. We had a captain and a ship, but no more than the skeleton of an untrained crew. The king poles were about seventy feet long and weighed nearly two tons each. They had to be raised into vertical positions and men were the only source of power for we had failed to provide ourselves with any mechanical device for this job. Somehow, with the aid of gadgets improvised on the spot, we got the poles up and what was to follow was easy until we came to the seating; it had come to us all jumbled up, had been painted and loaded and finding the right pieces at the right time was like doing a gigantic jigsaw puzzle.

Within a few days we had done what would have to be done in as many hours in future, and it was a really magnificent circus, but it had cost a fortune. Carmo stood a good chance of getting his expenses back, but ours had involved a huge capital sum; the tent could not be expected to last more than three seasons and it was for us to provide and pay the staff. One well known owner of a small circus was overheard saying he gave us about three weeks and that there would then be some useful circus equipment for sale.

The show opened on May 6th and received an even better reception from both press and public than we had dared to hope for. Everyone said it marked the beginning of a new era in the history of British circuses but the problem of how to get to the next town was one which fell squarely in my lap. Carmo had agreed to provide the vehicles, but although we played three weeks at Catford none had arrived three days before we were due to move. I had between seventy and eighty tons of equipment to deal with and it was impossible to plan how it should be loaded without knowing the size and weight-carrying capacity of the vehicles.

My worries about the transport before it arrived were mild compared with what I felt when it appeared. There were lorries which had been sold when they had served their purpose in World War I; steam wagons which were little more than scrap and three old steam traction engines which had been bought because they could haul three trailers each. In good condition they would only have been able to average about four miles an hour. Some of the vehicles had not even been painted.

How on earth could we move a big heavy show quickly with such equipment? And was this the sort of fleet which would produce a favourable first impression as the circus arrived?

Everything else was new or looked as new as the paint which had been used so generously and we had used all the movie-style adjectives to describe Britain's newest, biggest and most magnificent circus. It was no good saying anything, for Carmo had been let down and knew it and as soon as an opportunity occurred he had the vehicles treacled up with paint to make them more presentable.

We moved to Leyton and, although the journey took six times as long as it should, we just managed to open on Monday evening, but we had a bad accident during the build-up. We had been refused permission to employ foreign tentmen who knew how to handle tents like ours and although, in the meantime, we had provided ourselves with gear for raising the king poles we still needed at least five men, in addition to the tentmaster, who knew the drill and without these any one of five untrained men making a mistake could cause dire peril to everyone working on the site. And of course it happened; when the first pole was half-way up a mistake was made and it came crashing to the ground in a huge circular swing which could have mown down a dozen men and maimed or killed several. Only one man was injured but he had a broken leg and that was serious.

My father went straight to the Ministry of Labour and was given permission to have five Czechs and with their arrival ten days later we were far less worried. They were splendid workers and they knew every trick in the book and as they learned English quickly they were able to pass their know-how to the English tentmen.

Business with the Carmo show was by no means what we hoped it would be, but for that we only had ourselves and our lack of experience to blame. We stayed far too long in each place and to keep the mileage short we played a number of what we now regard as 'day tripper' resorts along the South Coast. In recent years we have preferred those seaside resorts where people stay a week or fortnight.

The tour was planned to end in the last week of September by which time we should have played only ten towns and covered the roads between London, Margate and Hove. The longest stay was one of five weeks in Margate and the shortest one of a week in St. Leonards. My fears about the vehicles were fully justified, for we had so many breakdowns that I lost count. A breakdown meant unloading another lorry and sending it back and transferring the load or towing the cripple in, but sometimes the towing vehicle broke down too and then two more had to be sent back. Whenever a lorry broke down my first question was, 'What is its number?' If it was the one with the king poles nothing could be built up until it arrived, but if it carried seating we probably had several hours to recover it. If it had the stable tents the situation was serious for the horses could not remain boxed up indefinitely in the railway horse boxes, and the grooms would have to take food to the station and feed and water them there.

In August Carmo asked us whether we would be willing to extend the tour until the middle of November as he, although about a year late already, realised that his tents and equipment could not be ready before then. The question appeared to be academic until, to our amazement, he said he intended to tent through the winter. We regarded this as pure folly, but it was no business of ours and he said he had ordered central heating plant and a tent which he thought was even safer than ours.

He was a kindly man and we agreed to his request though we did so reluctantly and for two very good reasons. First, it would only leave us four weeks to do all that had to be done before moving to Olympia and, secondly, Father had taken a winter tenancy of the City Hall, Manchester, and it was his intention to run a second circus there.

We parted company with Carmo on a Saturday night in Oxford and he planned to reopen at Wembley on Monday, but after a three day struggle to get the new type tent up he telephoned and from the tone of his voice I suspected he was on the verge of tears. Could we lend him our tentmaster? Of course we could, as by then all our equipment was stored in the winter quarters which Father had taken at Ascot. The tentmaster was rushed to Wembley and within two days tent and seating had been built and the circus was able to open.

Carmo's attempt to tent through a British winter was one

long series of misfortunes. Having played a few places on the outskirts of London he realised our show at Olympia would provide strong competition and decided to move to Birmingham for the midwinter season. The journey with his tired vehicles must have been a nightmare. Jimmy Breeds, who in the postwar years was our head linkman, was at that time a trombone player in Carmo's band; he had once been a miner and having acted as stoker on one of the steam wagons told me his was the first vehicle to arrive—on the seventh day.

During that winter Carmo had a fire in which the big top was badly damaged and we heard that Togare did a splendid job getting the lion wagons out of a burning tent. Another tent collapsed partially under the weight of snow and again the circus was closed while repairs were done. The next big project was to play Blackpool for the summer season and this was prompted, no doubt, by a desire to reduce road mileage and moves but Carmo's show was located on the outskirts of the town, and he had to drag people away from the sea whereas the Tower Circus was at the centre of the town and was already well-established in the hearts of visitors, and to the people of Lancashire and Yorkshire it was a must.

We always felt it unnecessary and unwise to take our circus to a town which had a permanent one when there were so many alternatives, but Carmo's greatest mistake was probably his attempt to tent through the winter. It was a brave attempt but I think it accounted for the short life of his circus and the next time I saw him he had an illusion show in the amusement section of the Glasgow Exhibition in 1938, but business then was not good, as we were in the middle of the Munich crisis.

Manchester had not had a static circus for years and we hoped to build up a good business there, but by the autumn of 1929 things were getting a bit out of hand. We had started tenting a year early so already had two circuses and Manchester was to be the third. We had kept the Carmo show open until the middle of November and were therefore pressed for time to deal with all the snags which arise when putting a circus into a strange building. Our biggest worry, however, was an unexpected one, for the owners of Belle Vue also decided to run a circus that winter and Manchester, having been starved for years, was to have two and both with good programmes. I should be guilty of false modesty if I did not say I think we had the better show, for it contained many of the best acts we had had at Olympia during the preceding years, but Belle Vue had the local knowhow and as we made little money considering the size of the risk taken we decided to retire gracefully after one season and leave the field open to them.

It was during the Manchester season that Coco had his first contract with Bertram Mills. Father had seen him in the Busch Circus in Berlin and given him a four-week contract as a run-in clown. Little did either of them think that the contract would be renewed over and over again so that it eventually covered all the ensuing summer and winter seasons over a period of thirty-seven years. Coco was then less than half his present age, and was unknown in Britain, but over the years he has endeared himself to the children of this country in a way no predecessor of his ever did. Grimaldi and Whimsical Walker are the two names that always come to mind when thinking of great British clowns, but they both spent the greater part of their lives working in theatres in London. Coco, on the other hand, worked for us in nearly every town from Inverness to Penzance and his almost countless appearances on television made him known in places too small for us to visit.

It may be worth noting that he is always referred to as Coco the Clown, but in circus terminology this is incorrect. A clown is the white-faced man in the magnificent spangled costume, but the man who, like Coco, is always at the receiving end when water and custard pies are flying is an Auguste. Several writers have offered explanations of the derivation of the word but they have little in common and I have no idea where the truth lies. In any event to children of all ages Coco will always be a clown.

Chapter Four
Bertram Mills takes the road
The first blow-down

In the early months of 1930 we were busy putting the finishing touches to the first show that was to take the road under the name of Bertram Mills. It opened at Luton on the 9th April and went straight into territory which had not been visited by the Carmo show. Our vehicles compared with those of Carmo were good, but we had economised in this department as the result of lessons learned in 1929 for we realised that before long we should have to consider other methods of transportation. Among the lorries were some 'petrol-electrics' with which we generated electric current; they did this job well, but where getting off a boggy ground was concerned they could not pull the skin off a rice pudding and it was then that ultra-modern equipment was needed. We bought first one and, later, two more caterpillar tractors which could pull almost anything out, but when things were at their worst we had to hire steam ploughing engines with long winch wires.

For the reason that our transport was not perfect we tried not to stray too far from home and having gone as far north as Nottingham and Derby we turned east towards Norwich and on the way there a lorry ran off the road and landed upside down, dumping five hundred chairs in a river. Fortunately they were of wood and floated—unfortunately I arrived just after it happened and was one of those who was drenched to the skin by the time we had fished them out.

Leaving East Anglia we crossed the Thames and headed for the South Coast towns where the Carmo show had been the previous year. We planned much shorter stays in each place, but even so going to that area was a big mistake for business was poor compared with what it had been in the early weeks. In Hove we had an excellent site on the sea front and for the first time spent a whole day and night keeping the big top up in the teeth of a gale. It was the 13th September. So successful were we that we began to believe the tent would stand anything nature could give it but we were soon to be disillusioned. The following week we were on Southsea Common when a gale hit us on Friday evening. We managed to get through the performances but by eleven o'clock were having gusts of up to eighty miles an hour and although the big top was taking its punishment and there was no sign of stakes pulling, the stable tents were a cause of grave anxiety and the whole labour force was concentrated on them. If anything had to go it must not be the stables for the thought that horses might be killed or injured was one which horrified anyone named Mills.

Every man from the manager to the cooks was helping Kral, the tentmaster, and his five Czechs who were working like slaves and trying to tell others what they should do, for none of us had the vaguest idea how to deal with such an emergency. When some of the stable tent stakes pulled it was common sense to drive them in again, but few of us even knew how to tie the side ropes to them. Everything had gone so well in the past that we had not appreciated the need to know about these things and old circus men who looked upon us as 'jossers' had good reason to do so.

At about 2.30 a.m. I heard a sickening thud, but it meant nothing to me beyond the fact that it came from the direction of the big top so I made my way to the front where, to my utter dismay, I saw the roof was rent from top to bottom. Kral came running at the same time and when I spoke all he could say was, 'Nothing to do'. That meant the tent had had it and it was the only one we possessed. A dozen ghastly thoughts went through my mind but the one which was uppermost was that we should have to close the circus until the end of the season, and pay the artistes unless we were lucky enough to get a second-hand roof quickly. Father had put a great deal of money into this venture and although the show was paying expenses the margin was not big; if expenses were to continue for any length of time while there was no revenue the loss would be enormous and Bernard and I had allowed this to happen.

Kral's words were only too true, for within a minute there was a second rent as bad as the first and the wind could get inside the tent; we wretched dwarfs of human beings now had to try to cope with an umbrella large enough to cover four thousand people in a force ten gale.

Within ten minutes 25,000 square feet of best quality canvas had been ripped to ribbons and these, like the tentacles of some giant octopus, were flaying everything within reach. When they touched the seating they wound themselves round it and then with the next gust a whole section was raised fifteen or twenty feet and then allowed to crash to earth. It looked very much as if the seating too would be destroyed, or so badly damaged that it would take months to repair.

The gale continued at full force another three and a half hours, but we managed to keep the stable tents standing although the staff and the artistes who were helping had a very rough time and we were lucky that nobody was injured, for bits and pieces were flying about like paper. I had a near miss when something flew past my head just before dawn. When it landed I went to see what it was as it did not look like anything belonging to us and it was not painted with the red and green triangle design, which was to become known everywhere almost as a trademark.

The thing measured about eight feet by five feet and turned out to be the roof of a small shed belonging to a builder on the Isle of Wight. This sounds like a fisherman's tale, but I do not suggest it had flown from Ryde to Southsea; I think it was blown into the sea, drifted across with wind and tide and then, when lying on the beach adjoining the circus ground, was picked up and blown to where it landed.

By morning we were all exhausted and the circus was one huge scene of wreckage. Before opening we had done everything possible to eliminate the mistakes and deficiencies of the previous year. We had generating plant capable of producing enough current for a town of five thousand inhabitants, about three miles of electric cable, two thousand lamps and even flashing electric signs. The stables were elaborate to a degree never seen in an English circus and every horse had its own stall with its name on a metal arch overhead. We had built up a first class team of executives so there were qualified men in charge of every department; Wallace Gibson, who had proved his great ability with the Carmo show, was general manager and Stanley Franklin, who had spent years with Keith Prowse, was box office manager. It is fair to say we had created a business organisation rather than just another travelling circus—and now it virtually lay in ruins.

By seven in the morning Father had been told by telephone. He took the news in his stride for he was always easy to deal with in times of adversity and if he was ever difficult it was when we were riding on the crest of a wave, for it was during these periods when there were no worries that he believed everyone had time to work and plan for improvement.

Within an hour he telephoned us. He had spoken to his old friend James Sanger, whose biggest competitor he had become, and without a moment's hesitation he and his brother George had said they would lend us a spare roof which was at their winter quarters. Father was to collect it and we were to wade through the wreckage, sort it, load it and move to Poole which was our next town.

By that time we had things organised to the point where we could pull down and load the circus in five hours, but with the collecting and sorting of the wind-scattered bits and pieces we now had a job that took a whole day. By evening we were all ready to drop, but a drop of rum was the only thing anyone had, and by nightfall we were on the road. In the meantime

Father had collected the roof and was in Poole awaiting us.

Before the gale the five hundred-odd stakes had been driven and the king poles erected in Poole, but all this work had to be undone for, whereas our tent was circular and had a diameter of 150 feet, the Sanger one was oblong and less than a hundred feet wide. The only way to find out where to put the stakes and king poles was to lay the roof on the ground and measure, as there had been no time to get drawings and it is doubtful whether any existed, for tentmasters have a way of keeping vital statistics in their heads—some think that others could do their jobs if the information is committed to paper.

Getting the roof up and enclosing it with our side walls which did not fit in a dozen ways was bad enough, but the real headache began when we tried to build the seating. It was like having to squeeze a three-inch orange into an egg-shaped space only two inches wide—and wooden seating is not to be squeezed. Instead of taking five hours that job took a whole day and we were not able to open until the Tuesday afternoon, which meant most of us had worked almost non-stop since the previous Friday morning and I doubt whether anyone had had more than six hours' sleep. We were all out on our feet like punch-drunk heavyweights and the artistes still had two performances to do although we had insisted on their getting a little sleep on Monday night.

It is on occasions like this, and I have seen only too many of them, that circus people display something I have not seen anywhere else. Once you have spent a year or two with circuses you become infected with something nobody has ever been able to explain or define. It does not matter how rough or how tough things are you cannot quit until the job is finished. Some people may attribute such determination to the old saying 'the show must go on' but that is a saying in which I do not believe. A show should go on provided it can be produced properly, and provided its production does not entail suffering or unreasonable hardship. When you are part of a circus you are a member of a big family and even an artiste, who has been a member of other circus families, becomes one of us as soon as he joins our circus. For some reason being a part of a circus means something more than just having a job and getting a living, but none of us knows the reason.

The ways in which the spirit of co-operation manifests itself are legion and, although we become accustomed to it, it is in times of stress that it is seen more clearly. When the weather is ghastly and the circus has to be dragged out of one quagmire and built up in another overnight; when it rains or blows incessantly the circus people are in trouble and that means all of them. If floodwater is flowing through stables where the horses and elephants will be in a couple of hours it is the job of grooms and those who own horses to divert the water but you may be sure every acrobat, juggler and aerialist will be there with a pick or shovel digging trenches. If the whole circus has been delayed on road or rail and there is still four hours' work and only two in which to do it the artistes' wives, the secretaries, usherettes and box office girls will all be there, carrying anything they are able to lift, and it is a job to prevent them tackling things which are far too heavy for them. They are there not because it is part of their jobs, or even because anyone has asked them to be, but because our circus is their circus and nobody wants to be late for an opening—above all everyone is determined that a performance shall not be lost.

In an age when so many people couldn't care less and when so many only want to be sure of their pay packet and don't give a cuss whether the employer loses money or his reputation, this is something of which every circus man is proud. It makes the trials with which we are beset and our climate not only tolerable, but easy to bear. The British climate is about the worst for circuses and we open as early in the year and close as late as those which operate in more favourable climates. We cannot afford to wait for good weather in spring, or close before the bad in autumn, as the idle winter months are already too long and too expensive.

The borrowed tent served its purpose well during our stay at Poole and by good fortune Stromeyers had a good second-hand one in store and this was rushed to us by passenger train and was in Salisbury when we arrived the following Sunday, so the

Sanger tent was dried and returned with a letter of sincere thanks.

In the Foreword which she wrote for the 1932–3 Olympia programme Lady Eleanor Smith said she wondered how many people realised how near the British circus had been to extinction when Bertram Mills took a hand in the matter. The circus, as we know it, was started in 1768 by Philip Astley on a piece of ground near the present site of Waterloo Station. The son of a cabinet maker he preferred the army and was a cavalryman in the Seven Years War. He came out as a sergeant, with a white charger given him by General Elliott as a war gratuity. With this horse and three others, one of which he bought for a few shillings at Smithfield, he announced that he, his wife and three others would 'execute extraordinary feats on one, two, three and four horses'. For a ring he had a roped off circle, for the simple reason that only in a circle could they show their skill continuously.

The belief that what we now call a circus is a descendant of the circus of ancient Rome is nonsense, although the word circus is clearly borrowed from the Latin word meaning ring.

Astley thrived and the following year was able to present his show in Astley's Amphitheatre, which he had financed and built with the profits of the first year, and in that show there appeared the first clown who ever worked in what is so often called the sawdust ring. That a circus ring is so described probably stems from the fact that small circuses do not go to the expense of making a proper ring with earth because they stay such a short time in each place. Big circuses mix sawdust with earth to dress the ring before each performance and to dry earth that is too wet.

By the time Astley died at the age of seventy-two he lived in Paris where he established a circus, and the English circus to which he had given birth was to spread throughout the civilised world. He was followed by others among whom the most famous, perhaps, were Sanger and Hengler; Hengler's last circus in London was at the Palais Royal near Oxford Circus where the London Palladium is now. And after these came Mills, of whom Lady Eleanor Smith wrote: 'Mr. Mills is to the English Circus what Mr. Charles B. Cochran is to the English Theatre and in saying this I am paying great tribute to the two most magnificent showmen of my time.' Eleanor Smith was a great lover of the circus and spent many weeks travelling with us and at Olympia, although the book for which she was best known in her circus writings was about a small family circus.

The results of the first two seasons on the road indicated that the average provincial town, unlike London, was not yet ready for a big circus once a year and by the middle of 1931 we had decided we must extend our field of operations. Scotland was the logical place to go, but the great distances and the hilly roads were frightening, as all the heavy equipment still travelled by road, although horses and elephants went by rail. Against this, neither Scotland nor the North East had seen a big travelling circus for a long time, so we started booking sites there for 1932.

The tour opened at Slough and the fourth town was Luton, where our arrival coincided with an outbreak of small-pox which made headlines in the press. Business was shocking and we thought of pulling out and playing the rest of the week in some small town. But that would have been madness, we should be unable to advertise our coming and curiosity would be aroused; inevitably people would discover we had fled from Luton and some would assume we had brought the disease with us. So we had to sit it out and go, as planned, to Cambridge the following week. Our guess was that if we arrived when expected and kept our mouths shut it was unlikely that anyone would be interested in whence we came.

That, indeed, is just what happened. Undergrads in those days had more money and less work to do than now and, as during our first visit in 1930, they poured into the circus. Some had the idea that it would be fun to sit on the ground between the boxes and the ring fence and very soon the whole of this area was packed. By the next day they were trying to buy tickets that would permit them to sit in this space, but although we refused it was packed at every performance. We did not like this, for if a horse stumbled over the fence somebody could be hurt, but there was no way of preventing it so the situation which existed was the rather absurd one that what was not allowed was permitted. Nothing of this kind could ever happen in Germany for the *Feuerpolizei* would be called. I always have a feeling that the German national motto should be 'Everything is forbidden unless it is expressly permitted'.

By this time the landlady of my Cambridge days had a house opposite the circus site on Mid-Summer Common and during the build-up she and her elderly maid, who still wore starched cuffs and a little white cap perched on top of her head, sat at a window watching our every move. I had been what she called one of her 'young gentlemen' when any of us were about, but I suspect we were referred to as 'her boys' when we were not within earshot. She knew I had not over-exerted myself during my time at the university and was quite shocked to see that I was now capable of hard work. I drove tractors and helped the tent staff—I had to because we were having a serious labour shortage, particularly during the early weeks of each tour. We were a seasonal business and had to recruit and train several new men each spring.

Every evening when work ended one of these dear old ladies came over and said the other was running a hot bath and that a meal would be ready by the time I had bathed. They knew I could dine at the circus but felt they could do better—and indeed they did. We had not yet provided ourselves with caravans with bathrooms with hot and cold running water and it was nice to get inside some bricks and mortar when the alternative was a two-wheeled caravan at a time of year when the weather is unkind.

Leaving Cambridge we headed north and by the time we reached York we were in what to us was virgin territory and business improved in a way for which we had not dared to hope. During the second week in Newcastle-on-Tyne box office receipts were nearly double what they had been in any week during the previous two and a half seasons; in Edinburgh they were even higher. We began to feel the time was approaching when we could make what might be a costly experiment, but one which, if it were successful, could be of inestimable value in future. Our worry was that there were not enough big towns where we could stay a week or fortnight without having to visit them at too short intervals. If we could go to towns like Truro, Abergavenny and Kilmarnock for three days without losing a day for the move, there would be more than enough towns to make up a three year route.

We had originally planned to play a week in Perth, which had the smallest population of any town we were to visit in Scotland, and to miss Stirling; but here were two places in each of which we might play three days and they were only thirty-five miles apart. In 1967 it is easy to say only thirty-five miles, but in those days it seemed a frightening distance for a big show with heavy equipment to move by road. Nearly all the vehicles were still on solid rubber tyres and if a lorry averaged twelve miles an hour with a trailer it was doing fairly well. However, we decided the experiment had to be made as we wanted to know the result quickly so that we could plan the 1933 route, which was then full of holes that could be filled with a number of the smaller towns in Somerset, Devon and Cornwall where, once again, we should be opening up new territory.

We set about organising everything from the movements of the advance department to those of the circus on a three-day basis; there were snags galore, for even the billing unit could not cover two towns properly in one week. But this problem was not as serious as expected for our arrival in comparatively small places caused far bigger impact than we had dared to assume.

The receipts in Perth were larger than those in many towns where we had stayed a week the previous year and those in Stirling were still larger. The experiment had been an enormous success, but at the same time it had demonstrated that so long as we moved by road a mid-week move imposed a far greater strain on the working men than they could reasonably be expected to bear—other than occasionally. Between the end of the pull-down at about 3 a.m. and the start of the build-up at 7 a.m. the only sleep they could have was on the lorries as they travelled and that was not proper rest. There was an even bigger problem with the drivers, for a good deal of vehicle movement takes place on the last day; each vehicle has to be placed correctly for loading and, when loaded, it then has to be got on to the road—and that can involve a battle with a quagmire. On arrival the vehicles have to be placed in the right places so that nothing has to be carried far and when unloaded they must be taken to the parking area, with the result that the drivers were hard at it with practically no rest from one morning until the evening of the next day. The build-up had to be done much more quickly and therefore a larger staff was needed, but one of the worst factors was that journeys from town to town had to be undertaken in the dark. The drivers were in strange country and if they did not lose the way or end up in a ditch it was a matter of good luck.

The obvious answer was that we should have to travel by rail. I knew a little about this as during visits to the States I had watched the Ringling Circus being loaded and unloaded when travelling as the guest of John Ringling in his own coach, which was part of one of the four circus trains. John had discovered that the president of an American railroad was, as a matter of courtesy, allowed to have his private coach hauled free of charge on any railroad in the States and had provided himself with a magnificent affair with kitchen, complete with chef, sitting and dining rooms, four or five bedrooms and a bathroom. Whether it is true that he travelled free I cannot say, but I was told he bought a small railroad company which owned a few miles of track and made himself president of the company. I should hate to vouch for the story, but circus men often do curious things and I am tempted to believe the tale which has been told about Sanger, who was said to be so upset when Barnum brought an albino elephant to England and advertised it as 'white' that he white-washed one of his own elephants so that he could advertise the same thing.

In the course of time we, too, were lucky enough to find an albino elephant in Burma where some people regarded it as the reincarnation of Buddha. It appeared at Olympia and then we let Ringling have it, but for a limited period, as we had only obtained permission for it to leave Burma against a guarantee for a very large sum for its safe return.

The Ringling, Barnum and Bailey Circus seldom stayed more than one day in each town and an over-night jump of a hundred miles was regarded as normal. This, coupled with the evidence I had seen on the Continent where circuses play a seven day week without losing a day during a move, had convinced me that the only way to move fast was by rail. I had heard a few years earlier that the railway trucks which had been built specially for Barnum and Bailey were still in existence and believed to be lying somewhere near Stoke-on-Trent. However, after endless enquiries and many false clues I learned to my dismay that they had been cut up for scrap a few years before. At the Railway Clearing House I had better luck, for the Southern Railway had a number of trucks which had been built for carrying railway lines and had carried tanks during World War I.

All we should need in future would be a large fleet of trailers and enough tractors to take them to and from the stations, but railway technicians then gave me a lecture on Board of Trade Regulations. Each of our trailers would have to be secured on the truck with seven strands of rope at each corner and they thought it would take at least fifteen, and perhaps twenty, minutes to do each trailer. To load sixteen trailers would take five or six hours and the unloading another hour and a half, even in goods yards where shunting facilities were good.

At that time we were only thinking in terms of one special train to carry the heaviest loads in 1933, but we intended to move everything by rail in 1934 and there would therefore come a time when all the circus vehicles would be on rail and we should need three or four special trains.

The railways said they could not provide staff to load and unload the trains and that even if we did so, the work would take so long that we should move more quickly by road. It looked as if we were back at square one; all the rosy pictures of quick, safe and easy travel were shattered. The possibility of playing great numbers of small towns no longer existed—until a thought occurred to me. I had seen railway coaches coupled together and if whole trains could be safe with chains as couplings we ought to be able to secure our trailers in the same way.

All we needed was the same type of chain incorporating a screw device to tighten the chain and I rushed back to the railways to ask what they thought of the idea. They approved, but said the scheme would have to be submitted to the Board of Trade, though they would do their utmost to get approval as they wanted our traffic badly.

Within days the good news came; the railways agreed to provide trains and trucks, but we must load and unload and one of their inspectors would see our men did their work properly. The next thing was to produce the trailers; they could only be seven feet six inches wide and if no more than twenty-one feet six inches long we could load two on each truck. To pass the tunnel gauge the top of the load could only be seven feet six inches above the floor of the truck, so they had to be low-loaders and every known device had to be used to keep the loading platform as low as possible. The wheels must be as small as we dared make them, but not so small that they would be unable to move on very muddy ground and of course twin tyres were essential.

Those who were asked to quote were told they should design the vehicles as if they were going to war, rather than normal road haulage. When the prices and drawings reached us I considered Cranes of Dereham were offering by far the most rugged vehicles, but their price was the highest. It was my father's money, of which a large sum was to be spent, so of course he was consulted. The result was that Cranes got the order and we did something which has paid good dividends ever since, for all the trailers lasted until the end of the touring days of Bertram Mills Circus and, apart from paint and grease, they cost almost nothing to maintain.

That year we made one other change which was to produce big economies. The wooden undercarriage of the seating required a great deal of maintenance and kept a couple of carpenters busy nearly all the time, so it was replaced with steel sections which were no heavier, were mass produced and which could be welded easily and quickly if damaged. Another step had been taken in the modernisation of the circus and one which nobody else had thought of.

Glasgow was one of the last cities we visited in Scotland in 1932 and it was there that we had some anxious moments. We had brought the Great Wallendas, the best high wire act in the world, from the States for the 1931–2 winter season and had wanted to keep them for the summer, but they already had another contract so Karl, the head of the troupe, suggested we should take Willi, his brother, who had a similar act in Germany. In fact Willi's act was not as good as Karl's, but we took it because our tent enabled us to be the first to show acts of this kind working at a great height. Karl was meticulous about his rigging, but Willi was not and one day, as the fourth member of the troupe stepped from the rope ladder to the little platform at the end of the wire, the platform collapsed and four people were left scrambling to get hold of anything they could reach. Somehow they all managed to hang on by hands, legs or arms and nobody fell, but it was no use scolding Willi for he was a man who was sure everything would be all right in the future. Unfortunately, however, he was killed a few years later on the Continent. According to a newspaper report the wire had been attached to something not strong enough to take the high tension and that something broke while Willi was doing a trick and he and the wire crashed to the ground.

It was a condition of the contract that we should provide and drive the eighteen long stakes to which their wires were attached, but as we were always in a hurry on move nights they had to draw and load them. One night, just as the big top was about to be lowered, I heard a stake being driven. As this was a time for drawing rather than driving I went to see what was going on. A junior member of the troupe was busily driving our stakes, which cost fifteen shillings each, into the ground. I, rather meanly, let him continue until the last stake disappeared and he started to smooth the earth with his foot to cover evidence of his naughtiness and then I told him to go and get a spade and dig them all out—he was not to use the mechanical stake puller as it was needed to draw the stakes of the big top.

When I passed through New York on a war job in 1943, the Ringling Circus was playing Madison Square Garden, so of course I went. I knew my stake-driving friend had joined Karl after Willi's death but the Wallendas were all Germans originally and I was therefore a little surprised when he came to speak to me wearing something very unlike the German sailor costumes in which they had always worked. I could not resist the temptation to say they had changed their costumes pretty smartly when the States came into the war. His rather shocked reply was: 'Mr. Cyril, I am a Lieutenant in the United States Marines.'

When we started tenting in 1930 things were no better in the provinces than they had been in London in 1920. Circuses generally were not welcome and their credit rating was low; it was normal for tradesmen to insist on cash on delivery even for a loaf of bread, but by the time we had made a couple of tours we had established our credit to the point where it became difficult to get bills quickly and we needed them to ascertain our day to day expenses. During a visit to Edinburgh the man who had delivered the earth for the circus ring said we still owed for the earth supplied three years ago. To think we had owed a small man money for three years was shocking, but he cut my apologies short by saying: 'It's not your fault—I have never sent you a bill—I knew you would be back in three years.'

Low credit rating in the early years was not only embarrassing, but it had a serious effect on business. In London advance booking had grown to the point where it accounted for about fifty per cent of all seats sold, and of course we hoped to achieve the same sort of thing in the provinces. We had built an elaborate advance booking office which arrived on the site one or two weeks before the circus, but its takings did not pay the wage of the cashier. Who ever heard of advance booking for a circus and what guarantee was there that the show would ever arrive? The very fact that our coming was heralded by an expensive advertising campaign only made people more suspicious. They had been caught before; no circus that spent so much money advertising could possibly afford to pay a good programme as well.

As soon as the circus had been built up the horses, ponies,

zebras and elephants were walked from the station; no attempt was made to stage the type of street parade which had once been the fashion, but the fact that we had half a dozen elephants attracted big crowds along the route and many people followed the animals to the circus. As soon as the animals reached the stables the menagerie was opened and those who passed through it realised we had a good deal more to offer than they had expected and as they left the stables they could peep into the big top, where they saw something far more impressive than they had seen in any other circus. Even the big top itself looked a giant compared with any tent they had seen and soon there was a queue on the box office and the circus was in business in another town. Nevertheless, it was all very hard going during the first visit to each place, especially as we were concentrating on large centres of population to cut down mileage and the number of moves, for we had to rely to a great extent on word of mouth publicity which travels more slowly as the size of the town increases. If we had to wait for the effect of this kind of publicity it meant three days' bad business at the start of each week and business had to be very good during the last three days if we were to do more than just cover expenses. We therefore had to publicise the coming of the circus in every way both before and after its arrival; if we could ensure that everyone knew the show was in town we had achieved all we could hope for and if, knowing we were there, people did not come it was just too bad.

It is too easily overlooked that we had started tenting during the century's worst period of depression. The bottom had fallen out of the stock market in Wall Street and London and there were more unemployed than there have ever been since. To the masses even the cheapest seat meant going without something else and that something could be food. For many a working man with a wife and two or three children a visit to the circus was miles out of reach. On hundreds of occasions when the show was about to begin there were from one to two hundred of the poorest children in front of the entrance; they had come penniless, but hoping they might catch sight of strange animals, or perhaps a clown in make-up going from the dressing room to the big top. That sort of thing was more than many of us could stand and there must have been countless occasions when, with a half empty matinée house, either one of the managers or Bernard or I sneaked a bunch of these children in by a side entrance and let them see the show.

From the earliest days Father had entertained underprivileged children at the dress rehearsals at Olympia on the day before the opening. The Mayors of London boroughs allocated tickets to the children of men who were out of work and even to those whose fathers were in prison; all the big charitable institutions sent parties and in this way thirteen or fourteen thousand children were entertained, but the demand for seats always exceeded the supply, and we had to find seats for the overflow at public performances during the days before Christmas, so that there was some sort of Christmas outing for anything up to twenty thousand children who otherwise would have had none.

There were times when none of us could bear to go in the tent; with cripples and orphans it was one thing, but there were times when the circus was near a home for blind children. It may sound absurd to invite children who are blind to anything as essentially visual as a circus, but some of the children had a little sight left, even if only in one eye, and the teachers paired them with those who could see nothing. Before they came the teachers explained what a circus is and tried to give the children a mental picture of its geography, and during the show those who could see a little explained to the others what was happening and they did it so well that those with no sight at all could, with the aid of their hearing, follow the movements of people and animals in the ring. I watched this for a few moments one day, but was never able to enter the tent again on a similar occasion.

Chapter Five
The tigers escape
Fire in Gloucester

The year 1933 produced more than its share of worries. The trailers had been built to carry the heaviest equipment and the train was loaded at Ascot in the first days of April; the Board of Trade had had second thoughts and insisted that in addition to the four chains each trailer must have wooden chocks in front of, and behind, all the wheels—which even some of the railway people thought superfluous, but it had to be done. The train left just before dawn, as the haul was a short one to Guildford, and having seen it off I motored over to take care of the unloading. By the time it arrived about two hours late I was all but desperate with anxiety in case there had been a wreck. It crawled in at about two miles an hour; most of the chains were broken and in many cases only the wooden chocks were preventing the trailers rolling forward or backward into the spaces between the trucks.

Between them the guard and driver had nursed the train to its destination without damaging a thing, but how we should move to Reading in ten days' time was not at all obvious. It had taken months to make all the chains and now seventy new ones had to be made; but all the railway companies wanted our traffic and it just had to be done, and was.

Business in the small towns was excellent which was encouraging, for there were forty-one towns on the route compared with a maximum of thirty in previous years and by the time we reached Devonport for a ten-day stay we had just done five small towns in two and a half weeks, and were to have a little rest before tackling another string of seven three-day towns in Cornwall and Devon.

In the programme we had the wild animal trainer Togare, who by now had reached the peak of his career. He had been a 'find' of mine, for in 1928 I was asked to produce a lion trainer at short notice for Carmo when he was in Ireland and it was Togare that I brought over from the Continent. He was a big success with Carmo and again when he appeared with Carmo's lions at Olympia a little later; his approach to his work was different to that of others and with his exotic make-up and costume and an infectious ring personality he had become the glamour boy of the circus. I always felt the public, especially the female section, was far more interested in the man than the lions.

In the meantime, he had bought a group of young tigers with his savings and had trained them and it was only to be expected he would devise some new way of presenting them. Instead of entering the ring by a door adjoining the animal tunnel beneath the bandstand he used two gilded doors on the opposite side. Two employees of his, also in magnificent oriental costumes, stood to open the doors when he made his entrance escorted by a bevy of girls. The way in which the tigers entered was also unusual and spectacular for, having passed through the tunnel, they climbed a ramp and then jumped down into the ring through the mouth of what looked like a huge Chinese dragon.

One evening in Devonport I was standing inside the main entrance watching the last few members of the audience arrive when Togare walked past me but having my back to the ring did not see him enter. A minute later one of the usherettes shouted: 'Mr. Cyril, look what's happened!' I turned and to my horror saw three tigers walking towards me and they were all fully grown ones. The cage door was wide open and on the far side of the ring Togare was bringing the fourth tiger from the mouth of the dragon with his back turned to the dreadful situation on our side.

In moments like this it is anybody's guess how people will behave. Whether my action was foolhardy, or just stupid, I don't know, but for some reason which I have never understood the one thing I did not feel was fear. Bravery can be ruled right out, for it involves the capacity to recognise danger and to overcome the fear which it produces. If faced with a similar situation today I should run as fast as I could, but in this case I opened my arms as if to indicate the way was barred and made some kind of 'Sch' noise, which I suppose was to persuade the tigers to turn and go back to the cage. Of course none of them got the message! One made his way to the stables, hoping to be able to get back into the wagon, but found that impossible and went and lay under a caravan. The second walked slowly up a gangway towards an exit; all would have been well, but for the fact that a woman took fright and stepped into the gangway hoping to reach the exit first. Had she kept her seat as others did nothing would have happened, but the tiger also wanted to be first and she received a nasty scratch and had to go to hospital.

It has always amazed me that the audience seemed to regard tigers walking about in their midst as a perfectly normal thing. Certainly we were running a big and well-equipped circus and we may have been doing most things in a more business-like way than they had been done in other shows, but it was surprising that the public should be so confident of the hands it was in, that it should accept such a state of affairs without anxiety.

We knew where two tigers were, but were still one short and feared it might have strayed into the street where, if it was not captured quickly, the police would have every right to shoot it. Fortunately we carried about four hundred yards of portable fencing with which to enclose the sites we occupied and if anything was worth its weight in gold that fencing was, for the third tiger was found walking along inside it being stroked by people standing on the side-walk. Getting the other two tigers back to the wagons was fairly easy for all we had to do was surround the caravans under which they lay with spare pieces of fencing and leave them there until we could return with a moving den (a strong wooden box with a barred door used for moving animals from one cage to another). Dealing with the tiger near the road was a very different matter, for we had to be careful not to scare the animal away while we formed a ring of men around it and we had to plead with members of the public to remain quiet and still. A safety net, which would be used later in the performance for the high wire act, was fetched, but none of us had had any experience like this before and we were not at all sure how to get the net over the tiger without frightening it into jumping into the road and going into the centre of the town.

With men on three sides of the net we approached as quietly and slowly as possible and when the tiger was covered the net was dropped quickly. The poor animal was scared by this and began to fight and we were worried lest the wooden fencing which formed the fourth side of the enclosure would hold. Once the animal threw itself at the fence with all its 450 lbs and there were sickening creaks as the wood cracked, but nothing broke and we were able to get the net round the tiger on all four sides so that it was pinned down. The next thing was to get the net under as well as over the animal, but in this its struggle to free itself helped and inch by inch the net was wrapped round the body until we could carry it back to the menagerie.

During all this the ring cage had been dismantled and the performance had continued and the question now was whether the tigers should appear at this performance or not. Once back in their wagons the tigers were as quiet as usual and Togare walked back and forth in front of the cages stroking them and giving them scraps of meat. He had kept in the background while the animals were recaptured, as he did not want them to associate him with the break in normal routine, and he assured us that when things had been restored to normal for about an hour they would forget and he would have no trouble with

them. So the cage was rebuilt and the tiger act ended the performance and Togare received the kind of ovation usually
reserved for home-coming heroes. Indeed he showed courage
in going through the act so soon after such a major upset, but in
doing so he displayed the knowledge which is inherent in dedicated trainers; the sooner the animals got back to normal routine the better. If there were any heroes about they were the
electricians, lorry drivers, grooms and tentmen who, never having had anything to do with wild animals, came forward to help
catch the tigers without thought of their own safety so that an
accident should not become a tragedy.

Late that night I had Togare on the mat and reminded him
that his employees were responsible for closing the doors; it was
his job to see they did theirs and if anything of the same kind
happened again he would have to look for a new employer.
Events of this nature are highly damaging for they destroy the
confidence of the public and produce sensational stories in the
press. That evening and again the following morning we were
headline news; one paper said 'Tiger hunt in the streets of
Devonport' and there was the usual crop of eye-witnesses'
accounts of what they saw or thought they had seen. The over-
all effect of the event was exactly what we expected; business
fell off in Devonport and I am convinced our receipts suffered
for several weeks, after which time people were able to forget.

In September we were in Gloucester and our site adjoined
a football ground with a wooden grandstand. The day after
the opening everybody went about his normal business until
about three o'clock in the afternoon, when we heard the one
word which every circus man fears more than any—FIRE.
Here we were, in the centre of a big city in 1933, and in spite
of all the precautions we always took an alarm had been raised.
The ground was a small one and the tents and vehicles were
packed together between the grandstand and the other side of
the site. In fact the circus was not on fire, but the grandstand
was and the local fire brigade had been summoned by telephone. It seems that earlier in the year hay had been mown
and stacked under the tiered seating and now some work was
being done in preparation for the football season. Perhaps

somebody smoked, but by the time the fire brigade arrived the grandstand was a blazing inferno; some of our lorries were on fire and the stable tents with horses, ponies, zebras, elephants and wild animals were threatened seriously.

Everyone grabbed an animal or two and led them into the road; fortunately there was a large playground surrounded by an iron fence on the opposite side so all the animals were turned loose there. In the meantime drivers took tractors to the stable tent and towed the wild animal wagons to safety. But another danger exised, for some of the closed lorries, being between the big top and the grandstand, were forming a bridge over which the fire was creeping. It only had to reach one petrol tank and the whole circus would go up in flames.

Drivers were now asked to move these lorries into the street to break the bridge, for although we had a great number of fire extinguishers, all but a few had been used. A few burnt out lorries did not matter and what fire extinguishers remained must be used to try to save the tents and seating. It is bad enough to drive a lorry through a sheet of flame, but far worse when the vehicle is on fire and the petrol tank likely to explode at any moment and at such a time nobody could be blamed if he or she acted on the *Sauve qui peut* principle. But from top to bottom of the circus family there was but one thought; save the animals at all costs and then if possible save the circus.

While the lorries were being moved I saw a large brown patch on the roof of the big top. Scorching, of course, and it meant that the tent could burst into flames at any time. A fireman nearby was directing his hose to the grandstand; the effect was about as useful as it would be to spit in the ocean to raise the level of the water and I asked him to give the big top a drenching to prevent further damage, but as the tent was not on fire he was not interested. A slight argument followed and I eventually had my own way. When we examined the scorched parts later they were as ripe as old bananas and it is almost certain that if the scorching had been allowed to continue the whole circus would have been destroyed.

When the animals were caught not one had a scratch but some of the lorries looked pretty sad although they were still runners. Then we found the harness room trailer in the road; the side of the body was burned, but a fire extinguisher appeared to have done a good job until we opened the doors. Rugs and harness, starved for air, were smouldering, but burst into flames as the doors were opened and there was nothing left worth salvaging. Fortunately, however, all the best harness and rugs had been hanging in the stable tent and were undamaged.

One would expect the resulting mess and disorganisation to be the cause of a lot of lost time but everyone worked like slaves to clear up and although we missed the matinée we opened punctually in the evening.

The newspapers made headline news of the fire, but they were kind to us for the circus itself had not been on fire and everybody seemed to realise that the trouble was not of our making and that all those connected with the circus had done a good job. I also am sure that was the case, for I know that two of the wives of artistes were in town shopping when they heard the circus was on fire; they could so easily have taken the safe course and gone for coffee, but they ran back and were among those who took animals to safety.

Never again was the circus threatened by fire, but my father decided we should have our own fire brigade and ordered a fire engine to be built; its presence produced an amusing sequel a year or two later. The circus was on a common during a hot spell and somebody set fire to the gorse about five hundred yards away. We were in no danger, but thought it our duty to do something until the local fire brigade arrived.

Our engine was driven by the duty fireman, but for the rest the crew was composed of any bodies that were handy and one of these was a cook in chef's cap, white jacket and apron. He looked as if he belonged in an old film comedy, but even more stupid when he returned smeared from head to foot with water, mud and soot. The fire was put out in about four minutes, which was just how long it took the locals to arrive in a machine which had cost the ratepayers a packet and which was on its first outing. We were not popular with the local crew, who turned tail without saying a word and left us to roll, dry and clean the two hundred yards of hose we had used. We thought they could at least have offered to hang it to dry on their mast, but circus people have to learn to be self-sufficient and we put up some poles and dried it ourselves.

That season we had a unique act. Arturo Manzano, the Spanish High School rider, had persuaded us to let him have and train four young steers and they did a short version of the kind of act Liberty horses do, but the act did not last long. The steers soon became bulls and bulls will be bulls. Although farmers put rings through their noses it would never do for a circus to do that sort of thing and as our bulls became unmanageable they had to go to a cattle market—presumably for beef.

As the move over to rail transport was to be completed the following season a large order for more trailers was placed with Cranes and since the petrol electric lorries which produced the show's current could not travel by train they were replaced by modern diesel generators.

A couple of years earlier Father had been to Poland and had engaged Charlie Mroczkowski as a permanent horse trainer. He had bought sixteen very beautiful young Anglo-Arab horses for him to train, so we no longer had to find horse acts for any of our programmes. At the same time he had bought a big horse of the kind which some people call a Palomino and others an Isabella. It was an animal of outstanding appearance, but had never worked because it had not been possible to find a match and a one-horse act was not considered important enough. At about this time Father was in Warsaw again and from his bedroom in the hotel he saw exactly what he wanted drawing a milk cart. He dashed down but, speaking no Polish, could do no more than make a note of the name on the cart. With that and an interpreter he went to see the owner and offered a big price, but it meant nothing until translated into zloty and then had to be increased. The first offer had been so good that the owner probably realised he had a customer who was willing to buy at any price. When the horse arrived in England he and the other one were such a perfect match they were named Castor and Pollux and were the first to do a routine with traffic lights.

If rail travel was the perfect answer for heavy circus equipment it was not such a joy for those of us who travelled in two-wheel caravans on loose-coupled trucks hauled by goods engines manned by goods drivers. Many of these men had never handled anything but freight and gave us some very rough rides. It was Arthur Sowler, the Master of Horse, who stuck his head out of the window one morning and, having hurled a stream of abuse at the driver, told him the journey had been like being hauled over cobble stones on square wheels; the fact that the driver was 150 yards away at the other end of the train did not matter—the complaint had been aired.

When I took over Schumann's job at Olympia I had been booking acts but as time went on this work fell to me much more and it was fortunate that I knew enough French and German to make my way round, and even negotiate contracts with people who spoke no English; but my knowledge of other languages was very small and this was a handicap. On one occasion, when I was trying to book a Hungarian, I had to enlist the help of a Czech, but as he spoke no German, French or English I had to find a German who spoke Czech and could tell me in his own tongue what the Hungarian was saying through the Czech. Travelling was not as easy then, for there were comparatively few airline services and, as I had to go to places large and small to find the circuses, I had to do most of my mileage by train and that bored me.

I have always enjoyed ski-ing, for it provides thrills of the kind I got with motor bicycles when at Cambridge, but at best I could only ski for a couple of weeks each year, so in 1933 I decided to take up flying for fun. There were snags as usual, for I was sure every member of the family would disapprove and I was spending nearly all my time with the circus in summer. I therefore had to find time without being missed at the circus or by the family.

The frequency with which the number thirteen keeps cropping up is extraordinary. We lost Willy Schumann during the thirteenth season, the circus ring is thirteen metres and I had my first flying lesson the 13th May at Stag Lane, a tiny aerodrome where every landing had to be just right to miss the houses during the approach and avoid running into the hedge on the far side. By October 13th I had done thirteen hours' dual control flying and moved to Hatfield, where I was lucky to become the pupil of Geoffrey de Havilland, a brilliant pilot and one of the most charming men I ever met. Having instruction spread over such a long period it was easy to forget the last lesson by the time I had the next and the Gipsy I Moths had to live through some rough landings even though I managed not to break anything. It looked as if it would be months before I should be safe to go solo, but during my second lesson after a couple of passable landings Geoffrey climbed out of the aircraft in the middle of the aerodrome and told me to go it alone.

I had watched several other first solos and noted the anxiety on the faces of instructors who had authorised them—one man was so sure he would crash he stayed up until his petrol tank was almost empty so that the fire resulting from the crash would be a small one. Having all this in mind I decided to put Geoffrey out of his misery quickly and my circuit lasted just four minutes. I then made fairly rapid progress and by the time I had done eighteen and a quarter hours I had my 'A' licence and was supposed to be fit to go anywhere in that type of aircraft, although I had had no instruction in navigation. The only other instruction I ever had was in aerobatics, which was more for fun than anything.

I bought a second-hand Gipsy I Moth for £250, but soon tired of the scenery round Hatfield and wanted to stretch my wings. The first trip was to Kettering and back, during which I did a couple of circuits over my parents' home at Chalfont St. Giles. It all seemed too easy for words.

The family now had to be told and the news was accepted moderately well, although Mother was sure I should kill myself and was even more convinced a few days later when I landed in a small field within sight of her house, but having started in a very small aerodrome I knew what space I needed and this knowledge was useful later when I followed the circus round Britain, landing alongside the big top whenever the ground was large enough.

My first long distance trip was also my first business flight, as I went to Blackpool to see the Tower Circus. During the show the manager asked whether I would like him to book me a room for the night and when I said I was flying back to London directly after the show he assumed I had chartered a plane, and was playing the millionaire circus man. When I said I was piloting my own aircraft there was amazement, for there were few private flyers then and I was the first circus man either to own or fly one. He drove me to the airport, but had tipped off the local press and I was met by photographers and reporters and very soon became known in the circus world as the 'Flying Director'.

Chapter Six
Loch Ness Monster and the Indian Rope Trick
Searching for talent

One July morning in 1934 a headline in the *Daily Mail* gave me a shock: 'Bertram Mills offers £20,000 for the Loch Ness Monster.' By the time I had read what followed my father was on the telephone, wanting me to insure the risk with which he had landed himself. He told me he had read something about a monster in Loch Ness in a Glasgow paper the night before and had telephoned the Editor of the *Daily Mail*, who was a friend. During the General Strike the *Mail* had printed a one-sheet paper in Paris, had flown it to Lympne and the Mills family had helped bring it to London by car. We also had excellent relations with the *Daily Mail* because they followed us at Olympia each year with the *Ideal Home* Exhibitions and we were often able to help each other.

No doubt this relationship had something to do with the editor's readiness to make big news of the offer, for few people could have heard of the monster then, and I doubt whether anyone had taken the possibility of its existence seriously. My job was to make sure the publicity did not cost £20,000, so I contacted Fred Hearn who handled all our insurance and he in turn went to Lloyds. Several leading underwriters listened patiently and then said they were very busy and would be glad if he would go and play somewhere else. By noon the evening papers had taken up the story and some underwriters were assuming there was a monster, and that it might be caught, but it was not till late on the second day that one was willing to give the policy a start. Thereafter it was fairly easy going, but the policy, which I think would have cost a fiver before the offer was made, was marked with a £100 premium and with the aid of the editors of two national newspapers and two fellows of the Zoological Society we produced a definition of the monster which read: 'An animal and/or reptile and/or fish either hitherto unknown or believed to be extinct, measuring not less than twenty feet in length or weighing not less than one thousand pounds.'

That sounded fair and meant nobody could land us with a dolphin or sealion, but the hunt was on and one newspaper published a photo which could have been of anything from a submerged whale to a shadow on the water. Whether there is a monster is anyone's guess, but it became a big tourist attraction and I have spoken to one Provost of Inverness and his wife who both assured me they have seen it. So far as I am concerned it goes into the same pigeon hole as the Indian Rope Trick. I will believe it when I see it. For me the most interesting thing is the Lloyds policy, which my father allowed me to put in my collection.

Mention of the Indian Rope Trick reminds me that we once offered £10,000 to anyone who could do it in the ring at Olympia but we did not insure as we doubted whether there would be any takers, and were surprised when we had a letter from a man offering to give us a demonstration. I went to Plymouth station where I was met by two rather unsavoury characters who took me in their car up on to the edge of Dartmoor. I rejected the cigarettes they offered as I did not want to go home having agreed to pay £10,000 for a trick which was no more than a hallucination. Eventually the car turned down a narrow Devonshire lane and stopped in a small wood. From there we walked along a winding footpath at the end of which was

F

a clearing about a hundred feet wide and squatting in the middle of it was a man who looked like an Indian and wore oriental costume. There were three other spectators, one of whom I knew, as he was a director of an important newspaper group, and they were as surprised to see me as I was by their presence for we both thought we were the only ones in the know.

Next we were handed a piece of rope about eighteen feet long, which I examined carefully from end to end to be quite sure it had not been doctored. It was then carried down the slope and one end was given to the Indian and the other laid out where we could see it, and I was pretty sure there had been no hocus pocus so far. The Indian started to feed his end of the rope under a rug which was draped over his knees and as the visible part shortened there came up from beneath the rug a corresponding length of rope which went straight up in the air.

Ever since leaving the car I had wondered why it was necessary for us to come to this spot; there must be something here which could not be found in anybody's back yard in Plymouth. The trees were suspicious, as a wire might be stretched between high ones, but having long sight I was sure this was not the answer. By the time the rope had risen to a height of about five feet I was quite sure it was not the one I had handled; my days with the circus had taught me a little about ropes and the twist of this one was not the same. Then I noticed that the soil on which we stood was light and sandy and knew immediately why we had been brought here. The sandy soil would enable them to sink a six inch diameter tube and the next step would be to wind a rope round a steel rod and drop it into the tube.

My newspaper friends seemed well impressed; they had not spotted the different twist in the substituted rope, but I had to tell them the trick was worthless. All I told the Indian's manager was that he would have to go through about seven feet of concrete if he tried to do the trick at Olympia and that closed the matter, but I have always wondered whether or not something along these lines may have been done in India. If the substitute rope had been wound round the rod correctly the truth would have been anything but obvious, but this does not answer how the small boy who is supposed to climb the rope disappears in a cloud of smoke.

During 1934 and 1935 we added so much to our rail-borne traffic that almost everything travelled by rail, although the artistes continued to move their caravans behind their cars. The 1936 programme was a strong one which included Tiebor's Sealions and Bombayo, the Indian slack-rope walker, both of which had been brought from America, and, for the first time, the six baby elephants we bought from Hagenbeck the year before. The route took us along the South Coast and, having been in Bournemouth for nine days, we were ready to move on a Saturday night when a gale sprang up during the matinée. It had reached force eight by the time the evening show was half over and we were in a park where there were neither houses nor trees to afford protection. However, we had gone through this sort of thing before and decided to carry on, although the velocity of the wind seemed to be increasing all the time. The bare-back act was working and the show due to end in about six minutes when a gust hit the tent with the force of a cannon-ball. It had been raining earlier so the canvas was tented out as tight as a drum, but something had to go and the roof was rent from the ridge to the sidepoles. As Kral had said at Southsea five years before, 'Nothing to do', and the band played the National Anthem. But we had a job in getting people to leave the tent as they wanted to stay and see what we should do about it. Within a few minutes the roof looked like shredded wheat and there was the usual mess to clear up, but by 4 a.m. the last train had been loaded and, as we were now carrying a spare roof, we re-opened on time in Bognor on the Monday. The blow-down could not have happened at any other time without costing at least one performance.

My searches for talent have produced a mixture of finds, frustrations and flops. At times they have been rewarding, but the job is hard work when the novelty has worn off, especially so when what you are looking for does not exist and you have to make do with something which you know is second best. I was still depending on public transport, but by May 1936 I had over two hundred hour's solo flying in my log book and, having followed the circus from Penzance to Inverness, decided to go further afield. I had sold the open Gipsy I Moth and Father had given me a single-engined cabin de Havilland Hornet, so flying had become comfortable; flying suits and goggles were no longer needed.

My first flight abroad took me to Rotterdam, Hamburg, Copenhagen, Berlin, Düsseldorf, Cologne, Brussels, Paris and Caen and lasted only nine days, during which I saw as many circuses and did what would have taken sixteen days by any other means. In those days the *Plaza* and *Winter Garten* Theatres in Berlin were good sources of talent, for their stages were so large that almost any circus act could work on them and the competition between them was so fierce they always had the best and most expensive acts. They changed their programmes each month, so by spending two days there at the end of each second month I could see four first class shows— and this I had done for a long time. By the end of the year I had been to Berlin three times and flights to France, Holland and Switzerland had become routine affairs. During the year I covered seventeen thousand miles in the Hornet with only one mishap. Having left Prague one evening in July I was headed for Vienna and had been told the weather would be good, but after an hour I ran into a much worse thunder storm than we see in this country. I had not flown to Vienna before, but the map showed that my only chance of finding it without radio in conditions of such bad visibility was to make for the Danube, upstream from the city, and follow it, so that I avoided the fairly high hills on either side at the point where it turns south about ten miles before the aerodrome. When I reached the river I was down to less than a hundred feet; it was nearly dark and as I could barely see through the windscreen I knew I was in a tight spot. When the Danube turned south I knew I was on the straight run home and then I had a ghastly thought. There were the bridges of course and I could fly over them, but I remembered having seen high tension cables crossing the river and I had no idea how high they were. If I went high enough to be sure to miss them I should be in cloud, should lose the river and would not even know when it was safe to come lower. The only sensible thing to do was get my feet on the ground as quickly as possible and wait for the storm to pass. The east side of the river was the flatter, and therefore the most hopeful, and within half a minute I saw what I was looking for—almost praying for—a huge green field where a forced landing would be a piece of cake.

Having flown over it twice at a height of ten or twelve feet to be sure it really was flat and had no ditches I came round the third time to land. The aircraft settled down nicely, ran five or six yards and then did a forward somersault. I had landed in a cornfield and the corn was 'as high as an elephant's eye' and the wheels of the machine were too small to run through it.

The people of Stockerau were soon on the spot with offers of every kind of help including a car to take me to hospital, as I had a nasty cut on my head, but it stopped bleeding quickly and my concern was to get the aircraft to Vienna to have it repaired. Fortunately there was a de Havilland agent there and by noon the next day he had taken the plane by road to the aerodrome and had arranged for spare parts to be flown out, so I continued my journey to Budapest, Belgrade, Sofia and Bucharest by commercial airlines. When I returned a week later my machine was ready, but when I asked if it had been test flown the answer was : 'No. You must do that yourself.' By the time I landed in England after that trip I had done over 3,000 miles and my reward was one act which I found in Budapest.

My father was much luckier when he made a quick trip to Spain in 1924 and found Charlie Rivels; he was working with his brothers in the family circus owned by his father and his best act was a parody of a flying trapeze act, in which he dressed and acted like Charlie Chaplin did at that time. It was the funniest act I have ever seen, but when my father tried to book it the old man was hurt. The salary offered was £120 per week which, at that time, was a fair one for a little-known act but instead of grabbing it with both hands the old man said : 'Mr. Mills, you are a big director from London and you should not make a joke at my expense, for you know that is far more than I earn with my whole circus.'

A contract was signed and within a short time Charlie had become one of the highest paid circus artistes in the world. Such is the road to stardom, for even as long ago as this a Bertram Mills contract was looked upon as the blue riband of the circus and anyone who had appeared at Olympia was assured of a long run of good contracts. When Charlie appeared at Olympia for about the sixth time just before the war I thought I had done well to get his signature at about seven times the salary his father had thought too much. Charlie and his brothers also produced some very funny clown *entrées*—their father had created a character for each one and they made a splendid team, but in recent years they split up and formed three separate troupes and things have never been quite the same. They all took new partners who tried to step into parts which were not created for them and in some cases the result was not very successful.

By the time Charlie had reached the star salary bracket he was accompanied wherever he went by a tutor and a music teacher for his children with the result that Paulina—who married Albert Schumann and who has been largely responsible for converting the wonderful Schumann horse acts into magnificent spectacles—and her brothers play several musical instruments, speak almost every European language and can calculate salaries in any currency as quickly as a computer.

A contract of quite another kind was signed in 1927 with a man named Wall, who swam in a huge tank with half a dozen crocodiles. The act was offered by an agent who booked for the two other London circuses and for once my father broke his rule and booked it without seeing it. His publicity people were excited about it and it sounded too good to miss—or perhaps too good for a competitor to have—and it was plugged hard in the press hand-outs.

Getting the tank and its four tons of water into and out of the ring took three minutes, so the show lost momentum, and the wheels made deep ruts which had to be filled before others could use the ring. Even if what Wall did was sensational and unusual it was difficult to see through inch thick glass and water and the act was as big a flop as I remember.

This booking emphasised how essential it is for an act which has been given the full treatment by the publicity boys to live up to what the public has been led to expect of it. In this case everyone had been led, albeit innocently, to expect a sensation and they just didn't get one.

I was more fortunate in 1937 when I found Koringa, 'the only female fakir in the world', working in a small circus on the Continent. I had had one disappointment after another and by the time the winter programme was complete I was not at all happy about it, even though it contained King Tuffy, the first wire-walking lion, which was coming from the States. It had always been our policy to project the Bertram Mills image in preference to anything else in all our advertising and publicity; acts were just part of the show and their names were usually unknown and did not matter. Posters were made to be symbolical of circus and the only name that mattered was Bertram Mills. If either Cyril or Bernard Mills had a mention in a paper nobody would know who they were unless their names were coupled with the circus; they belonged in the background and liked being there.

In the autumn, however, I suggested to Father and to Bernard, who was in charge of all publicity, that there should be a change in policy. I thought I had a real 'find' in Koringa and asked that she should be given the kind of treatment the seventy lions had had twelve years ago. If Koringa was the success I hoped she would be, she might carry a programme in which I had too little faith. My request was granted and in due course London was flooded with advertisements which said Koringa as loudly as they said Bertram Mills Circus. After the dress rehearsal Father made only one comment on the programme: 'I would never have booked Koringa but I think she will be a success.' And indeed she was; within hours he asked me to negotiate a contract for the three following summers and he wanted it done quickly, for her success would mean other circuses would be after her at any moment.

At the dress rehearsal I as nearly came unstuck as I ever

wish to be. After playing with giant pythons Koringa mesmer- ised fully grown crocodiles into immobility without touching them. She then had a granite paving stone broken with four- teen pound sledge hammers while it lay on her chest; this was followed by rolling with a naked back on a heap of freshly broken glass, and walking up a ladder of swords with bare feet. For her last trick she was buried in sand; when I saw this done on the Continent it had lasted twenty minutes, which was far too long, although it was helped along by someone who described Koringa's background over the loud-speakers. I had cut this part to five minutes which I thought long enough to convince people she was not just holding her breath. When her manager arrived at the ring entrance I asked for the script of what had to be said; I was prepared for something in a foreign language which, being cut and translated roughly, would pass at a rehearsal, but it was a shock when he said there was no script and that I should have to make one up. That, apparently, had been done elsewhere, but the thought of con- cocting something out of whole cloth and palming it off on a London audience was shocking and to make matters worse several press men were present.

As the trick began I took the microphone and started. 'Ko- ringa was born in Bikaner in the heart of India and at an early age she was given to the fakirs. . . .' The rest escapes me, but I kept going for the full five minutes, at the end of which I was in a cold sweat for I realised that I had done something for which I might have sacked anyone else and, worse still, some- thing of the same kind would be needed at the opening the next day and I had only the vaguest recollection of what I had said.

I was saved by my private secretary, Connie, who later mar- ried our post-war ringmaster Tony Yelding and who, when her children reached boarding school age, came back and re- mained my private secretary as long as I had anything to do with the circus. She was sitting behind me with a stop watch, timing the acts, and had taken down every word I had said.

After the rehearsal I dashed to my office to study a map of

India to see if there was a place called Bikaner and, if so, whether it was in the heart of India. To my relief I had scored two bull's-eyes, although I have never known how or when I ever heard of the place.

The script was used at every performance in London and the provinces and I made sure that Koringa had, and learned, a copy in her own language, so that she could play her part at interviews.

I could not let Koringa do that part of her act in which she stuck large needles into her body without bleeding, as it is not the sort of thing on which British audiences thrive and is most unsuitable for children. I do not believe in the supernatural and therefore regard these things as tricks, or illusions, but knowing how they are done is embarrassing if questions are asked, so I never made any attempt to find out. Koringa had appendicitis when she had been with us about a year and her doctor struck a bargain with the surgeon to be allowed to witness the operation and when it was over he told me Koringa bled 'just like a human being' wherever the knife touched. That left me as much in the dark as anyone else.

Fortunately nobody ever asked a question about the Koringa script, so I have been able to keep the secret until now.

There are many ways to get a circus programme together; the easiest is to give the job to an agent and take whatever he offers, or wants to get rid of, and pay whatever he asks; the hardest is to see all that is available; that means seeing all the European circuses each year and going to the States every year or two. Europe produces the majority of circus acts and the States is one of the biggest consumers except where 'thrill' acts are concerned, for there is a big market for these at State Fairs where it is quite normal to see six or seven of these acts in one show. The sky is the limit for every thrill act and it is only reached when there is no more room for the guy wires which support the rigging. On one occasion I saw a couple do a jitterbug dance on a platform two feet square on top of a steel pole 120 feet high swaying in the wind. The first few seconds were as much as I could stomach and I did not book the act, although other performers told me the man and his wife were quite safe and it did not worry them if they had to work in a rain storm.

Another of my 'finds' was Rudi Horn, the German boy, who was the first to throw half a dozen tea-cups and saucers, catch them on his head, and then add a lump of sugar and a tea-spoon for good measure. He was doing it standing on the ground and I was not much impressed, but after the show his father asked me if I would be interested if he did it on a uni-cycle. Indeed I would and we made a gentleman's agreement that I was to have the first option on the act as soon as it was ready.

About seven months later the father wrote to say the trick was ready and I went to see it at once; a contract was signed, but before that happened I had to fight off the efforts of some agent who wanted to take him over, even though he had only found him a few days before. Rudi played one winter and three summers with us; since then he has played almost every top-ranking establishment in the world and is still one of the highest paid circus artistes. His tea-cup trick has been copied by people who have done it on tight topes, slack ropes and unsupported ladders; but nobody has done it as well, although I am convinced it is more difficult to do on a uni-cycle than on any other apparatus.

When he was at Olympia, Rudi had a lot of fun in the fair, for some of the concessionaires were giving cigarettes, which were in short supply, as prizes and where throwing balls or hoops was concerned he could win nineteen times out of twenty, so twenty cigarettes only cost him sixpence, until it was realised who he was and then he was barred from every game in the fair.

If you go about finding talent the hard way it helps to have friends all over the world and I soon saw the possibility of creating a chain of people who would give me a tip whenever they saw a good new act. Circus owners do not boast about their 'finds' to competitors, but there are circus lovers everywhere and they spot anything new quickly and can therefore be very useful. Among those upon whom I could rely for information were people in almost every walk of life who had two things in common—a love of the circus and a desire to help us to produce good programmes.

Before the war my private eye in Paris was an antique dealer, but during the last twenty years I have relied on Jacques Fort, one of the most wide-awake fans I have ever met, and it was from him that I received an urgent message one day. I must go to Paris at once to see a new aerial act that had only been working three days; but we were in the middle of an Olympia season, so I replied that I could not go over before the week-end.

Jacques met me at Le Bourget and my first question was: 'Are you sure Johnny has not booked them?' I knew that John Ringling North had been in Paris for ten days and was looking for talent for the Ringling, Barnum and Bailey Circus and it seemed certain he would have got in before me.

During the first half of the show Jacques asked all his friends whether J.R.N. had been to the circus. They all said he had not and the owner confirmed this, but I still felt insecure. When I saw the act I wanted it badly and asked Jacques to arrange a meeting with the head of the troupe directly after the show. Just before midnight we went to the hotel and the business of bargaining began but I was in a difficult position. When an act has worked in other circuses it is possible to know the kind of salary it commands simply by knowing in which circuses it has worked, but in this case there was no such yardstick. Also the head of the troupe knew that Johnny was in Paris and that that meant the possibility of a long engagement in the States at a big salary in dollars. It was nearly five o'clock in the morning when the contract was signed.

As I was due to fly back to London to be there for the Monday matinée I took three hours' sleep and then telephoned Johnny and said I was going round for breakfast at his expense. He was an old friend and going to Paris without seeing him was unthinkable. He asked me what I was doing in Paris and I said I had come over to see whether there were any good acts about. Of course he asked: 'Are there?' to which I could only reply: 'There was one until about four hours ago, but I have taken it on a three year contract.' When I said I had booked the De Riaz he was disappointed, but took it well; he had realised I was a potential buyer, but had not thought I would leave London during an Olympia season and did not know I had a good source of information in Paris. He had therefore gone about his other business first, or may even have delayed his visit to the circus so as not to appear too keen.

One of the worst trips I ever made was to Belgium, Holland and France during the winter of 1945. The morning after my arrival in Brussels I went to the *Cirque Royal* where the Strassburger Circus was playing. It was about noon and Karl Strassburger was exercising a dozen Friesian horses in semi-darkness, as the use of ring lighting was forbidden except during performances. As I walked through the main entrance and towards the ring Karl stood still, dropped his hands and let the horses get jumbled up. Wilke, the ringmaster, pointed towards me and there was dead silence. I had no idea what was wrong, but as nobody spoke I too remained silent just to be in step with everybody else. Everybody in the circus was staring at me, so eventually I felt I had to do something and called out, 'Hello, Karl.'

The spell was broken and they all came forward to shake my hand, explaining they thought they had been seeing a ghost. They all knew I had been a pilot before the war and had assumed I would go into the R.A.F.; but in 1940 some chair-borne Group Captain had said that at thirty-eight years of age I was far too old for any job off the ground. I suppose someone named Mills was shot down near a circus, that the name got out, someone assumed I was involved and started a rumour that I had been killed and this had spread through all the continental circuses.

Before leaving England I had sent a note to H. J. Lijsen, an old pre-war friend and private eye, and had asked him to meet me at The Hague. He too had heard the story and had assumed he had confused names and that it was Bernard who would visit him. When he arrived my appearance shocked him as it had done those in Brussels and he was in no shape to be shocked, for he was an elderly man and had walked the five miles as his bicycle was beyond repair. During the latter stages of the war he had worked in a Town Hall, where his salary was probably a pittance, and had often ridden twenty miles out and twenty miles back after work to get three or four pounds of potatoes for his wife and himself. Before going to the circus at Scheveningen we had a big chicken lunch in the best restaurant—I am sure it was the first decent meal he had had for months—and before leaving I promised to send him a bicycle from England. That sounded simple, but it took three months and endless form-filling; officials seemed to be convinced that, on account of the small amount of foreign currency I had been allowed, I had incurred some debt which the bicycle would repay. When I said it was just to enable an elderly man to go thirty or forty miles to get a few potatoes they gaped in amazement.

The next stop was Paris, where I booked three really good acts for the first postwar Olympia programme, but the food there was horrid and the coffee worse. I was glad when, after seeing the show at the *Cirque d'Hiver*, Joseph Bouglione invited me to lunch with him the next day, for there was plenty of good food in Paris if you knew where to find it and he did. There was nothing more to see in Europe, as I could not go to Germany or Italy and the circuses in Switzerland and Scandinavia were closed in winter.

The whole trip had produced six acts and, considering its length, was one of the most fruitful I ever made, but it proved to me that the war had taken a heavy toll in the ranks of the younger circus artistes, for they were just the types to be useful as commandos. On the other hand, I learned that there was a great deal of new talent, even if most of it was not of the same quality as before the war, and that Scandinavia would be a good hunting ground in the spring. A large number of artistes from the occupied countries, and even some Germans, had managed to escape to neutral Sweden, where several circuses flourished. Even in Denmark the Germans had encouraged them to continue, as they provided amusement for the occupying troops; in Copenhagen the Schumanns had been able to carry on so that their stud of horses had remained intact. The one problem which would make things difficult was that the British Variety Artistes Federation had put a bar on all ex-

enemy aliens and it would therefore not be possible to get labour
permits for them.

In addition to the information I received from known friends
I continually received letters from people of whom I had never
heard telling me about good acts they had seen, and these were
not easy to deal with. My own experience had taught me how
easy it is to be taken in by an act that is only fairly good when
the rest of a show is absolute rubbish. Such an act might be a
sensation in a little show, but when appearing among a galaxy
of stars it could be ordinary in the extreme. It was only too
easy for my informants to be impressed by an act seen at a
casino or night club, but what that act would look like in a big
circus was another matter. Whenever I heard about an act
from one of these untested sources I was curious to know where
it had been seen, and what circumstances prevailed at the time,
as I wanted to save making fruitless journeys.

A question which is often asked is : 'In what country do you
look if you want a certain type of act?' Germany produces
more than its share of acrobats and animal trainers; in the latter case there is good reason, for it was the Hagenbecks who
introduced the training methods which are in almost universal
use now. They ran a big circus and the zoo at Stellingen-Ham-
burg, but they were also the biggest animal dealers in the world
and, having soon discovered that rather than buy untrained
animals circus owners liked to buy ready-made acts and wanted
the trainers to go with them, they started what in fact was a
school for trainers. All their trainers used the same methods
and cues so they could present any act containing animals of
the type to which they were accustomed, if it had been produced
by a Hagenbeck trainer.

France and Mexico have produced many of the best flying
trapeze acts and, while most springboard acts come from Hungary, jugglers, at least since the days of Rastelli, have usually
come from Italy. None of this, however, answers the question,
because the one country in which I would not expect to find
an outstanding act is its country of origin, and the reason is
simple. It takes a man or woman many years to reach perfection in circus work and during all the early years the artiste

is at home in small shows but when stardom is reached the act is a saleable commodity anywhere except at home, where it has been seen by too many people during the making. This reasoning cannot be taken to a logical conclusion, for if it could there would never be a 'find'. Such a thing occurs when an artiste, having reached near-perfection in a little circus, is living for the day when he will be seen by someone from a big circus. Therefore, to find these new acts one must make a note of the people who show promise and then hunt for them on the motorways and village greens. Whether by train, car or air one must go wherever circuses go—and that means just about anywhere.

During the last twenty years talent has become scarcer, even though television has increased the demand. Circuses had to become more competitive and this meant spending more on programmes; but the laws of supply and demand have not worked, for the big salaries that the good acts can earn have had the effect of discouraging those with good acts from producing anything new. A new act might not be as successful as the old one and as long as there were countries where the old one had not been seen it was good enough and no risk or expense was involved. We have been in an epoch when full employment and big salaries have had a stagnating effect and circuses everywhere are suffering from it.

By 1951 a single-engined aircraft with no radio was no longer practicable, for I could not enter any of the controlled zones round airports and there were few private landing grounds, so I gave up flying, and since then the annual search has meant one long journey round the Continent and a number of short ones by airlines.

The car trip would begin towards the end of April, after a sea voyage from Harwich to Esbjerg, which enabled me to see all the Danish and Swedish tenting circuses and some of those in Norway before going to the opening of the Schumann Circus in Copenhagen. This, coinciding with that of Tivoli, marked the opening of the season. After the first performance each year the Schumanns give a big party for the press and people who are prominent in the life of the city and I was always lucky enough to be invited to these, but they went on until five or six in the morning and if I had seen an act I wanted the night before I was not as well rested as I might be by the time negotiations began.

Hamburg was the next stop and after seeing the matinée at the *Hansa* theatre, and a near-by circus in the evening, I sometimes went to the *Reperbahn* 'to see how the other half lives'. Some of the shows there are pretty near the knuckle but they are run in an orderly fashion and nobody has ever tried to clip me there, although that often happens in so-called night clubs in other countries.

After a trip along the autobahn to Berlin, which involved the Russian zone and all the tiresome formalities connected with it, my journey took me through the rest of Germany. From there I went to Switzerland, Austria, Italy, Spain, France, Belgium and Holland and when I came home I had driven between nine and ten thousand miles and had seen at least fifty shows in from forty to forty-four days. If the trip took three or four days longer it was because I became bored and stopped somewhere in Italy for as many days' sea and sun bathing.

It was difficult never to become bored, for I saw about eleven hundred acts during each trip; if I went to a circus where there was only one act I wanted to see I still had to sit through the whole show, however bad it was, and as I was always given a front seat I had to appear interested in everyone and applaud at all the right times. Even keeping awake was difficult sometimes and all this is more like work than fun when it continues for weeks on end and is repeated every year. A pit into which any newcomer can fall arises from the fact that the circus world is almost one huge family and, in Italy especially, everyone seems to be related to everybody else. Having seen a good act there it is a temptation to dash round to the artiste's caravan after the show and offer a contract, but those who expect to be welcome at that circus in future go first to the owner and put their cards on the table. If you don't do that and are not a walking encyclopaedia of circus personalities and cannot remember and place every face you have ever seen it is almost certain that your 'find' is a close relation, even the son or daughter, of the owner; if that is the case there will be a stall until you leave and then it will be blurted out that you have tried to pinch an act. This sort of thing has happened only too often and some people who have tried to be too clever now have to send agents to do their business.

One year, before starting my long trip, I made a quick one to Seville, as five circuses were there at the same time during the fair. They were so packed together that the side ropes of one tent were interlaced with those of its neighbour and two were so close that my only way out of one was through the menagerie of another, without paying. The programmes were a far cry from what an English audience would expect, for only one show had an animal act—one horse. The circus rings were raised wooden stages, so no tiered seating had to be built. There were four or five performances each day and they were all an hour or more late in starting; the last one I saw began just after 4.40 a.m. and when I returned to the hotel, worn out, 'tomorrow's' festivities were beginning.

My host, the owner of one of Spain's biggest circuses, had used his considerable influence to get my wife and me a room at the magnificent *Alphonso XIII* hotel and had announced he was taking us to the bull fight on the big day; as I knew he would have bought the best seats, which cost a small fortune, we dared not say we did not want to go. I had been once before and was so sickened that I walked out amid jeers after about twenty minutes and the thought that my wife and I would have to sit through a whole afternoon, and pretend we liked it, was worrying.

The weather was glorious and the spectacle before the *corrida* included a High School horse which would have been a sensation in a circus. Compared with what is to follow the early stages of a bull fight are tolerable and the bull was still in good shape when a thunder cloud rolled up and it began to rain. By the time things got bad for the bull it was pouring and the water running down our faces made it impossible to see what was going on. It rained so hard the matador could not kill the bull in the orthodox way and it had to be finished off

G

with what looked like a butcher's knife—disgusting, but it got the animal out of its misery quickly. Still it poured and the whole sad business was gone through with the second bull by which time, according to custom, the public had had its money's worth; there having been two *corridas* the remaining ones could be cancelled and no money need be refunded. We left feeling as grateful as the other bulls would have done had they known what was in store for them.

I expect coals of fire will be heaped on my head by those who like bull fights and are able to appreciate the skill of the man, to the extent that they can overlook the torture of the animal, but I am convinced the part taken by the *picador* has no purpose other than to reduce the bull to a state of weakness through the loss of blood and to damage the muscles in its neck and shoulders so that it lowers its head and exposes the vulnerable spot at which the sword can enter. Even if this is not technically correct I still regard the whole business as cruel and degrading and the fact that there is some kind of altar or chapel behind the scenes at which the contestants pray before the *corrida* only makes matters worse.

I must be fair to the Spaniards, however, for they are charming people and they can earn good marks even at a *corrida*. One of the ladies in our party was expecting a baby and after the second *corrida* there was a rush for the exits and we were feeling anxiety for this lady when our host shouted something in Spanish which I did not understand. Instantly everybody stood still and our party walked out as if it had been Franco and his entourage.

As we drove away in the car I asked my host what he had said. 'I just told them this lady is *enceinte*,' was his reply. I am still wondering what would be the effect of such an announcement at the end of a big football match in Britain.

Chapter Seven
Behind the Iron Curtain
Moscow State Circus

One of my favourite cities before the war was Budapest, which had a permanent circus and the *Margareten Insel,* an island in the Danube, with night clubs where the floor shows were as lavish as anywhere; but it had changed a great deal by the time I first went there after 1945. By the time of my arrival the Iron Curtain had fallen this side of Czecho-Slovakia through which I passed, and soon after leaving Prague airport I realised I was being followed by three men who went everywhere I went with the infallibility of shadows. Having signed in at the hotel and gone to a café, I saw them sitting two tables away so told the waiter to take them some beer. When being followed like this I was tempted to keep looking over my shoulder to see if they were still there, for I had made up my mind they were secret police and not just men who had an eye on my wallet. When the beer was served they all raised their glasses to me but even if it had relieved the tension they had orders to follow me and did not seem disturbed by the fact that I knew about it. At the circus they split up and took seats at three strategic points in case I planned to give them the slip.

After the show I was the guest of the manager, who was some kind of Commissar; in fact it was V. Trubka, the famous wild animal trainer, whom I had known for years and who, whilst being in the top class at his own job, knew little about how to run a circus. Later, however, he did one good job for he secured an engagement for himself and his tigers, which in the meantime had become state property, in a foreign country. His political bosses were so keen to earn foreign currency that they let him go and neither he nor the tigers ever returned.

When I told Trubka about my shadows he said there was nothing for me to worry about; the only people who need worry were those with whom I spoke and therefore all my conversations should be carried on in a loud voice so that the shadows could hear everything said. He also gave me a piece of good advice. I should probably be approached by people offering valuables, including diamonds, at absurdly low prices if I paid in foreign currency; I should have nothing to do with such people as they would probably be *agents provocateurs* and if I were tempted I should find myself in the local cooler.

The Iron Curtain had not yet come down on Hungary, but the Russians, though inconspicuous, were there and everyone was nervous because Communist influence seemed to be gaining strength. Great damage had been done during the so-called liberation and practically nothing had been done to remove the rubble of what had been a palace.

After the circus the owner said we were having a big party at the best restaurant, but to be in possession of enough money to be able to afford this sort of thing was a dangerous occupation. The only people who could go to this restaurant were foreigners and those from the neighbouring Embassies and therefore the party was to be 'mine' and he gave me a huge wad of forint notes with which to pay the bill. There were twenty-six of us and when I was handed the bill it looked as if the date had been added. It appeared that a rich foreigner was being given the full treatment and, as German was the only common language we had, they probably took me for a German and decided to make me pay well for being one.

The next night I went to see an act at the big Variety Theatre and again was the guest of the owner of the circus at dinner before the show, but this time things were to be very different. We should not go to the very best restaurant and the guest of honour was someone to whom I should be most polite and in whose presence I should refrain from any expression of political opinion—a high-ranking officer of the Secret Police who controlled the admission to Hungary of foreign performers. A more villainous looking character I have never seen; half Mongolian, he would have been a casting director's joy if he had been looking for a thug for a James Bond film, but if Bond had met him I think he would have decided to go out of business. He was about fifty years of age and accompanied by a twenty-year-old blonde who was patently of very easy virtue; probably an employee of his organisation who, when at work, was planted in the hotels used by visiting foreigners, but who in her spare time was one of his perks.

I am not aware that I was followed in Hungary; if I was, it was done far more professionally. In any event, I had nothing to hide and in perspective it is amusing if people have nothing better to do than waste their time with this sort of thing. My circus owner friend was clearly apprehensive, as he was regarded as a Capitalist. When the Iron Curtain dropped a few months later he, although over sixty, was sent to work in the mines, where he died after a short time.

The visit to Budapest produced one big dividend, for when a number of us were having drinks in the circus restaurant someone asked whether I had ever seen Borra. The name meant nothing, but they said the man was a pick-pocket and that he had packed the circus for a month. My thoughts turned to Giovanni, who had done this type of act before the war, and I was not at all sure this was an act for a very big place, but everyone said Borra began where all the others left off and that he was a must for us, particularly as the act was so amusing.

Nobody knew where Borra had gone and I had to be extremely careful in making enquiries because, if I made them in the wrong places, other circus owners and agents would join the hunt. For several months the search was fruitless, until I saw the name in a Gothenburg newspaper a few days before I was going to Scandinavia. The *folksparks* of Sweden provide far more than we expect to find in an amusement park and Liseberg, the one in Gothenburg, is probably the best; like Tivoli, in Copenhagen, it has first class restaurants and two theatres. In the newspaper there was a list of acts appearing that month and among these was that of Borra. No star billing or anything to indicate it was anything more than just one of the acts booked.

I arrived on the last day of the month and, having seen Borra work, went to his dressing room to try to negotiate a contract. He was busy packing and asked me the time, but my wrist watch had gone as we had shaken hands. He gave it back and when I asked him where he was going he said Stockholm. I was going there too and as he was short of time we agreed to meet there and when he said 'Good-bye' he added, 'and I'll give you your watch there.' It had gone again.

Having had some experience behind the Iron Curtain I was never too keen on going to East Germany, but a year or so before the Wall was built there was an act I wanted to see badly in the Russian Sector of Berlin. Most British subjects who go to Eastern Bloc countries are sponsored by the Board of Trade, or are representatives of big British companies involved in international trade and there are usually important people to meet them and play host, but in my case I had to make my own way. There was still free passage for Berliners between the four sectors, but it was not quite so easy for foreigners to enter East Berlin, so I consulted the daughter of a man with whom I had done a lot of business before the war. She was perfectly willing to take me to the circus, but there were conditions. I should go hatless, as an English hat would be spotted; I should wear her husband's German raincoat, keep my mouth shut and let her do the talking, if any.

At the *Brandenburger Tor* we were surrounded by *Volkspolizei* who looked us over and searched the car to see we were not smuggling; then we were allowed to pass. Not a word was spoken, for West Berliners did not speak to the frontier guards unnecessarily. The commissar of the circus was a decent sort of chap who had owned a small circus which had been taken over by the state, but he had had the sense to appear, at all events, to be well-disposed towards the Communists. In fact, he and another man were at that time planning to escape and some months later, having routed a small 'State Circus' along the zone frontier through small towns, they succeeded—elephants and all. They must have had good friends among the guards who probably went with them. If they did not, I expect they would have been shot.

It was a wild animal act I had gone to see, but although the trainer would have liked to do what Trubka had done, the authorities would not let the act go beyond their reach so the journey produced nothing. However, it gave me an idea, for I passed the *Friedrichstadt Palast,* a huge new variety theatre in the Russian sector. I knew that in one of the Eastern Bloc countries there was an artiste doing a new and very interesting act and, having heard a round by round description of it, I wanted it for Olympia. The artiste could travel between East and West Berlin, but the props would never be allowed to go and they were essential. The plan was a simple one; if it had been complicated there would have been too many chances of somebody slipping up and landing the artiste in trouble. I must keep repeating the word artiste, for a mention of the name or even the sex might still result in repercussions on parents or relatives.

First, we had to find out whether the artiste was well-disposed towards escape to the West. If so, we must arrange a booking at the *Friedrichstadt Palast,* which could be done by sowing the seed of an idea in a certain man's mind and leaving him to work things out so that he got the credit for booking an outstanding act. From East Berlin the artiste would take the *U-Bahn* (Underground) to the British sector and then be flown in a British plane to Hamburg. In the meantime, we must have drawings with full dimensions of the props so that new ones could be ready by the time the artiste arrived. The plot took some time to hatch but it worked like a Swiss watch; a highly talented artiste was freed and the success of the act in London made all the trouble worth while.

But one can also have disappointments, for a year later I

booked another act belonging to an Eastern country. Those individuals who are considered politically reliable are allowed to leave though it seems they all have to leave close relatives at home. The engagements are negotiated through a government agency and contracts have to be prepared in triplicate; the artiste signs one copy, but the signature is worthless and it is that of the agency upon which one has to rely. In this case the contract was signed in May and I heard nothing until November when I had a telegram announcing, without a word of apology, that the act would not fulfil the contract as it was going to Moscow.

If, when this sort of thing happens, you have already advertised the act and will be breaking faith with the public you can do nothing. In recent years I have tried only to book East European acts which were already this side of the Iron Curtain and I have made it my business to see any that came from the East as soon as possible after their arrival and before other circus owners came on the scene. One of the problems with these acts was that, on arrival, their costumes were deplorable by our standards and they paid little attention to make-up. If they played a season with a continental circus they earned money of a kind they had never had before and were able to have new costumes made so that they could feel in the running with other artistes and not look like poor relations. Their props were often bad, too, and I have never understood why artistes coming from countries where their training and everything they need is provided by the State should be so badly equipped. Some of the props are ingenious and reflect considerable credit on their designers, but they are badly made. The Szogis who came to Olympia had a complicated mechanical prop the whole of which had been built with scrap from a junk car dump and it broke so often that our welders spent many nights repairing it to make it fit to use the following day. Some of the Russian acts that have come to this country have been outstanding, but it is worth remembering that when the first Moscow State Circus came here we had not seen Russian acts for about thirty years and the Russians, with a population about as great as that of the rest of Europe, had a large supply of what was new mater-

(*Left*) *Charlie Rivels*
(*Right*) *A corner of Tiny Town and the miniature hansom cab*
(*Below*) *Gargantua*

OVERLEAF *Yvonne presents a group of lions in the Mills Type Wild Animal Cage at Olympia*

The Elephant Balloon

Coco as a young man

ial to us and of course they sent a lot of the best. Even so, if we had been able to put together in one programme all that was best in Europe at that time it would have been just as good a show, but our audiences would not have wanted to see it since it would have been composed almost entirely of acts which would have appeared at Olympia in recent years and they, so far as London was concerned, were old hat.

The Moscow State Circus was offered to us a long time before it came to Britain, but I turned it down for two reasons. In the first place, I was required to take a complete show, but was given only the vaguest indications of what it would contain. Secondly, it was not offered by the Russian Ministry of Culture, which I think would have been the proper procedure, but by a representative of a Communist Front organisation and I visualised the possibility that what we were asked to pay, or at least a part of it, would find its way into the pockets of the Communist Party. From a purely business point of view I probably did the wrong thing, but I believe I did it for the right reason. For a business that had always steered clear of politics this would have been no way to begin.

Chapter Eight
Thrill acts
Accidents. Ticket touts
and others

Some time later I heard that the Moscow State Circus was appearing at the recently re-built *Cirque Royal* in Brussels and went to see it. On arrival I presented my card, but was told if I wanted a ticket I must buy one. Now I am not a ticket scrounger and whenever I go to a place of entertainment other than a circus I buy my ticket and enter anonymously. At a circus it is different, for if anyone who is well-known buys a ticket and enters without announcing himself, it can only give rise to the suspicion that he has in mind business of a kind which may conflict with the interests of the owner of the circus.

I was far from happy with some of the things I saw in Brussels and glad the show was not coming to London for us. The conditions under which animals were housed did not compare favourably with those in British or continental circuses and the artistes were not treated as we should want them to be. Most of the acts were good, but everything seemed to be done to a set pattern, which brought soldiers to mind, and if any individual had personality it had been suppressed completely. One of the acts was of a kind which the Russians have done often and which annoy me intensely. Five men worked on a high wire without a net and one of the tricks attempted was sensational, but at the same time impossible. By that I mean the chance of its being done successfully was about one in ten. To make it possible each man had a 'lunge'—a belt to which was attached a wire which went through an overhead pulley block and the end of which was held by a man on the ground. When I saw them attempt the trick all five men ended up hanging from the wires like puppets and I just laughed.

The difference between a 'lunge' and a safety device is this. A safety device or a safety net is to protect the lives of performers if anything goes wrong while they are attempting a trick which they are able to do nineteen times out of twenty, because they have practised it for months or years. A 'lunge' is a device which artistes use while they are learning tricks; every bareback rider uses one while he learns to do somersaults on a horse or from one horse to another. It is my belief that the use of the 'lunge' should be restricted to the place for which it was meant and that to use it at public performances is unfair and improper. When tricks with 'lunges' are shown on television they can be most effective, for if the director knows how to use lights and cameras the wires do not show. If the trick is missed there can be retakes until it is done successfully and the artiste therefore gets credit for doing something which is more a fluke than anything else and which he would never be fool enough to attempt without the 'lunge'.

At the end of the show I presented my card again, as I would have liked to have had a word with a few of the artistes, but the way to the dressing rooms was barred by a sentry in private clothes and after a few minutes the whole troupe was marched down the stairs and into a waiting bus by two more men in civilian clothes. When they had gone the Belgian gate-keeper told me this was the daily routine and that the ride to and from their hotel was all they ever saw of Brussels unless they went for walks accompanied by N.K.V.D. escorts.

The Moscow State Circus is the name of the circus building in Moscow and most Soviet cities have such a building. All artistes are employed by the State and whatever programmes appear in Moscow are called the Moscow State Circus, just as any programme we presented was called Bertram Mills Circus, and therefore the Russians have been able to export several different programmes under the same title. Having engaged none of them I have no experience of dealing with the Soviet Ministry of Culture, but others have said they are difficult people and it is often hard to find out what acts will be included until a few days before the troupe arrives. In other words, one has to book a show with a minimum of information and hope for the best. By and large I think the programmes have satisfied people, but whereas some of the acts have been outstanding others have been far below the standard we expected.

I have always felt British circus interests were badly served when the first Moscow State Circus came to London. At that time there was in existence an agreement between the Association of Circus Proprietors of Great Britain and the Variety Artistes Federation that at least twenty-five per cent of the acts in any static circus should be British and it was an agreement enforced by the Ministry of Labour when issuing labour permits, for its purpose was to protect British artistes from cut-price foreign competition. However, when the Russians came here with a show which was a hundred per cent foreign, both in acts and ordinary personnel, no protest was heard except from the Circus Proprietors and theirs was ignored.

Surely, if there was to be competition between British and Russian circuses in Britain, both should have had to compete on an equal footing, but as things were it looked as if there was one law for them and another for us—and nothing was done to protect the British artistes.

Now that I am no longer in what is essentially an international branch of show business, I can express freely opinions on things I dislike, whether they concern Capitalist or Communist countries.

It has been customary to describe 'thrill' acts, especially those working at great heights, as 'death-defying' and to give pictures such captions as : 'He walks on the brink of eternity'. Some of these phrases have been lifted from the blurbs of Hollywood publicists and others are no more than the boasts of showmen who want to persuade someone that they have something more sensational than their competitors. In any event, I am sure nobody in this country wants to see an accident, but motor racing and some other things prove that many people will pay to see men expose themselves to great danger if they feel sure they have the skill and experience to overcome it. The problem is, where to draw the line, for during my circus days there have been a few performers who have taken risks of a kind which are certain to prove fatal sooner or later.

Before the war two men did an aerial act which included a trick which I thought was sheer madness, but they cornered me after the show and were very surprised when I said I was not interested. They were doing something nobody else had dared, or was fool enough, to attempt and thought they were a must for a circus like ours. I told them frankly that I was afraid a catch would be missed and the flyer killed and it is not nice to tell a man this sort of thing. Not very long afterwards it happened, but the catcher made excuses and said freak conditions had intervened. He recruited another flyer, who was killed doing the same trick, but even so the catcher produced another act in which there was a different, but equally suicidal, trick. This time the flyer was lucky and what looked like poetic justice was done, for the catcher, while doing nothing more dangerous than climb his rigging, fell off and was killed.

In 1936 we had a girl named Fritzi Bartoni who did one very difficult trick in which she fell forward from a trapeze and caught herself by her heels on the cross bar and she had been doing that without a net, but it was a new act she had just practised. When she arrived I noticed that there were sores just above her heels caused by too much practice and the resin she used to give the heels a grip. We insisted that she should use a safety device, which she attached before this trick only, and she worked the whole season without falling or being saved by the gadget.

Our season over, she went to the *Winter Garten* Theatre, Berlin, where I happened to be on the day she opened. I had a word with her before the show and she announced with obvious pleasure that she was going to do the difficult trick without the safety device and added, 'You can't stop me here.' There always has to be a first time and it sometimes coincides with the last and I begged her not to be silly, but nothing I said made any impression.

Two hours later she crashed on to the stage and was carried off with a broken pelvis. As she passed me on a stretcher on the way to an ambulance, obviously in great pain, she tried to smile and gave me a look which meant she knew how foolish she had been and would not do it again. Fortunately, she recovered quickly and was back at work with us the following April and, although she continued to do the trick in one circus or another until the outbreak of war, just once without any kind of safety device had been enough.

Accidents of the kind I have described are few and far apart and the great majority are caused by rigging failure or sheer carelessness. Lilian Leitzel, who had worked at Olympia in 1921–2, was, by 1931, the wife of Alfredo Codona, the first man ever to perform the triple somersault on the flying trapeze. At that time he was appearing in Berlin while she was in Copenhagen and it was the first time since their marriage that they had worked apart. Lilian's act was not one involving great danger to anyone accustomed to working thirty or forty feet above ground, but one night she fell in front of a crowded house and her death added another name to those who have died because of the failure of the rigging upon which their lives depended. Ropes and even pieces of metal are subject to fatigue and must be inspected and renewed often; it was the failure of Lilian's apparatus that caused her death and the loss to circus of one of its brightest stars.

Frances Duncan, a charming Australian girl, died in very similar circumstances, although the distance she fell was very much less. In her case a splice broke in her rope; the fact that the splice was perished and should have been renewed was concealed by a new piece of bias binding, which had been put over it only a few weeks before.

Elizabeth, the Belgian girl who fell at our circus in 1947, was very lucky, for she dropped about forty feet into the ring and although her injuries were serious she was working again a few months later. It was another case of rigging failure, but an unusual one. Just before coming to England her father, who was her rigger and a first class workman, bought some new wire, but unfortunately he did not know how to differentiate between steel and galvanised iron wire. He said he had asked for steel wire, but it was galvanised which broke and caused the accident, so we showed him how to be sure he was never caught again.

The Katyanas was an act of five girls who worked at a height of about fifteen feet and did pretty tricks, rather than difficult ones. Two of the girls were twins and, during a part of the act, all they had to do was sit on the ends of a long trapeze bar while the three other girls worked in the middle; it was while doing this that one of them fell off. The results were so serious as to be unbelievable—a broken leg, arm and pelvis and several teeth knocked out, but although she was working again in a few months she paid dearly for her carelessness.

What upset me nearly as much as the accident was what I found going on between the matinée and evening performances. The ring and seating were deserted, but a local free-lance photographer had dreamed up a picture which, if it had been taken, would have fetched a big price. He had persuaded the injured girl's twin to get into costume and some of the ring boys to hold a net below and of course the twin was to do a fake fall into the net. Every newspaper carried the story of the accident, but what a scoop it would have been if one had been able to publish a photo of the accident as it happened. Even the picture editor would have been deceived, but, fortunately, I had been tipped off just in time by a member of the staff who did not like the taste of what was cooking. Never before or since has an empty-handed photographer left Olympia in such a hurry.

In a business which is not without its elements of danger one would expect to hear 'Good Luck' said very often, but it never is. The circus way of saying it is : *'Hals und Beinbruck'*. This, believe it or not, means : 'Break your neck and leg.' That is accepted by everyone and there would be trouble if anyone said anything else to a superstitious artiste.

Many people ask why aerial artistes do not work over nets

always. There are two answers. First, there are often safety precautions which are far more effective but not seen by the public; secondly, some tricks look dangerous, or are made to appear dangerous to the inexperienced eye, but are less hazardous than the average crossing of a busy London street.

Everyone connected with circuses does everything to prevent accidents, for we do not want to see our friends hurt and we are closer to each other than a master builder is to his men who work on very high buildings; and of course no circus artiste can cover himself by insurance—the salary he is paid includes an element in respect of this.

When I had an artiste who did one dangerous trick I used a hand net held by eight or ten men below; if this went in just before the risky trick, in a black-out, few members of the public spotted it and most of those who did were grateful. On the other hand, performers who were accustomed to working without it often objected and I had to 'bend' the law in my favour to justify what I was doing.

There was a time when some people were telling a story about an accident for which I was said to be to blame. A man had said he had a new act. Others had dived from the roof of Olympia into tanks of water but he could do it into a barrel of saw-dust. It sounded interesting and I arranged an audition, including drum rolls and all the trimmings to make it look like a real performance. Sure enough, he landed head first in the barrel, pulled himself out and ran sideways out of the ring waving one hand and holding the other under his chin. A few minutes later I sent for him and said I thought the trick was very good, but he would have to cut out all the sissy business with his hand under his chin as he left the ring. 'Sissy finish be damned,' he replied, 'I've broken my ruddy neck.'

Running a business which involved having millions of people pass through our hands placed a heavy burden of responsibility upon us, for so many unpredictable and unavoidable little accidents can happen. Just after the war, when the tenting circus was looking spick and span in the new paint which had been applied so generously, everything went well until the first hot spell when, during the matinée interval, three thousand people found their bottoms stuck to the seats. Post-war paint, lacking essential ingredients, had melted and since the paint was bright red the appearance of the home-going audience was not a pretty sight when viewed from the rear. That cost us plenty of dry cleaners' bills, but for once we gave thanks for clothes rationing as there were no claims for two hundred guinea dresses.

Not so easy to deal with are the spivs, which any large and regular gathering of the public attracts. Among the worst were the ticket touts; these men, working in teams of anything up to twenty, bought the cheapest tickets for Boxing Day and Saturday performances and sold them, at six or eight times the price paid, to parents who did not want to disappoint their children. Over and over again I saw mothers and fathers take crying children away because they simply could not afford the outrageous prices demanded and I made up my mind to break the racket. But it wasn't easy, as there was nothing illegal about it —the spivs said they were only doing what theatre ticket agents did and there was no law to limit the size of a booking fee. The only question was, therefore, when does a booking fee become extortion?

We put large notices up to warn the public and even hinted that the tickets might be forgeries, but still they found buyers. Anyone who wanted to buy more than six tickets was asked to prove bona fides; no tickets were sold to known touts—who then sent women to do their shopping. We made a black-list of names and then one of addresses, but still they managed to get tickets, for they realised we could do nothing to vet orders for twos and threes through the post and that produced an even worse situation. People who bought six or eight tickets had no time to check them in the rush, just before the performance, and when they arrived at the circus they found they had seats in three or four different parts of the house. Then parents came and begged us to do something so their children could sit with them, but there was seldom anything we could do as the spivs only operated when they were sure we should have a full house.

Eventually I consulted the local Superintendent of Police who was as anxious to protect the public as we were and he came up with a splendid idea. The next day every tout who offered a ticket to a woman was arrested and charged with using insulting behaviour but a few days later, having paid small fines, they were all back but only offering tickets to men. Perhaps it was coincidence but there had been one case of bag-snatching and one of pocket-picking in the last few days, although nobody had been caught. It could well be that the ticket racket was, in some cases, a cover for pick-pockets and when this occurred to us we decided to go to town in a big way. The next time the touts appeared they were all arrested and charged with loitering with intent to commit a felony and when the magistrate knew there had been cases of picking pockets he bound them all over not to go within half a mile of the circus box office for two years. We had won at last and were never to be worried again, but the thing which surprised me was that only one man ever threatened me. The others took it in good part and whenever I went to a big fight or Wimbledon they all offered to sell me tickets at the normal price, but of course I had them already.

One afternoon we saw seven suspicious looking characters hanging round two of the circus exits; it was clear they were waiting for somebody and were up to mischief. A local C.I.D. officer was asked to come and look them over. He immediately recognised two as known pick-pockets, so I went into the seating to try to see who might be involved. In one of the boxes there was a woman wearing a diamond and emerald necklace worth thousands. It is not nice to have to admit that the place for which you are responsible is seething with thieves, but being straightforward always pays. I therefore told the woman who I was and said that if the necklace was as valuable as I thought it to be she would have little chance of getting through the crowds at the end of the performance with it and suggested she should go up to the office with me and put it in the safe. To my amazement she took it off, gave it to me without even asking for a receipt, and said she would collect it later.

A few summers ago, at the tenting circus, a patron said his wallet had been stolen. He was quite sure the thief was a young man who was sitting with a woman a few seats away and he wanted the C.I.D. called in. The couple was watched during the whole performance and when they went through the menagerie afterwards, but they never betrayed the slightest suspicion that they thought they were being watched and both the detective and I were convinced it was a mis-deal. However, the patron insisted they be questioned and the officer agreed to tackle the job. I wish I could remember how he managed to suggest there had been a theft without even hinting that the people he was interrogating were thieves. Instead of saying, 'Search us if you wish,' which would have put the onus on the policeman, the young man said, 'We wish to be searched.' Nothing was found and we all parted good friends; innocent people have nothing to fear from the police if they are co-operative and use their common sense. The end of the story came some hours later when a very apologetic man told me by telephone that he had found his wallet on the dressing table at home and asked me to let the police know, as he had not the courage to do so himself.

On another occasion I heard the telephone ringing in the office well after midnight; when I answered it a woman told me her two small children were missing. She was clearly in a state of extreme anxiety and was relieved when I told her we had found the children alone after the show and, as nobody had collected them after half an hour, we had asked the police to take care of them. When she told me what had happened I could hardly believe her, for she had allowed her children to come to the circus with two of their friends and the mother of the friends. When the show ended the woman took her own children home and went to bed, having forgotten she had taken the two other children.

In the post-war years labour problems were severe. We often had to rely on local labour exchanges to fill unexpected vacancies and of course we were a sitting target. If a man was a layabout who never kept a job, who could blame a clerk if he unloaded such a character on a Saturday, just as the circus was leaving town? But there were worse dangers than that. There was an occasion when two men were sent to us during the afternoon, and by 1 a.m. C.I.D. officers came to the circus to ask if we had blankets. It sounded a silly question and I said so, but they were serious and said that if the circus owned blankets they were probably the ones which were being flogged in the town at that moment for five shillings each. The blankets turned out to be exactly like ours, so the following morning the police came to arrest the men. It was early in the season and the ground was a quagmire and when brought to the police they were standing in several inches of mud. They were told to remove their gum-boots, inside which was stencilled the name of a well-known firm of constructional engineers; this, coupled with the fact that the blankets were identical with ours, landed them back in prison within thirty hours of their release.

Very late one night an electrician came to my caravan and said an electric cable had been cut in the mess tent. I supposed the damage had been caused by carelessness, but a man who has been pulled out of bed to repair what he thinks is malicious damage cannot be expected to be in good humour, so I felt I had done all I could when he had agreed to repair the cable and I had promised to investigate the next day.

Two hours later I was awakened by the paymaster, who said, 'Someone is slashing the walls of the big top with a knife.' Slipping into some clothes I went with him; in this case there was no room for doubt. There were about thirty rents, each between two and four feet long, and all the Paymaster had seen was a pair of dark trousers—for by the time he arrived the body had disappeared under the side wall.

I gathered four men who had been with us a long time and we began a search for an intruder. After a few minutes we passed the head fireman, who was on duty that night, and I asked him if he had seen a stranger. He replied: 'No, but there must be one about as the walls of the tent have been cut.' I told him to stay where he was and keep his eyes open, but I was wondering how he knew what had happened and why he had not been the first to report, unless he was responsible for it. I told those with me of my suspicion and we returned to the fireman, saying we thought we had heard someone in the vestibule tent. When we reached it I said I was satisfied there was nobody else about and I should therefore search all those present.

The first man searched was one of excellent character and knew I was only going through a formality; the second man was the fireman and the only thing in his trousers pocket was a kitchen knife about nine inches long. It could have been the one used, but there was no proof until I saw that the blade bore two charred spots and the distance between them was that between the two wires of a fifteen amp cable.

Before I could say anything the old hands let fly and if I had not asserted my authority quickly the man would have had a beating up he would never have forgotten. To old hands the circus was theirs; if the roof had been cut instead of the side walls the damage would have run into two or three thousand pounds' and we should have lost several performances while temporary repairs were done.

The man was taken to the local police station and charged, but I had a nasty feeling about the whole affair, for I had to assume that somebody in a high position had done or failed to do something which had given rise to a grouse. The following day, however, the man pleaded guilty and when asked whether he had done it because he had a grudge against his employers he gave us a reference of which we could be proud. He had no reason at all, except that he had been in gaol for nearly everything in the book including attempted suicide. He was sent to prison, but was clearly a schizophrenic and I have always felt a mental institution would have been a more appropriate place.

Chapter Nine
The worst year of all
and then the war

Apart from a bus strike lasting three weeks, 1937 was an un-
eventful summer, although we visited forty-seven towns—a record which was to stand until 1954, when we did forty-nine in
thirty-one weeks. The early weeks of 1938 were busy ones in
the winter quarters, for we had a new programme and there
was a great deal to do in the preparation of 'house' acts. There
were ten people and six horses in the bareback act; John Gindl
was producing an act in which the six elephants were to play
football; Charlie Mroczkowski was perfecting a routine with
twelve Arab horses and Coco, Alby Austin, Percy Huxter and
Bob Beasey were working up some new slapstick nonsense in
which they would appear as bill-posters who were sure to finish
drenched to the skin. On the other side of the road, on what
we always called the mechanical side, about a hundred tradesmen were working long hours overhauling equipment and
vehicles.

On March 24th, just before the circus was due to take to
the road, the B.B.C. produced the first of a series of one hour
programmes entitled 'Showmen of Britain'. Bertram Mills was

the subject of the first and Charles B. Cochran of the second. It was a magnificent programme which, using a coach horn blower and the circus band, covered the whole of my father's activities from hunting and coaching to circuses and politics.

After a quick trip to the Continent to see some acts for the following winter, I returned to Ascot in time to see the circus trains leave on April 11th. But by then we were all worried as Father, who had been out with the hounds three or four days before, was ill in bed and that was most unusual for him. The build-up of the big top at Luton began on the morning of the 13th and the artistes were due to arrive for rehearsals that day, but as Mother had telephoned to say Father was very ill indeed, Bernard and I motored over to Chalfont St. Giles. He had pneumonia and I am not sure that he recognised us.

We spent an hour or two at the circus during each of the next two days and the rest of the time at Pollards Wood, the family home, but as the illness gathered momentum and the crisis approached it became more and more doubtful whether he would have the strength to survive.

He died on the morning of April 16th. The circus was due to open that afternoon.

Even now I do not know what would have been the proper thing to do in such circumstances and at the time we were all too heart-broken to be able to make a sound judgement. My feeling was, and still is, that we did the wrong thing, but we did what we all believed he would have insisted upon. He would have said people had booked seats and gone to the circus expecting to see it and it was our job to please them and not upset anyone's plans.

Bernard and I motored back to Luton and I cannot remember a word being spoken; we told what had happened and said the circus would open as advertised. Those who had been with us a long time, and there were many, were stunned, for if ever a man was loved by his employees he was and even if no one was worrying about his job everyone saw a huge blank space, one which no other man would ever be able to fill.

How they got through the performances that day I shall never know, for Bernard and I returned to be with our mother.

We had realised that Father's death would be recorded in the papers the next morning, but when we left the circus within five hours of his death, the contents bills of the evening papers outside every newsagent's said one thing only, 'Bertram Mills Dead'.

Three days later he was buried in the churchyard of the village in which he lived, having been borne there on one of his farm carts drawn by one horse. Friends from all over Britain came to pay their last tribute and there were so many flowers that a large part of the churchyard was paved with them. We all knew he had been respected, but I do not think any of us had realised how much—how very much.

The circus was closed that day and then continued its journey towards Scotland, but on the following Sunday there was a memorial service in the circus tent. It was conducted by the vicar of the local church and the music was played by the circus band. Although the circus had moved over-night everything was ready and everyone, to the last working man, was present. They had worked non-stop through the night to be ready in time. For many of the foreign artistes it was their first engagement with Mills, but the name was as well-known throughout the circus world as it was here and they too knew that his death meant that something had gone out of the circus.

The circus carried on and business was good during the early weeks, but by the time we reached Edinburgh things were looking bad, for Hitler had helped himself to Austria and the clouds of war were gathering fast. People were becoming jittery and business was not nearly as good as during previous visits to the North.

The other big worry was the Olympia programme; for the first time I had doubts about my ability to produce a good enough show. Everything in the past had been Bertram Mills, and it was obvious that comparisons would be made and there were sure to be those who thought the standard might not be maintained. On the other side of the coin, we believed that if we did our best many people would welcome any sincere attempt to carry on something that had become a part of life in London at Christmastime and that indeed is what happened;

but what may happen six months hence does little to relieve today's worries.

In Europe things went from bad to worse and by the time we reached Glasgow we were in the middle of the Munich crisis. Having travelled so much in Germany I should have been blind if I had failed to notice the rate at which preparations for war were progressing, but I saw no such signs in this country although at the luncheon we gave in Glasgow, which was attended by the Lord Provost, one notable guest was missing. Patrick Dollan, who became Lord Provost later, was in charge of air raid precautions and was busy supervising the filling of sand-bags. What a way to prepare for a war that could have started the next day!

That Glasgow luncheon presented more than enough problems, for Father had presided at the last and Bernard, who had organised these functions, was away ill; so I was completely on my own. We had the Old Berkeley coach and a team of horses with the circus and on such occasions the Lord Provost and his party rode to the circus in it after the lunch and either Father or Bernard always drove. This gave publicity to the circus and it seemed a pity to miss it so, although I had never driven a four-in-hand and am as poor a horseman as is possible, I persuaded Tom Tagg, the master of horse and a first class whip, to give me a few lessons. When the day came I managed to drive the coach from the centre of Glasgow to the circus without wrecking anything.

The next town was Ayr, during the autumn race meeting, and as I had the aeroplane at Prestwick I decided to go to the races by air and landed on the centre of the course. Nothing new in that, but between the fourth and fifth races Tom arrived with the coach and I drove our party away. Quite a lot of people had been reminded that the circus was in town.

I have less happy memories of Prestwick now, for it was from there, in the middle of the 1942 winter, that I began my first war-time crossing of the Atlantic in the bomb-bay of a Liberator. We were in darkness all the way, smoking was not allowed and for five hours the temperature inside was thirty-five degrees below zero. When coming in to land at Montreal the aircraft stalled, as the result of ice on the tail plane, but we were saved by the skill of a brilliant pilot and landed safely two hours later when the ice had been shaken off. I was only one of twenty-three men who had been terrified, for we all knew what the trouble was.

From the first week of September until the 8th October, when our departure from Glasgow coincided with Neville Chamberlain's arrival waving a piece of paper, business was ghastly. We were losing money hand over fist which was not encouraging for two brothers who were trying to run a circus on their own for the first time.

During the previous two years I had tried to persuade Father to turn the business into a private limited liability company, but he had been reluctant to do so as he feared it might make the circus less personal. However, by the time he died he had instructed his solicitor to 'look into it'. After his death Mother, to whom the circus had been left, wanted to have no more to do with it than in the past; she was not a business woman and did not think she belonged in a circus any more than a textile manufacturer's wife belongs in a mill. She simply wanted Bernard and me to take over and get on with the job and, as we both agreed about forming a company, it was done.

When the last edition of the 1938 summer programme appeared the caption below Father's picture read 'Founder' instead of 'Proprietor' and when we opened at Olympia the programme said: 'Administration—Cyril & Bernard Mills Limited' in small type, but the big type still read 'BERTRAM MILLS CIRCUS'.

At the opening lunch we had 1,363 guests, who were as representative of the nation as those at any previous one. On my left sat the Earl of Athlone and on my right, Her Royal Highness Princess Alice, and a few places along the top table there were the Soviet, Brazilian and Turkish Ambassadors. These, and all the others, assured us by their presence that they were giving the Mills boys the same support they had given their father. Lord Lonsdale was there in the chair of the Honorary President, but all this, whilst being very encouraging, did nothing to quieten the butterflies in my stomach. We still had to produce our own first circus and the afternoon would show whether we were capable of doing so.

When coffee had been served Lord Lonsdale made a speech in which he paid a memorable tribute to his old friend Bertram Mills and then said some very kind things about the effort Bernard and I were making to carry on in the tradition which we had inherited. It was then my turn and I was as nervous as a kitten and I am sure Princess Alice realised that. She was kindness itself and there must be few men who have had a word of encouragement whispered to them by a member of the Royal Family at such a moment. I had never made a speech anywhere and was facing an audience containing many of the most eloquent speakers in the land and the senior representatives of every national newspaper.

I made it short, under the pretext of giving everyone plenty of time to reach the circus, but in truth to give myself a few minutes to regain my balance before the start of the show into the production of which I had put everything I had. My audience could not have been kinder, for it realised that filling the space left by a man who was so well-known and respected was an unenviable, if not an impossible, task. I happened to be the elder of two brothers and the job landed squarely in my lap; Bernard would not have wanted it any more than I did.

Business that winter was decidedly sticky on account of the threat of war, so we felt we had not done too badly when at the end of the year there was a profit of over £21,000 even though it was less than half that made the previous year.

In 1939 we took an inland route which brought us to Plymouth towards the end of June. Business had been thoroughly bad almost everywhere, although we had the same strong programme which had done so well in the early weeks of 1938 and were hoping things would improve during the holiday season in Devon and Cornwall where business had always been good. One disappointment followed another; we were only just paying expenses and as, during the tail end of the season, we were routed along the South Coast the outlook was not good.

We reached St. Leonards on August 28th and were due to

stay a week, but at 4 p.m. on the 31st a representative of the railways walked on to the ground and told us that all the circus trains had to be surrendered at nine o'clock the following morning. They were wanted for the transportation of tanks.

My only question was 'Where?' for this was something we had feared for weeks; if they were not willing to get us back to Ascot we should have to go by road and we were not equipped for this. The man said they would accept the trucks at Ascot, but we must start loading at once. The matinée was due to begin in forty minutes and it went against the grain to have a day's expenses and no receipts, so we said we would load as usual during and after the evening show. We were told, however, that it would be impossible to free the trucks in time if we delayed so long. As usual the word 'impossible' stuck in Mills throats and fortunately the railway man was an old friend of ours. He knew that we could be determined and sometimes stubborn, but that somehow or other we always managed to do things on time, so he agreed to the delay despite the orders he had been given.

By six the next morning the animals were in their stables and dens at Ascot and the freight trains had been unloaded and surrendered to Thor by half past eight. We had told the artistes we were trying to make plans to carry on, but with only four or five road tractors long jumps were out of the question. The obvious thing to do was to make for Slough and then play some London suburbs, but we should have to keep away from places within easy reach of Olympia as we could not have the cake from any area twice. Stanley Franklin had been rushed to Slough, but had no luck and so turned to Eton and Windsor.

If ever I could have been knocked over with a feather it was when he announced he had been given permission to use a field belonging to Eton College opposite Agar's Plough. To this day I do not know whether this kind gesture towards people in difficulty was made because Bernard and I were Harrovians, or in spite of it, but somebody at the top had come to our rescue.

We set about building the circus up and although it took so long to move all the trailers with our small number of tractors it was clear by Sunday that we should be able to open the next day. Of course we had done no advertising, but our arrival out of the blue was on most tongues and we hoped to do a little business.

That Sunday was September 3rd, 1939, and at eleven o'clock in the morning we heard we were at war. It looked as if the circus had had it and nobody was sure we should not be bombed that night. Everything was torn down and we began the trek back to Ascot. Tents and equipment were packed into the sheds where they would remain for the duration of the war; animals went to their stables and dens but what would happen to them was unknown. On the fourth day, when our work was nearly finished, a man in uniform walked in and told us the place had been requisitioned and that we must get out at once. It was to become an internment camp.

Fortunately, Mother was still living at Pollards Wood, where there were loose boxes for thirty-five or forty horses. There had been a sale after Father's death and about twenty of his coaches, all his hunters, jumpers and hackneys had been sold, so by making each loose box into two stalls and a coach house into an elephant shed we were able to house all the domestic animals. One of the two large riding schools housed the wild animals and the other provided an exercise ring for the horses, ponies and elephants and space for a dozen of the more valuable caravans.

They left us a few sheds adjoining the railway siding at Ascot and in these there was enough space to store tents and most of the equipment but the rest of the caravans and trailers had to go to Pollards Wood where we scattered them in the woods so they would not be seen from the air or from the road in what was essentially a residential area. Again, everything had to be dragged through Windsor.

For the moment the artistes were out of work and, although we told them we had a plan, several jumped at the temporary work the military people offered which was to turn the place at Ascot into a huge cage, by surrounding it with barbed wire. One of those who worked hard at this was Wenzel Kossmayer who, since he had been with us some time, was not interned as were the recent arrivals and it must have been a blow when, at a later stage of the war, he found himself encarcerated in the very sort of place he had helped to construct for his fellow countrymen.

Our plan was to run a stage circus during the winter, for in a discussion with Olympia Ltd. everyone had agreed there could be no winter show in London. With the black-out and the threat of bombs it would have been madness to have anything up to fifteen thousand people in the building at the same time, especially as it had a glass roof.

I went to see George Black, the head of Moss Empires, and offered him as much of the circus as could be put on the stages of his Empires and Hippodromes. He jumped at the idea and within six weeks we were a going concern again. Starting at New Cross we played nearly every big variety theatre from Portsmouth to Glasgow, but I never want to have anything to do with a stage circus again. Running a tenting show and battling with mud and gales was bad, but this was infinitely worse. Horses often had to be stabled two or three miles away and walked to the theatre in the dark through traffic, rain, fog and even snow. Few of the stages were large enough for a ring more than about thirty feet in diameter and in some the distance from front to back was so short that the ring was oval.

We had to be sure the stages, many of them old, could bear the weight of six elephants and where they could not they had to be shored up. We had to use a coconut mat in the ring instead of earth and the horses slithered about as if they were on skates until rubber pads were fitted; even then, they were blinded by the foot-lights every time they approached the front of the stage and there was the risk that they would go over into the orchestra pit. Quintillia, the wire-walker, Frederico and the Willows, the aerialists, had been interned, but the programme was still adequate for we played twice nightly and the show had to be cut to an hour and forty minutes. Emmett Kelly, the American 'hobo' clown, had not liked the idea of spending a period of war in England and had gone home even before war broke out, but we still had Coco and seven other clowns.

The stage tour lasted until the middle of February and although business was good by variety theatre standards it was poor by ours; however, our expenses were much lower than when we needed the huge staff to move the tenting show and we got through the winter without losing money. There were a few unfortunate episodes; a horse went through a plate glass shop window in the black-out in Nottingham and one of the lady artistes was attacked by a thug, also in the black-out, in Glasgow, but both escaped without a scratch. The circus train was derailed on the outskirts of Liverpool and everything, in-cludings the lions in their shifting dens, had to be carried two hundred yards through eighteen inches of snow and then dragged through a hedge before they could be loaded on a lorry.

At that time our agreement with Olympia still had two or three seasons to run and I made a proposal that it should be subject to a standstill until the end of the war, provided both we and the building still existed then. Frankly, I did not think I had much of a chance as I assumed there would be inflation, but the then directors were only too willing to have a ready-made tenant for the first post-war years and the proposal was accepted.

At the end of the stage tour we took the animals back to Pollards Wood and, as we were still in the period which people call 'the phoney war', we decided to have one more go with the tenting circus. The railways could provide horse boxes, an elephant truck and enough flats to make one train, so with fewer horses, less caravans and only the equipment that was essential we set out again at the beginning of May. We had delayed the start until the longer evenings enabled us to get the evening performance nearly over before the black-out. Musso-lini came into the war while we were in Swansea and all the Italian artistes were bundled off to the Isle of Man, but there were not many of them so we could carry on. We were headed for the industrial towns of the Midlands as they were the most likely ones to be prosperous and even if the risk of bombs was greater there it was worth taking, for there were few places where we should have to pitch our tents near an important military or industrial target.

The circus was built up in Worcester on Sunday June 16th and opened the following day, but by this time there was nothing phoney about the war. Denmark, Norway, Holland and Belgium had all been overrun and the situation in France was appalling. The circus continued to exist, although only just. I was motoring to London listening to the radio when it was announced that France had capitulated. I turned back and Bernard and I had a short conference with Wallace Gibson, the general manager, and decided this really was the end.

We had all the artistes and staff together in the big top; although they must have known what was coming they still had to be told, as neither Bernard nor I like avoiding unpleasant jobs by putting a notice on the board. There was a considerable amount of advance booking for the next two days so we decided to stick it out until the end of our scheduled stay and on the Wednesday night we did the last pull-down. Everything went back to Pollards Wood or Ascot, but what had been married quarters, stables, canvas shed and wardrobe department six months before was now a huge cage full of enemy aliens.

Our struggle against heavy odds had come to an end and we knew we were beaten at last. The whole future was a vacuum and what had begun almost as a bet and in twenty years had been built up to Britain's biggest ever circus had been destroyed overnight. For one brief moment I was glad my father had not lived to see everything falling to pieces, but then I realised that if he had been alive he would have known what was the best thing to do. Very soon, however, I became convinced that, if there could be any compensation for his death, it was that he had been spared the sight of what was no more than the wreckage of all he had built.

His mantle had fallen on Bernard's shoulders and mine and it was for us to decide what had to be done; the answer came quickly enough. The country would now need every man and woman and the most we could hope was that we should be able to keep the animals alive; that vehicles and equipment would not be destroyed by bombs and that one day we might be able to gather all the pieces together and start again.

Even without rationing we could not afford to keep horses and ponies in stables for long periods as the cost of food and grooms, if they were available, would be enormous, so horses and ponies had to be turned out to grass in good weather. From all sides friends came with offers of pasture and by the time the animals were in their temporary homes it was difficult to remember what was where. The Shetland ponies were in a field near Northolt aerodrome until the commanding officer telephoned to say they had just missed being machine-gunned by a low-flying Italian raider, who had sprayed the aerodrome.

Tom Tagg, who was then over seventy, and I went to collect them and it is hard to imagine being more exhausted than we were by the time we had rounded them up; it took nearly four hours and was like trying to catch eels with bare hands in a very large pond.

At about this time John Gindl, our elephant trainer, was interned, even though he was Austrian and as anti-Nazi as we were. Bernard took up his case but, by the time he had persuaded the authorities that a bomb anywhere near six elephants would be a bigger risk than one loose Austrian, Gindl could not be found. He had been put in a bus and sent to a camp which was full, so he was sent to another and then another and it was five days before he was released. In the meantime his wife, Gertie, never left the elephants for more than a few moments, for she was the one other person they knew really well. A few weeks after John's return a big bomb dropped in the heart of Buckinghamshire, miles from any kind of target, but only about forty yards from the elephants. They were terrified and, with trumpeting that could be heard half a mile away, tried to break loose, but John only lived twenty yards away and he dashed out shouting to them; as soon as they heard his voice they were as quiet as lambs. What was good enough for him was good enough for them. Animals are creatures of habit and are scared by the unknown or the unusual, just as children are, and we always had to have the trainers and grooms standing by on Guy Fawkes night. The bangs were bad enough, but there was also the risk of a stray rocket falling on a tent and the tent-

I

master and firemen had to keep a keen look out for anything of this kind.

One of the first things elephants are taught is to follow one another in correct order, with the one behind holding the tail of the one in front with its trunk. Apart from keeping them in their proper places it makes it easy for one man to prevent them straying when they are taken on the road. This gave rise to a tale about John Gindl during the short 1940 season when we were doing everything possible to economise. It was said that as the journey between two towns was very short we asked John to walk the elephants, but it was a foggy night and as they went over a level crossing a train crashed through the gates and killed one elephant. The train stopped and the driver came to say how sorry he was and that it was fortunate only one elephant was dead, to which John replied, 'Yes, but you have pulled the bottoms out of the other five.'

By the autumn of 1940 we had only two employees in an administrative capacity : Tom Tagg, who had charge of the animals, and Miss Moore. She had been employed by my father since she left school and at the time of his death was his private secretary and personal assistant. By this time she was secretary of the company and while Bernard and I were away doing our war jobs she had charge of what money there was and paid all the bills. One day she telephoned me to say she had a chance to let the Dorset Square offices for the duration of the war, but there was something very fishy going on and she did not feel safe in going ahead. When she explained how the negotiations were being conducted I could only think it looked like S.O.E. in its best cloak and dagger style and, having made enquiries through a friend and being informed my guess was correct, I was able to give Miss Moore an assurance that the rent would be paid. Dorset Square became part of the French Underground and the jumping off place for spies and saboteurs who were dropped in France. After the war a book called *The White Rabbit* told what went on there and in the tentacles which spread from there. Also in June 1957, an aircraft of the R.A.F. Transport Command brought over about forty men and women of the French Resistance to take part in what was called 'Operation *Croix de Lorraine*' and Her Majesty the Queen Mother unveiled a tablet beside the front door which reads : 'To commemorate the deeds of men and women of the Free French Forces and their British comrades who left from this house on special missions to enemy occupied territory and to honour those who did not return.' One Frenchman spotted the desk at which I still work and said he felt much easier now than when he had sat in front of it while being briefed just before being dropped in France.

With our circus closed for the duration of the war Britain no longer had a large travelling circus and it was only to be expected that the small ones would try to make a few trusses of hay while the sun shone, but unfortunately there was a crop of new-comers, some of which were run by people who knew nothing about the circus and cared less. Their only purpose was to get rich quickly and their shows soon earned the title 'Rogue Circus'. They were an embarrassment to the small family circuses which tried to carry on, for they left trails of unpaid bills and advertised things the programme did not contain and never had contained. The animal content of one amounted to an old pony and two dogs, but the limit was reached by the one which had three prices of admission and no seating. I suppose those who paid most were entitled to stand in the front, but in fact those who arrived first did so and late-comers had to take what space was left. Few of those who ran such shows believed in paying taxes and tickets were collected rather than torn so they could be sold over and over again. It would be no exaggeration to say that in some of these shows everything was a fiddle, but although some were in existence at the end of the war they disappeared quickly when the reputable circuses got going again. Still, they had left a nasty taste in many people's mouths.

One of the war-time circuses was in a different category; it opened near London and had quite a good little programme, but a big mistake was made. The circus was advertised as 'Jean [in small type] MILLS' Circus' and by the time I caught up it was within three miles of my home and it took me no time to tear down two of its posters, keep one, and send the other to our lawyers.

If the apostrophe had been placed so that the bill read 'Mill's Circus' it might have had a very wobbly leg to stand on, but no defence was entered to our application for an injunction and I heard no more of this show.

Only on two other occasions did we have trouble of this kind and it was given by the same man each time. Our circus was moving west during one of the very early seasons and a small circus was moving east and when they met, the two bill-posting teams got into conflict. There was an unwritten law that no circus covered the bills of another, but Charles Leighton, one of the best advance agents ever, telephoned to say his opposite number was covering all our bills. He was instructed to put more up, but they too were covered; we ordered an extra supply, but on the fourth day our pictorial bills had been slipped with the name of the other circus so it looked as if our acts were appearing in the other show. This meant that the public was being misled and it was going altogether too far, so I had the bills photographed and took prints to the owner of the other circus. He pretended to know nothing and tried to lay the blame with his advance agent, but I reminded him that that was not an excuse in law and said that if anything of the sort happened again I would give him good cause to regret it, as Bernard was in charge of our publicity and I did not intend to stand by while anybody tried to make a monkey of him. We had no more trouble of that kind, but a couple of years later the man had the cheek to advertise his show as the Olympia Circus. As soon as we had obtained an injunction he had new posters printed with Olympic Circus, so back to court we went and the judge told him he was within an inch of contempt of court and that he could expect to go to prison if he tried any more tricks of that kind.

In 1940 we were still running the Royal Opera House as a dance hall and had a fairly long tenancy, but neither Bernard nor I thought much of its chances and, rather than carry the risk of the big loss which one bomb could produce, we decided to shed part of what looked like a burden if we could find anyone willing to take it. Carl Heimann who, with Mecca, was still doing the catering, had teamed up with Alan Fairley and was running dance halls and it was obvious they were the ones to approach.

They liked the idea, as it meant nobody could be hurt badly and if the war did not last too long and we were able to hang on until it ended we should have a valuable business. No large capital was needed as the place was a going concern so Carl, Alan, Russell Pickering, Bernard and I put up a thousand pounds each, but in our hurry to get on with other things we acted on just about the worst piece of 'professional' advice any of us has ever been given. We formed a new company and, as it had no pre-war profits standard, all the profits were treated as surplus war profits and taxed 100%. If the business had been carried on by Cyril & Bernard Mills Ltd. the result would have been very different, as we had established a profit stand-ard which ran into many thousands of pounds. The first years were unrewarding, but by the time American troops had come here good profits were made; however, they all went to the tax-gatherer. Even that was not the end of a sorry tale, for in the late stages of the war there was an opportunity to extend the lease for a long period, at what should have been considered a reasonable rent, but again professional opinion was the cause of the chance being missed. When the lease expired soon after the war the Royal Opera House had been a 'half-crown-hop' dance hall for more than twenty winter seasons and the rents paid had played some part in keeping grand opera alive during the pre-war years, which were perhaps the most difficult in its history.

Chapter Ten
Getting going again

Although the staff was so small the cost of keeping the circus
dormant during the war was a big drain on our bank balance,
for horses and ponies had to be stabled, fed and groomed in
winter and the lions and elephants had to be fed and exercised
all the time. It cost about £11,000 just to feed the elephants
during the war and, as the new company had been in existence
such a short time, it was not long before Bernard and I had to
give financial assistance. Not a penny was earned for several
months, but by the time the worst of the bombing was over
Tom Arnold started a stage circus and Bernard was able to
secure some useful contracts for our animals. These produced
enough money to feed animals and pay the staff, but having
had so much trouble with the elephants when we ran a stage
circus we were not surprised that T.A. did not want them. We
were luckier at Blackpool, where Clem Butson was still running
the Tower Circus and Gindl and the six elephants spent a considerable time there. Even so, by the time the war ended our
bank balance left precious little room for manœuvre.

Bernard was released from the R.A.F. about the middle of

1945, but although I did not return to England before September we had decided to reopen the tenting circus in 1946. Olympia was still a Government clothing store and there was no hope of getting a programme and staff by December that year.

We contacted every pre-war member of the staff of whose whereabouts we knew and considered ourselves lucky by the time about fifteen per cent of those who had been with us in 1939 were on the way back—and of course all these people were destined for key positions in future.

Stanley Franklin was earmarked for manager. Davis, 'Dave' as he was known to everyone, was back in his old job as chief engineer as were Jack Lindsley, the musical director, and Mrs. Wilmer, the wardrobe mistress. Dick Taylor had been promoted to train master and Frankie Craig to property master and senior ring foreman. Tom Tagg, now over eighty years of age, was again master of horse and Tony Yelding, who had been a rider in the bare-back act before the war, was to become ringmaster for the first time. Very soon he was to prove himself a far better one than we had ever had and the most conscientious man the circus ever employed. Nobody restarting a circus could have had a better team. The only people we really missed were Wallace Gibson, who for health reasons did not feel able to return to such an arduous life, and Kral, the tentmaster, who died at the end of the war. But he and his number two, Vaclavik, had remained in this country and it was Vaclavik who was to be the new tentmaster.

One day when I returned to the office from Ascot Bernard told me that during the day he had booked an act called the two Cromwells; he had seen them working in a stage circus during the war. The news gave me a nasty shock, for it was an act I had turned down because it included what I had regarded as a suicide trick. I was soon relieved of my worry, for Bernard told me that the first thing they had done was show him a letter which I had written seven years earlier. They had carried the letter ever since and told him they had never done the trick which I disliked since they received my letter.

For the first post-war summer programme in 1946 we had

to rely on acts which were in Britain and those which we could produce with our own animals and people, but where horses were concerned we had had a crushing blow. Charlie Mroczkowski had produced outstanding horse acts for us before the war, but before we had been able to announce our plans he had received and accepted an offer of a long contract at a big dollar salary from Ringling. We were therefore with horses and without a trainer, but John Gindl came to the rescue. He, having been a Hagenbeck man, could train and present horses, ponies and zebras as well as he presented elephants, so he took over all the Liberty and High School horses as well. The fact that when he first came to us it was in order to present an act which included zebras reminds me of the small boy who saw one for the first time in the menagerie and asked what it was. When his mother told him he replied: 'Oh, I thought it was a pony in a football jersey.'

We were afraid, when restarting the circus, that we should have forgotten a great deal of what 'know-how' we had had before the war and were certain that in taking the road we should forget to take everything with us; with these thoughts it was only logical that we should reopen at Slough which was the nearest town to Ascot.

We applied to the Slough Council for a ground and thought we only had to await the next meeting of the Parks Committee to be told what rent we should have to pay; but our application was turned down because the ground had been let to some mushroom circus during the war and had been left in such a filthy condition that the council had passed a resolution that no corporation property was to be let to circuses in future. We were told it was almost certain the resolution would be rescinded in our favour, but that would mean waiting for the next council meeting and be too late. We immediately thought of the ground Eton College had let us have before the war, but it had been ploughed and we should never be able to get our heavy vehicles on and off it. Only one place was left and although I never believed Bernard would have enough courage to ask for it he did so. In the first place the application had to be made to the Windsor Council, but then, although encouraging noises had been made, there was some delay and it looked as if somebody higher up had to be consulted. I shall never know the truth of the matter, but I suspect that it may have been His Majesty, King George VI, who gave the final word of approval for the site of the circus was just below and almost in the shadow of Windsor Castle in the Home Park.

We arrived at this most wonderful site on a Thursday, eleven days before we were due to open, knowing we must allow plenty of time for the build-up with only one qualified tentman and the rest of the crew untrained and far below strength. By erecting the stable tents as soon as we arrived we planned to open the menagerie on Saturday morning, knowing that the sixpences would be useful by the time pay day arrived. Saturday had therefore been advertised as the day the box office would open and as it approached we kept our fingers crossed, hoping a few people would remember our pre-war reputation and risk buying seats without waiting to hear what the press thought of the show.

We worked late on Friday night and I did not put in an appearance until about nine-thirty in the morning; the sight that awaited me was one to make any circus man's heart leap with joy. There, half an hour before the box office was to open, stood a queue of at least 120 people and more were coming along the road. This was no time to keep customers waiting but we had not dared to hope or plan for this sort of thing. We had only one cashier as yet and her job was to have been the sale of menagerie tickets so any of us who thought we could sell tickets had a go at it and how Franklin made the accounts balance at the end of the week, if he did, I shall never know. No box office man dreads anything more than having inexperienced people handling tickets and money. But if there were mistakes nobody cared; what mattered was that we sold a great many tickets and were able to go to the bank on Monday heavily laden for the first time in nearly seven years.

In the meantime the menagerie had opened. Our first two customers were small boys and I could not resist the temptation to tear their tickets myself and keep our halves for my collection —they represented the first shilling taken in an era when our receipts were to run into millions but we did not know that then.

The queues lasted all week and when we opened we had already sold most of the Windsor tickets and by Wednesday were selling tickets for Reading, the next town, to people who were willing to follow us. And all this happened in Holy Week when there is little business normally. Someone dared to suggest we should open on Good Friday, but that was trodden on with a big foot as something we had never done and should never do in all our days.

Either Bernard or I must have made a careless remark to Mother before we moved to Windsor, but even if our finances were at an all time low we did not want her or anyone else to know it. We believed we should just be able to scrape through, since the artistes would not have to be paid until the end of the first week and accounts from suppliers were not likely to arrive for a week or two, as we had placed all our orders with firms we had dealt with before the war and they knew our credit rating had been high then. Within a few hours of our arrival at Windsor the postman delivered a registered envelope addressed to us both and as it bore the Chesham postmark we guessed it was a letter of good wishes from Mother; in fact, it contained a cheque for several thousand pounds and a little note saying she hoped it would be enough to tide us over until the money started coming in. It was with a sense of gratitude and relief that we were able to hand the uncashed cheque back to her when she attended the opening performance.

The day the circus re-opened we were rewarded far far more than we deserved to be; we had two full houses and among the audience were hundreds of friends who, unknown to us, had bought tickets and made the journey to Windsor to give us a send-off. The next day the national press was wonderful and although in our view the programme fell far short of our pre-war standards it contained lots of things people had not seen for a very long time. Also, I think it had a good deal of the old Mills spit and polish, for everything had been rehearsed to the last degree and costumes and uniforms, most of which had been stored carefully during the war, were probably of better quality than those seen in theatres during and just after the war.

Getting things up to what, we had to admit, was a far call from the standards to which we were accustomed had been a long series of headaches for, with everything rationed, even a few feet of timber to make a part of the seating safe was difficult to obtain. Because we had not operated during the war we had lost the right to limited supplies of many things which those who had continued in business could obtain; we had even lost our right to a few gallons of ice cream and it was only because our suppliers were good friends that we had any—they let us have any surpluses there were. It seemed a strange way of treating a firm that had closed and tried to help the war effort.

Feeding the staff looked like being a major problem and I had to go to Colwyn Bay to get a licence from the Ministry of Food, but was told by one official after another that none of the licences applied to a travelling circus. To have accepted this ruling would almost have meant no circus, so I demanded to see someone at the top and fortunately got as far as a high-ranking civil servant who was intelligent enough to realise that if the rules did not cover a large tenting circus it was because no such thing existed when they were made. He promised to issue what he called a peripatetic licence, but said nobody would know what that was (I didn't) and I should have to send him our route in advance so that he could instruct local offices of the Ministry to see that local tradesmen were given supplies for us.

In the event, feeding the staff was not as big a problem as we had expected, for tradesmen who sold rationed goods were allowed a small surplus to compensate for waste and if they were careful there was always a little over at the end of the week. If they favoured a regular customer there was a risk she would boast over the garden wall and then Mrs. Smith would want to keep up with Mrs. Jones, but we had no garden wall and the tradesmen knew we should be gone next week.

Being in Windsor during Holy Week meant there was no possibility of a visit by any member of the Royal Family, even though they spent Easter at the castle and could hardly have failed to see the circus from the terraces. Nevertheless, the fact that we were there must have aroused some interest, for at

Reading the following week we had the honour of a visit from their Royal Highnesses the Princesses Elizabeth and Margaret one day and their Royal Highnesses the Duchess of Kent, Prince Edward, Princess Alexandra and Prince Michael the next. Both visits produced photographs in nearly every newspaper and did more than anything else to let the public know Bertram Mills Circus was back in business. We count ourselves very fortunate that Her Majesty the Queen and Princess Margaret have visited our circus so often, for their visits and those of other members of the Royal Family have given it prestige of a kind which no other has enjoyed. Perhaps it is due to the fact that all members of the Royal Family are animal lovers and understand animals. When they saw them in the pink of condition, housed as well as is possible in a circus and often better than in some static places, they may have realised that our animals were as well cared for as any. I am quite unable to convince myself that any member of the Royal Family would ever have come to the circus if they thought there was any truth in the kind of anti-circus propaganda which one or two subscription-gatherers publish.

During the first post-war tour we had our trains back, but the railways could only move us at week-ends and they said we should have to wait at least until 1948 before we could move overnight, as we had done before the war. If this was worrying in one sense it was a relief in another for, with so many un-trained men, we were as unready for mid-week moves as the railways. This meant big towns only during 1946 and it looked as if we should have to go to several large places which really ought to be kept for 1947 and 1948; if this happened there would be nothing left but three-day towns for 1948. Reading had been a three-day town before the war and Slough had been a four-day disappointment in 1940, but now the business was so incredibly good in both that we were able to make a hasty reappraisal of the situation and route the circus into a number of what we regarded as three-day towns, with the in-tention of staying a week in each. We even took the risk of stay-ing a fortnight in towns where, in the early years, a week had been enough or even too much.

It all worked like a dream and wherever we went the big top

was packed. But even such prosperity can bring its troubles, for there were invariably more people than the tent would hold and some wit suggested we should have an elastic one. In normal times it creates a good impression if a few people have to be turned away when the house is full, but our problem was that they were not prepared to be turned away; some tried to get in by offering big tips to the staff rather than have their children disappointed.

If we had been greedy we could have increased prices overnight between one town and the next, but even though we had to recoup our war-time losses our reputation was worth more than any immediate gain, so prices remained unchanged. One day in Liverpool the show was about to begin, the tent was full, but nearly two thousand people were still wanting to buy seats. Some unreasonable man shouted something to the effect it was a racket and that as we were turning people away at every performance we ought to have a bigger tent. He was accompanied by five or six of his kind and they announced they were going in and started pushing. Nothing can be more frightening when there is a large percentage of women and children present for, to resist the pushers and protect their families, other men naturally push in the opposite direction and the whole crowd begins to roll back and forth like waves on a beach and nobody can blame mothers if they panic in such circumstances.

For a moment things looked ugly and at one time the crowd swayed against the walls of the high vestibule tent and there was the danger that it would fall on them. Fortunately, there were several policemen present; they had been dealing with the abnormal traffic caused by the circus and they waded in and had things under control quickly. Nevertheless people still hung around hoping, until a police sergeant announced he had been inside the tent and was satisfied it was full and that we had taken a proper decision in refusing to admit anyone else.

The determination to see the circus at all costs manifested itself in a variety of ways, but perhaps the worst case, even if we laughed about it later, also occurred at Liverpool. I had been away for two days and when I returned my caravan was spotlessly clean as usual, but it smelled like a hospital and I thought my batman had been a bit over-industrious. Later, when I said I should find it difficult to sleep with such a strong smell of disinfectant, some of the managerial staff laughed, but gave no explanation for the giggles at first. When I tried to find what the joke was I learned there had been an emergency during the matinée that day; a woman had gone into labour and been put in my caravan to await the arrival of an ambulance, but by the time it arrived time had already run out and the baby had been born. When it was all over mother and child went off to hospital and the mother's only comment was that she knew she only had about forty-eight hours to go, but she wanted to see the circus and knew it would be gone by the time she came out of hospital.

Until about that time all circuses drove stakes manually; as we had over five hundred and many of them were more than five feet long, it was a job which took twenty men a day using fourteen-pound sledge-hammers. It was hard work and, being done before the arrival of the circus, most of those who did it were casuals who had neither the skill nor the stamina needed. Hammer shafts were broken by the dozen and very often men hit their own legs or feet and had to go to hospital. It occurred to me that if those very noisy pneumatic hammers used on roads could break concrete, they could drive stakes if adapted, but when I suggested it to some of the circus people their comment was to the effect that, if it would work other circuses would have done it a generation ago. However, I could think of no snag so had a hammer adapted and hired a compressor for one day. The job was done in five hours by two untrained men and of course the tentmaster and his staff were delighted, so we ordered a compressor and two hammers; thereafter the work was done by four men in about two hours. The machines saved time and money and eliminated accidents, but we had a lucky escape once. A very long stake was being driven when it struck an underground high tension cable; the man using the hammer was unharmed, as we had fitted the handles with insulators against just such a possibility, but half a fairly large city including three big factories was blacked out for a few hours. Fortunately, we were not to blame for we knew the cable existed and had insisted its position should be marked with a white line, but the line had been put in the wrong place. The news that we had found an easy way to do the worst job in the circus spread along the grape vine quickly and within a short time every circus that prided itself on being well-equipped was using a mechanical stake driver.

When the 1946 tour ended we had visited only twenty-four towns—little more than half the number we should have played on a similar tour in 1938—but over a million people had seen the show. In the meantime Olympia had been released from war service and the owners had promised to have it ready in good time but, apart from the problems there would be in getting essential materials for the build-up, most of the men who built the seating (the greater part of it belonged to the building) were no longer there and, just as we had wondered a few months before if we remembered how to run a circus, we were now wondering whether we and the Olympia people would remember all the details of the build-up in Olympia. We were to be the first post-war tenants and our landlords allowed the build-up to begin some days before our tenancy started, so their staff had about three weeks to do what normally had to be done in nine days. They were as anxious as we were to see Olympia a going concern again.

We were back in our offices at Dorset Square and although the agents were selling tickets like hot cakes, those who wanted to book direct with us could only do so by writing to the box office at Olympia. We moved the box office staff there a couple of weeks earlier than usual, for we had had a message from the local post-master that a large quantity of mail was accumulating. This was wonderful news, for it looked like a repetition of the pattern we had seen at Windsor, but the shock came when we asked for our mail to be delivered. Not just one big sack full of letters; not two sacks or a dozen; but three van loads and all the letters contained cheques, postal orders or cash.

A pools promoter would have been ready for this sort of thing, but we weren't. We bought a mechanical letter opener and everyone went to help the box office staff, but letters arrived far faster than we could deal with them so for some days the back-log increased. Then the real trouble began, for people telephoned and wrote to ask whether their orders and money had arrived and in most cases the letters had not yet been opened, so we did not know the answer. Several clerks had to be taken off more pressing work to deal with these enquiries, by explaining the flood, for it was essential to keep people happy; if they thought their letters had gone astray they would put a stop on cheques and that would have produced a tangle which nobody would have been able to unravel.

What really worried us was that people knew that if they wrote to us before the war they had their tickets in three or four days, so they now had every reason to wonder what had happened to Bertram Mills Circus, as there were delays of two or three weeks. Our mail had reached the dimensions of an avalanche and was making it impossible for us to live up to what the public was entitled to expect of us. In the long run, hours of toil by a splendid, but all too small, staff prevailed and by the time the box office opened for cash sales, eighteen days before the circus, we had broken the back of the postal flood and thought all would be plain sailing. So many people had booked by post that Boxing Day and Saturdays were all but sold out and other days so well booked that we were assured of a bumper season. We were, therefore, not entitled to expect an abnormal rush on the box office when it opened, but again we were surprised. It had been advertised to take place on December 2nd and by eight o'clock that morning an Olympia gateman telephoned to say a queue was forming and by opening time it stretched twice the length of the private road leading to Olympia. The normal quota of six cashiers was useless and help was brought in from other departments; every possible window was opened, but although we sold tickets faster than we had ever done the queue lengthened twice as fast as we shortened it. It stretched over the bridge and down Kensington High Street. Police reinforcements were rushed down to keep things under control, but still the queue grew longer. Jimmy Breeds, our head linkman, kept going down the line telling people we were selling as fast as possible, but those at the tail end would have a long wait unless they preferred to return another day.

All day, with only sandwiches and cups of tea grabbed while selling, the staff carried on and by six o'clock everyone was about ready to drop; but there were still two hours to go and something drastic had to be done. A man was posted at the end of the queue and new arrivals were told they could not be served that day. Eight o'clock—closing time—came, but still the queue was 150 yards long and four abreast and as they had been at it for ten hours nobody could have said less than a sincere thank you if the staff had said they were too tired to continue. But not a bit of it; there were *only* thirteen or fourteen hundred customers left and everyone volunteered to continue if only because these patrons had waited so long already. It was nearly ten o'clock when the last one had her tickets and everyone in the box office was dead beat, but if they had had a rough day they knew it had been worse for the patrons, for they had been out of doors and it had been a cold December day. For us, it had been a day to remember and it is doubtful whether anyone else in show business has seen one like it.

The strain on the staff and on those who came to buy during the next few days was only just bearable and as one performance after another was sold out we had to send notices to thousands of people to say there were no seats for the performance selected and offer whatever was left. Telephone bookings had to be refused when there were only a few thousand seats left and by the time the circus opened on December 20th we, with the help of the ticket agents, had sold well over half a million tickets and the only ones left were those we were keeping up our sleeves at each performance for V.I.P. guests and just in case there was any chance we might have visits from the Royal Family. What a good thing it was we kept those tickets.

The opening was preceded by a luncheon at which the Lord Mayor was the guest of honour, but Lord Lonsdale had died and our very dear friend Lord Burghley, now the Marquess of Exeter, had become our honorary president and was to continue to hold that office until my last circus. Compiling the list of guests was one of the worst jobs we ever had, for we knew that the National Hall would not be available for the lunch in a couple of years time. When that happened the number of guests would have to be reduced from about thirteen hundred to five hundred, which was the capacity of the largest restaurant in Olympia, so it was obviously better to make the cut at once as we should be helped by any wastage there had been during the war years. The result, whilst comparatively small, was every bit as distinguished a gathering as its predecessors and for the first time it became possible for the guests to be announced and received as they arrived.

I was no less nervous on this occasion than I had been at the last pre-war lunch and my embarrassment was only increased by the fact that in my speech in reply to David Burghley's toast to the circus I found it impossible to give proper thanks for the very kind things he had said about our parents, and the effort we were making to put Bertram Mills Circus back on its feet. When he had said these things he had his audience aching with laughter when he suggested some of the duties in which he might become involved in his capacity of honorary president of the circus and then he gave all those members of the Cabinet who were present, including Clement Attlee, a thorough going over on the way the 'Westminster Circus' is run.

When my turn came there was barely fifteen minutes before the circus was to begin, so I could do little more than try to express the thanks which were due to all those whose support had enabled and was enabling us to get going again.

At half past two there was a fanfare by four trumpeters of the Household Cavalry and the toastmaster made his announcement in the circus : 'My Lord President, your Excellencies, your Graces, my Lords, Ladies and Gentlemen, pray silence for the Right Honourable the Lord Mayor of London.' With that the Lord Mayor in his scarlet robes rose and, after making a charming speech welcoming the circus back as one of the things that was part of London, said : 'I now declare the circus open.' The band struck up, the parade began and we were back in business in the place of our birth and without a worry of any kind. All we had to do now was run the show for about six weeks knowing the 'House Full' board would be out at every

performance. If we had any anxiety it was whether the programme we had been able to put together was good enough for
the volume of patronage it was to have.

The next day the newspapers contained notices as good as
any we have ever had. One critic used the headline : 'Circus in
the Mills Tradition—a triumph of production.' Another, under the headline 'Greatest Show on Earth', said, 'Magic has
descended on the place . . . the great day the circus came to
town again brought out a crowd that nothing short of a
national celebration could assemble . . . a rare piece of pre-war
miraculously preserved—gay, colourful, exciting, unchanged in
a changing world.' And then : 'Show me the man who dislikes
the circus and I will show you a corpse or an unregenerate
Scrooge.' All this naturally increased the pressure on the box
office where there were no tickets to sell, so we had to do something to prevent the golden chances slipping through our fingers; what we did was probably one of the most cheeky things
ever done in the history of show business. We started selling
seats for the following winter simply by issuing receipts and
promising to post tickets when they came from the printers
several weeks later. And we got away with it. What amounted
to pre-advance booking was so great that we decided to extend the 1947–8 tenancy by four days and by doing this we
were able, during the following winter, to sell nearly 50,000
more seats than we had sold in a season which had been so
good that we had assumed the record set up would never be
broken. At this time the public's appetite for circus was in-
satiable and ours was the only big circus attempting to cater for
it and when our accounts for the first post-war year were ready
they showed we had wiped out our war-time losses, paid the
heavy cost of relaunching the show and made a profit of
£211,000.

We had had the fun fair at Olympia, but one of my big worries had been to find somebody reliable to provide the big
rides. By this time Billy Butlin was heavily committed to getting
his holiday camps open again and, although I did not fancy
my chances with him, I thought it was worth a try. We met
and, during a discussion which lasted as long as one drink, the

deal was done. As I left he said: 'It will be fun being back at Olympia and it's nice to be able to do business so quickly—I reckon we have done about £40,000 worth in five minutes.' As things turned out, it was a remarkably good guess.

We were still a private company and only obliged to reveal our profits to the Inland Revenue, but the business we had done both in London and the provinces could only be expected to produce green eyes—and indeed it did. Chipperfields, who had had a menagerie which travelled with fairs and later a small circus, decided to become big in a big way; Billy Smart, a travelling showman who had never been heard of in the circus world, added a large circus to his travelling fair and even if he made mistakes in the early days money was so easy to make that they were paid for quickly. Tom Arnold, having run stage circuses during the war, decided to run a winter circus at Harringay and Clem Butson left the Tower Circus at Blackpool and joined him as booking manager and producer of the show.

None of this worried Bernard or me for the time being, as there was so much money about for circuses that anybody who started one was sure to make money and there would still be enough left for others. What did worry us was that we had to divide and share equally the enormous profit we had made and by the time taxes had been paid, at rates up to nineteen and sixpence in the pound, our incomes would not be large. Worse still, there seemed to be no way in which a private company could put a sensible amount into reserve against a rainy day. There appeared to be only one solution to this problem, but it was one for which neither of us cared very much, since we felt —as Father had done—that it was important to maintain the personal touch the circus had always had. If we became a public company the public might feel the circus had become a machine run by financiers whose only interest would be the money they could get out of it. We feared it might be thought that the family spirit had gone out of the business, but it was still the only thing to do provided Bernard and I could retain complete administrative control as long as it was to be known as Bertram Mills Circus. Someone else might one day have a right to use the name Mills in connection with a circus—we might even sell our own name one day, but we never should sell the name Bertram. We considered, as Mother did, that we had every right to use that name so long as we controlled the business, but the idea of selling it to be exploited by anyone else was unthinkable.

Having decided what had to be done, the next thing was to find someone to do it and I turned to my old friend Sir Edward Reid, a senior partner in Barings. Nobody could have been greener than I was about the flotation of a public company and I don't think any circus in history had ever had a Stock Exchange quotation, but when Barings offered to do all that had to be done we knew we were in the best hands in the City of London.

The result was that, during the summer of 1947, Bernard and I each sold one third of our shares so that in future we should each hold one third of the equity. Bernard and I continued as joint managing directors with long service agreements and George Ritchie of Barings joined the Board.

In the meantime, the circus had gone to Scotland where it ran into a polio epidemic which affected attendances seriously for about two months during the height of the season. During our last visit to Glasgow we had had the international crisis and the big top torn to ribbons in a gale; this time it was polio, but history was to repeat itself, for we had another wind of hurricane force and again the tent 'went with the wind'. We were able to carry on with a well used pre-war roof while a new one was being made, but by this time I had had my fill of blow-downs. In twelve seasons we had lost four roofs each costing five or six thousand pounds and one only escaped narrowly in Scarborough, in 1934, where we lost two performances while the damage was repaired. We were still using two-pole big tops, but the best equipped circuses in Germany were using four-polers and nobody had lost one in a gale, so we had one made by the Gourock Ropeworks Company of Port Glasgow. The result more than justified the change for, although the four-poler takes longer to erect and strike, and costs more, we were able to operate during the last fifteen seasons of our tenting life without losing a single tent.

Although attendances during the 1947 summer were lower than those of 1946 we did even better than we had done the year before at Olympia, but our profits for the year were only £178,000—a drop of £33,000. The polio epidemic had cost more than that and the tour had been a more expensive one as we had travelled much further.

If there was one night in 1947 which none of us will ever forget, it was that on which Winston and Mrs. Churchill came to Olympia. They arrived when the performance had been in progress about fifteen minutes and as they went to the box the whole audience rose and cheered. The band and even the artistes in the ring had to stop while the cheering lasted. The expression 'he stopped the show' is one which has lost its true meaning by abuse, but in this case it is really true that the old gentleman did so.

If the first two post-war years were good, 1947–8 was even better, for we broke all our own records and probably those of every British circus before or since. Again over a million people saw the show during the summer and more than 600,000 saw it at Olympia and our profit for the year reached the enormous total of £243,965.

Even so, the year had not been entirely free from worries. We began the summer tour with a group of lions presented by Nicolai, a Greek, but his contract was about to expire and he was in the process of handing the animals over to Togare who, having lost his own animals during the war, had rejoined us as a house trainer. Each evening, after the last show, the cage was built and Nicolai and Togare entered first with one lion and then another, but there was one big male which did not take kindly to his new boss although he would do anything for Nicolai. Togare had been warned this animal did not take well to strangers, but he was a trainer long before Nicolai and was in too much hurry to get rid of his instructor. One evening he insisted on taking the lions through the routine alone, but we took the precaution of having the fire hose ready and Nicolai stood with his hand on the door of the cage. Half way through the act Togare, his back almost turned, went too near the big male while doing a trick with another lion. The big one took a swipe at him with his fore paw, but almost before we realised what had happened Nicolai was in the ring and there was peace. Nevertheless, the swipe cost Togare some time in hospital and deflated his ego considerably.

When he returned he had to take things more easily and when he took over the act he showed it well. On one occasion he passed some remarks to which Bernard took exception, as they were made in front of the ladies in the general office, and when he was warned this sort of thing would not be tolerated he announced he would stay till the end of the season and then tear up his unexpired contract. Bernard replied that he need not delay and could leave at once, so we were without a wild animal act in the show for the time being.

As soon as Togare had gone Alex Kerr came to the office. He was the son of a Glasgow police officer who had joined us as head elephant keeper because he wanted to be where there were animals. He had had a little experience with wild animals at a small zoo, where his first job had been to polish the shields of tortoises. He said he had watched Togare at every performance and, when nobody was looking, had made friends with the lions to the point where he could stroke them through the bars. Even so, to let him try to present the act looked a dangerous sort of proposition, but there was one thing in his favour: he was a serious man—there was nothing of the 'have-a-go-at-anything' type about him and Bernard agreed to give him a chance.

One by one and then two by two he had the lions in the cage with him, but this time there was no instructor and he was quite alone. All we could give by way of protection was the ever-ready fire hose but it was never needed; even the big male that had attacked Togare took to him like a duck to water and within a few weeks he was showing the act every bit as well as his predecessors. He remained with us twelve years and during that time produced, with different sets of cubs, three new wild animal acts one of which contained lions, tigers and a leopard.

It was during one of the early post-war seasons at Olympia that we had a reminder of the unusual troubles a circus can encounter. We had a sealion act and during the interval at a dress rehearsal some of the children who were our guests found their way through the unattended entrance of the enclosure where the sealions were. Under their tank wagon was a four-day supply of fish and they dumped the lot in the tank. Now sealions, like wild animals and fish, rely for their food on being fast enough to catch it and when they have eaten as much as is good for them they can no longer catch more. Therefore in a circus animals are rationed to the quantities that are good for them but naturally the sealions ate the lot. Within hours they were ill and unable to perform and nothing their owner could do would produce a movement of the bowels; after three days they were all expected to die, but Bernard had a brain wave. He telephoned a big chemist's shop and asked if they had any sea salt—which is normally sold by the ounce. When they said they had, he asked how much there was and the reply was, 'Plenty', but he insisted on knowing how much that meant. When told there was about forty pounds in stock he said he wanted the lot and sent a car for it. It all went into the sealion tank and within a couple of hours a result was produced and the sealions were back in the ring two days later. Their owner had never heard of such a cure and even though it looks like common sense at this distance somebody had to be bright enough to think of it quickly at the time.

Chapter Eleven
Early post-war years
The Hamilton affair

Ever since the opening at Windsor I had believed business would be enormous during the next few years, for consumer goods were scarce and even clothes were still rationed, but it was too much to expect that what, for us, was a boom period would last for ever. The job of keeping costs down was difficult, for when money is so easy to earn those who have no experience of periods of slump and little idea of values throw money about like drunken sailors. Newcomers to the circus business all over the world were no exception; with the result that artistes' salaries soared out of all proportion to the increase in the cost of living and some circus owners offered absurd sums for grounds they wished to occupy. They quite overlooked the fact that if they paid £250 for about an acre of land for a week they were paying rent at the rate of £13,000 a year for what had probably been bought for only a fraction of that amount.

Our new competitor in London, the Tom Arnold Circus, did not worry us. Harringay is a great distance from Olympia and we could do good business without having to draw people from North and East London and there were more than enough people living in the area served by Harringay to keep it full. Before the war there had been circuses at the Agricultural Hall at Islington and the Crystal Palace and people enough to satisfy us all. Nor did we worry for the time being about the big new tenting circuses of Chipperfield and Smart, although it was obvious they would become serious competitors before long in the provinces—if only because most places would have a big circus every year, whereas it had been once in three years in the past and our own early years had shown that few provincial centres could support a big show every year.

This, however, was a problem concerning the future and during each of the first four post-war years we were able to pay dividends of three hundred per cent on a capital of £30,000 and at the same time were able to put considerable sums to reserve and these enabled us, among other things, to become the owners of the buildings we occupied in Dorset Square and, from 1963 onwards, at Isleworth.

From 1950 onwards things became increasingly difficult and by 1955 the dividend was down to twenty-five per cent, but even so we were still playing to an average of over 1,200,000 people a year, which was good by anybody's standard. The trouble was that costs were rising at an alarming rate even though the huge demand for circus was proven. A circus is like a train; when a certain percentage of the seats are occupied expenses are covered and the proceeds on the sale of all others is clear profit, but it is wrong to assume that circuses always make huge profits just because hundreds of thousands attend; just as it is a fallacy to assume British Railways should make fabulous sums because they carry millions.

Before the war we could pay expenses and make a profit if we sold fifty per cent of our seats, but by now we had to sell seventy-five per cent of them to keep out of the red. Until then there had been only one price for adults and children for, even if we hate to admit it and have tried to combat it, a large section of the public regards the circus as an entertainment for children. On this basis our prices were those which parents should have been able to pay for their children and if they accompanied them they did so at children's prices. The one price rule had been maintained throughout the years, even though there is a saying that it takes five grown-ups to take one kid to the circus and in spite of the fact that an evening audience of seven thousand at Olympia seldom contained more than a couple of hundred children.

We were convinced that, with the demand for circus proven up to the hilt, the proper thing to do was to increase our prices a little each year to keep them in balance with the rise in the cost of living. Others believed that by cutting prices they could create an even greater demand and bring back all those who could now spend their money on much needed consumer goods. We refused to have anything to do with price-cutting for some time but eventually had to fall in line and once we had done so there existed a position from which no circus could retreat.

These were some of the things which were worrying us when we left Glasgow in the autumn of 1959, but we had no idea of what horror awaited us a week later in Hamilton. It is a story I hate even to think about, but it is part of the story of Bertram Mills Circus and it would be wrong to omit it.

As most people know, Hamilton has a large Southern Irish population and an almost equally large one which comes from the Six Counties and there exist there the same tensions as in other places where the two meet. Among our tentmen was an excellent lad who came from Belfast, but he, as we were to learn, was not averse to a scrap with a Southerner and soon after the arrival of the circus he picked up a girl in a café who had been going steady with a chap from Dublin. A fight resulted and our man came out so much the better that his opponent decided to get level with him.

All was normal until about eleven o'clock on Saturday night. We were moving to Ayr and the big top was down and loaded, and most of the stakes had been drawn, when a hail of bricks descended on our men from what had appeared to be onlookers. Within seconds our men were being attacked and there were fights everywhere and in some cases our men were badly outnumbered. Fortunately the diesel generators were some distance away and I was able to make my voice heard telling everyone to get into the circus ring. In fact, there was no longer a circus ring, but our men knew where it had been and very quickly eighty or ninety of us were assembled facing outwards and able to see the strength of the threat. Genuine onlookers had had the sense to move away and when the ruffians saw how many we were they, like the cowards they were, retired and we carried on with our work. The gate leading to the road was some distance away and just inside it was one of our tractors which had returned from the station and was awaiting another load; fortunately the driver had left it, for the next thing we heard was the sound of it being smashed up. Some of us rushed over just in time to see an elderly man waving his arms and telling a gang of hoodlums not to do that sort of thing. When I was still some yards away this man was set upon by eight or ten thugs, floored and kicked unmercifully. The whole thing only took a few seconds and then the attackers, realising they had gone too far, made a dash for the gate. Very soon the police arrived but some of us had been able to have a clear sight of most of those who had used their boots for there was good street lighting only a few yards away. When I saw the man on the ground at close quarters I knew at once why he had been attacked; he was of very similar appearance to our staff manager, Bill Wooll. Bill had never harmed any of these men, but he was part of the circus and I think any one of us who had been alone would have been attacked that night. If ruffians cannot find the man against whom they have a grudge they often take it out on the next of kin and as the old man was alone, and appeared to be acting in the interest of the circus, he was a good enough target for them.

By the time our last train had been loaded we were told the old man had died in hospital and realised that we had witnessed a murder; in the meantime we had given descriptions of the culprits and the police were turning the town inside out to find them. By 2 a.m. four of us were asked to attend identification parades which went on for several hours and at the end of which we had picked out six or seven men, but only those four who were identified by all of us were charged and some weeks later three of them were sentenced to death but the fourth established an alibi.

We assumed there would be no more trouble when we left Hamilton, but the following Saturday night in Ayr the pull-down was going according to plan just before midnight when two of the king pole guys were untied on one side of the tent and the roof and poles crashed to the ground. During pull-downs we had adequate lighting for our work, but it was concentrated on the area of operations rather than on the spectators, who were always present and to whom nobody ever paid any attention. When the tent crashed it could have injured anything up to fifty people, but only one man was hurt and he had a leg broken; however, Alan Bain, the superintendent of works, was missing and could not be found until somebody noticed what looked like a bundle of something under the canvas. Alan had been trapped there and was lying face down under half an acre of canvas, but not a bit worried as he had plenty of air and knew he would be released as soon as the roof was unlaced and folded.

Some untrained man might have untied one guy wire by mistake, but for two to be untied on different king poles at the same moment was too much to be treated as a coincidence and we always assumed this accident, the only one of its kind we ever had, was a sequence of the Hamilton affair.

We missed Hamilton during our next three or four visits to Scotland and although I was worried about going in 1962, as the convicted men had been reprieved, had served their time and been released, we went there; but happily there was no trouble.

Carlisle followed Ayr and by the time we arrived it was blowing so hard we could not even put the stable tents up during the Sunday so the horses, having been given a chance to stretch their legs, had to return to the horse boxes on the train where they were fed and watered until the next day, but we had to find somewhere to put the elephants and they spent the night in some boarded up railway arches. By noon on Monday we had the stable tents up, but the big top had to wait till Tuesday and we lost a day. On Tuesday afternoon we opened again, but by Wednesday the gale had returned and was so severe that it looked as if we should have to pull the big top down to save it.

Fortunately there was a river alongside the ground and by keeping the roof drenched and taut with our own fire engine and that of the local fire brigade we kept it up until the wind dropped.

By the time the post-war boom was at an end we had been able to improve programmes enormously, but when I first went back to Germany in 1948 the ban on ex-enemy aliens had not been lifted. The one form of entertainment which the Nazis had encouraged was the circus, for tents could be pitched away from targets that might be bombed; circuses were allowed food for animals and were even allowed to travel by rail, but they were expected to produce good programmes and that meant artistes from the occupied countries could get engagements where they were paid little, but had enough food, and this was better than going to forced labour camps.

Getting permission to go to Germany was not easy, but as there were a number of displaced persons who had been performers and were in resettlement camps run by the Allies the Foreign Office let me go to explore the camps as a source of new talent. I flew to Hamburg with the R.A.F. and there the F.O. provided me with a car and chauffeur who took me first to the Hagenbeck Zoo at Stellingen where I was welcomed by my old friends Lorenz and Heinrich. The destruction in Hamburg and around the docks was my first sight of what real bombing means and I said to myself: 'And we thought we had been bombed!' The zoo, also, had taken a heavy beating, for it seems a pathfinder had dropped flares about three miles off target and the bombs that followed killed many animals.

I soon realised there was little talent in the resettlement camps and decided to see as many circuses as I could find, in case there were still artistes from what had been the occupied countries in them. That meant going off the beaten track and miles from the so-called transit hotels run by the forces of occupation where I could get a meal; when the German circus owners offered food it was tempting, but I knew they would have to go short if I accepted their hospitality. I was the first English circus man they had seen for nearly ten years and, as I arrived with an army car and a corporal as my chauffeur, I think they believed I must be a very important person. Since I was not in uniform they knew I had not come to take their shows over and run them for our troops, as some others had done a few years earlier.

As a search for talent the whole trip was a failure and the only act I found was that of Jolly, the Austrian, who did the one finger balancing trick which had not been seen here; for the rest of the Olympia programme I had to rely on Hungary, Czecho-Slovakia, Scandinavia, France and the Low Countries. On the other hand, it was proved there was a great wealth of new talent in Germany and that the thing to which we had to devote our attention was the lifting of the very stupid ban on German and Italian artistes. I had no compunction about doing this, for with the liquidation of Mussolini the Italians had almost become our allies and already it was evident that Germany was to become an ally in the near future.

The ban was lifted in May, 1950, but as I had to attend an opening of the circus by the Lord Provost in Edinburgh my departure was delayed and one of my competitors got to Germany first. It did not matter, though, as he was an unknown quantity there and I had taken the precaution of letting those in whom I was interested know I was coming. I got the acts I wanted and by the time I had completed my tours of other European countries and the States I had a programme which could be compared favourably with those we had presented before the war. And it was high time for such a programme, as there were already signs that we must do better and better every year.

That first post-war trip to Germany brought back memories of the many I had made before the war—but what a difference there was. Among the countless things which were *verboten* during Hitler's time was the taking out of Germany of more than twenty marks and on one occasion, having booked one of Hagenbeck's wild animal acts, I asked Lorenz to allow his secretary to book me a seat on the next flight to London. He drove me to the airport where I picked up my ticket and we then went and had coffee. When the flight was called a customs officer asked how much German money I had; I showed

him about twelve marks and he then searched my suitcase and
went through the papers in my brief-case one by one. Eventually he said : 'Where is it?' I had no idea what he was looking
for, but was a bit worried in case something had been planted
in my baggage while we were in the restaurant and replied :
'Where is what?' His answer was : 'The twenty mark note you
were given in change when you paid for your ticket.'

Fortunately Lorenz had waited to see me off, so I told the
customs man to go and ask him the answer and while he was
doing so I told another customs officer what I had done with it.
When the first man returned he was invited to compare
Lorenz' story with mine. Having paid for the coffee I still had
the note and gave it to Lorenz, saying he could buy me a drink
next time I went to Hamburg. He had shown the note to the
customs officer and the number it bore was that of the one on
the slip of paper the ticket clerk had given to the customs.

As time went on formalities were piled on top of one another and I got heartily sick of having my passport taken away
at every port of entry and having to wait about ten minutes
for it to be returned. I could only imagine the photo was being
copied, so I had a dozen copies made and gave one to the im-
migration officer each time and then there were no delays.

Bureaucratic efficiency may be impressive, but it is often as
full of holes as a net—which after all is only a lot of holes tied
together with string—and if anything unusual happens the
whole system can fall to pieces, as it did for me in 1939. I was
in Prague, having booked a very good comedy act called Lapp
and Habel, and was sitting in my hotel room puzzling out how
I should present it in London as some of the comedy depended
upon one man being suspended on a piano wire. It was easy
to manipulate the lighting on a stage to conceal the wire, but
doing so at Olympia was going to be difficult. As I looked over
the square I had a splendid view of the beautiful cathedral
founded by the man known in our carol as Good King Wen-
ceslas, but it looked as if something was wrong. People on the
Platz were having urgent discussions and every newspaper was
being read by five or six people at a time. It was March 13th
and the Nazis were on their way in. I telephoned the airline,

but all planes were grounded and the frontiers closed. Neither the British Consulate nor our Embassy could help, beyond saying I should probably do best to sit tight until the occupation was complete and that would take anything up to three weeks.

I did not like the idea of having to stay in an orderly country while the Nazis substituted their kind of orderliness and was determined to get out if I could. I had an idea which might work because it was the sort of thing which appeals to the over-methodical German mind. They probably would not think there was anything wrong about my being in Czecho-Slovakia at that time, or any need to detain me if I handed myself over to them, so I packed my bag and took the first train going in the direction of Dresden with a ticket to Decin on the frontier.

The track running south was one long convoy of trains packed with troops and all the paraphernalia of war, but although our progress was slow we kept moving. In the first class coach was one other passenger, a Norwegian who spoke a little French but no German and very soon we were in the same compartment discussing our chances.

He had gone to Prague to buy glass and, as the situation between Germany and Czecho-Slovakia was so tender, he had been able to get a far better rate of exchange in Norway than he would have been given in Prague. However, owing to the turn of events he had bought nothing and was trying to get home loaded with Czech money which would be worthless in a few hours. I told him that if he would give me the money and carry my suit-case when we reached the frontier I would try to help him. Luck was with us; the *bureau de change* was still open and the clerk was sitting waiting for somebody to come and tell him what to do. The Nazis had been too busy doing other things to put a guard on the place, so the clerk and I were alone. The till contained dollars, pounds, francs, marks and an assortment of other currencies and rather than give anything to the invaders he gave me the lot in exchange for a handful of worthless Czech notes.

As I had hoped, we were allowed to cross into Germany without any difficulty and in the train on the way to Dresden we were able to count the money and found there was a substantial profit, which the Norwegian asked me to accept, but I settled for the best dinner he could buy me in Dresden. All that mattered, so far as I was concerned, was that I had got out of Czecho-Slovakia in time for the opening of the tenting circus and soon after that I sailed for New York to see the World's Fair and some circuses.

Chapter Twelve
Flea circus and other
side shows

An act called Little Fred's Football Dogs was the first of its kind at Olympia and we should have liked to have had it with the tenting circus, but were unable to do so on account of the quarantine regulations. Having foreign dogs at Olympia meant that their quarters and exercise area had to be approved by the Ministry of Agriculture and when this was done the permit had to be rushed to the port, but the dogs could only be brought to London by a licensed carrier to ensure they did not come in contact with domestic animals. Once they were at Olympia the building had the status of a quarantine station; no strange dogs or cats could be admitted and notices had to be posted at all the entrances and the staff had to be briefed to watch for anyone who broke the rules.

With such strict regulations I was surprised when I saw an artiste who had just arrived leading a dog. I assumed he had just bought it and thought no more about it until several weeks later when he had returned to the Continent and one of the ring boys let me into the secret. The artiste came over with his car and, knowing nothing of the regulations, had had the dog sitting on the seat beside him as he went through customs. The only thing said was : 'What a nice dog.'

One would think there might be or even should be regulations covering the importation of fleas, but I have never heard of any. Some years before the war I heard about 'Flea Circuses' and when I saw one in Germany I booked it for the fun fair and thought I had a money-maker. During the first few days at Olympia my time was always fully occupied getting the programme running properly and I did not worry about the flea circus or even ask how it was doing but on the fourth day I was shaken by the news that the takings were averaging six and threepence per day. Normal prices of admission to side shows of this kind were then sixpence for adults and threepence for children.

That evening I went to see what was wrong; perhaps the 'Barker' was no good; perhaps the cashier and ticket-taker had organised a fiddle, but from the outside everything seemed to be right. Inside the show was as I had seen it, but there were only five people in the audience. I was ready to admit I had backed a loser and was leaving when I realised that it was not just an audience of five people, but one of three dinner jackets and two mink coats. That was it. These people had never seen a flea and some other types had their own flea circuses at home and had seen too many. At threepence and sixpence the show looked too cheap to appeal to mink coat types, so the next day the prices were doubled; the show became respectable and did good business until one day the man came to me and said he could not last much longer. Our climate was too much for German fleas and they were dying. At that time, during the early days every season, Olympia was frequented by a funny little man no more than five feet high. Who he was we never knew, but he spoke five or six languages and as the foreign artistes arrived he was always there to offer himself as guide, philosopher and friend. He helped them find hotels and lodgings and acted as interpreter between them and the ring boys.

When the flea trainer came with his troubles I suggested he should contact this little man, who always seemed able to produce anything from a piece of steel wire to the kind of sausages a Pole ate in Warsaw. The little man jumped at the job, even though it involved going to the East End where he asked the landlord of a doss house if he could search the beds for fleas. The approach had not been right and he returned empty-handed but with a black eye; the landlord had been a six-footer and had taken the poorest possible view of the request.

The German gave him a lesson; he had to begin by telling the tale, explaining what a flea circus was and how difficult it is to find good performers. The next step was to try to get the landlord's sympathy; he was a stranger and wanted advice. Could the landlord give him the name of some competitor who would be interested if he paid? He was to get half a crown a head and would pay a shilling for each catch he made. That usually did it; the chance to be de-flea-ed and paid for it was too good to be given to a competitor. Most landlords welcomed him and landladies were even easier—presumably they were the bed-makers. So the flea shortage was solved and the show made money.

Some years later I had an all-British flea circus which took nearly £1,500 in six weeks and that is big money for a couple of dozen fleas at half a crown each. It is the old story of human curiosity; most people will pay to see something they have never seen, especially if it is something the existence of which they will only credit if they see it with their own eyes. They feel rather as I do about the Indian rope trick.

Some showmen will stick at nothing if they can get away with it, but I drew the line very firmly when some man wanted to exhibit the de-frocked vicar of some small parish in a side show in the fun fair. The plan was to have him squat on top of a thirty-foot pole all day to be gaped at and it was difficult to think of anything more degrading. I just said we had no space for that sort of thing. It was not in the tradition we had inherited. Another, an American, ran a side show in the States having a huge sign reading 'Free Admission' at the entrance and a cashier at the exit and as the show was not too bad most people paid even though they knew they had been caught. Perhaps the cleverest thing of this kind was done by another American who considered people were spending too long in his menagerie and causing the sale of tickets to be delayed at the entrance. At the exit end he built a short passage at the entrance to which was a sign reading 'To the Egress' and everybody flocked through thinking they would see a female animal of which they had never heard before.

During recent years films and television have taught the public a great deal about the people of distant lands, but before this happened there was considerable interest in such people and one year we had a large troupe of genuine Red Indians whom the children loved; another year we had the plate-lipped women from the Oubangichari region of French Equatorial Africa who had been a big success in the Paris Exhibition but were a flop in London, whereas the so-called giraffe-neck women from the Shan States of Burma were the biggest side show attraction we ever had.

These women had been taken to the States by an American promoter on the understanding they would be returned by a certain date, but that had not been done and they had been posted as missing and we were pounced upon by the India Office the moment they arrived and ordered to send them home at once. Fortunately we were considered reliable and when we gave our word they would go home after the Olympia season they were allowed to stay, but we had to guarantee their fares on a British ship. All this upset the American, for we withheld enough of his share of the receipts of the side show to cover the fares as they were clearly his liability.

At the end of the season we hated to see the women go as they would be valuable with the tenting show so we set about getting our own troupe and Stanley Williamson, our P.R.O., was sent to Burma. Briefing him was difficult, as the only information we had about the area to which the women belonged was what we had picked up from Maung Suri, the male interpreter who had accompanied the first troupe.

Williamson flew to Rangoon and from there to the rail-head at Schweenung the journey was easy enough, but it then became a series of nightmares. The roads were no more than tracks through jungle, cut by the wheels of wagons drawn by oxen, and the only means of transport was an antiquated car with every ailment in the book, the hire of which cost seven shillings a mile. For the last twenty-five miles from Loikaw to Pekkong Williamson was in the hands of three guides who admitted freely they had never been to the place and only had a rough idea where it was.

We knew from Maung Suri that the village was in the hands of two masters who did not hit it off. One was the Swaba (head man) and the other a Roman Catholic missionary and that they did not see eye to eye was no fault of the priest, but of the Swaba, who believed his position would be in jeopardy if his people were converted. Worse still, both were opposed to letting the women leave as they feared they would become tainted by Western civilisation.

Knowing something of the Far East I had told Williamson that baksheesh—a tip in the East, but bribery to our way of thinking—was acceptable in those parts and had suggested that the priest, in return for acting as unpaid interpreter, would probably appreciate a few bottles of Scotch toddy and some canned foods and that the Swaba would like a watch and a few bits of junk jewellery. Williamson was to buy these things in Rangoon, but not to overload himself as he might have to do the last few miles through the jungle on foot.

The negotiations with all the people involved would fill a book, but there were two things in Williamson's favour; the women wanted to come to England, for Maung Suri told them the first troupe had been happy and made a lot of money and he also wanted to come as interpreter, for his only job was that of district postmaster which involved about fifty letters a year and his salary was only about £6 per annum. In the East you can get anything if you are prepared to haggle long enough, but Williamson had a dead-line as we wanted both him and the women to arrive before the opening of the summer season.

When the women left Pekkong they were as thin as rakes, their clothes were rags and they had never worn shoes, so they had to be properly fitted out in Rangoon and on the ship they were stuffed with food so they would be presentable.

We never found out how the two spiral coils of brass were put round their necks, for even Maung Suri did not know. He said it was done by an old woman of the tribe and that no man had ever been let into the secret; Williamson brought back a piece of the brass, which could not be bent when cold, but the job could not have been done with hot metal unless the neck was first encased in some kind of mud or plaster mould which could be broken away later. The woman's beauty and presumably her value on the marriage market was a function of the number of rings round the neck and its resulting length, so none of them would discuss the subject.

We provided them with a double-decker motorised vehicle, the upper deck having three bedrooms and the lower, a dining room with kitchen adjoining, and although the chef did his best there was always trouble at mealtimes the first few days. The first to be served emptied the pepper pot and if it was re-filled a couple of times they were still not happy—until Maung Suri explained that only red pepper was strong enough for them. So a couple of ounces of cayenne pepper was bought. Everyone was delighted, but it was all eaten at the first meal and henceforward the man who bought catering stores had to clean every town we visited out of cayenne pepper.

Another side show, the Ross mechanical man, was brought to Olympia from the States and did so well we extended the contract for the summer season. The figure was a man who had perfected eye control to the point where he could resist even an involuntary blink for ten or fifteen minutes; but he had to resist more than that, for a few nasty members of the public, unable to convince themselves that a robot could do what the mechanical man did, tried to prove their point with pins, but even when this happened Ross failed to react—he just said it happened much more frequently in the States. One evening the manager of the show came to the office in a panic saying the gaff was blown and we must close the show at once. It was one of those damp, cold evenings when one's breath condenses and every time Ross exhaled his breath looked like a cloud of smoke. There was only one thing to do and within ten minutes the sign-writer had produced a notice reading OUT OF ORDER for the entrance of the tent and as half a dozen people in

The author and his private secretary
Mrs. Yelding during an undress
rehearsal at Olympia
(Left) The author, left, with his
brother Bernard at the Tenting
Circus

OVERLEAF *Victor Gaona coming
out of the triple somersault to the
hand of his father, the catcher*

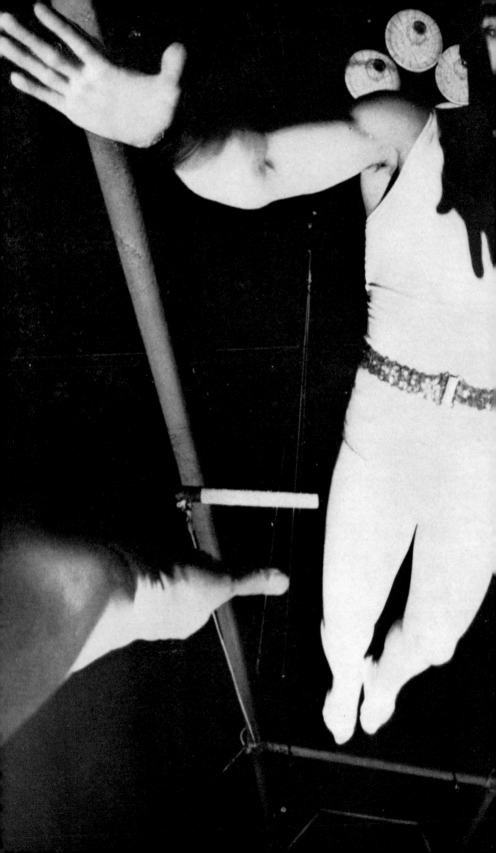

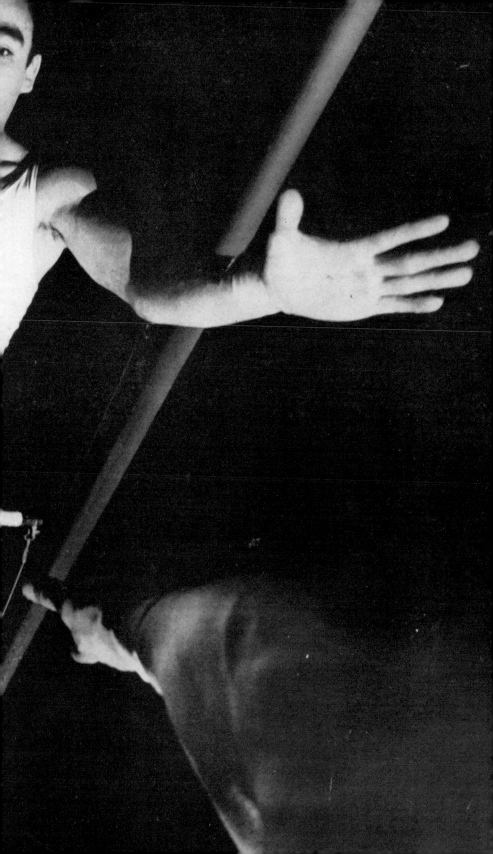

Circus on the move

A stilt-walker unhooks the side walls

The tentmaster supervises the loading of floorboards

Each scrap of litter must be removed before the Circus leaves

Everything has to be loaded in the same place every move

Quarter poles are lowered just before the big top comes down

Lowestoft had discovered the truth the show remained out of order till we reached the next town.

One of the most interesting side shows we ever had was Gargantua, a giant gorilla owned by Ringlings. They had bought him as a baby and, by using air-conditioning plant which controlled the temperature and humidity of the air, had raised him to the age of seven. His height was five feet six inches and his arm span nine feet and he weighed a quarter of a ton and was thought to have the strength of from twenty-five to twenty-seven men.

The wagon in which he lived was a huge affair enclosed first by thick high tensile steel bars and then by bullet-proof glass nearly half an inch thick and, as no human being could go within his reach, it was divided into two compartments so that he could occupy one while the other was cleaned. Gargantua was a vegetarian and treated a case of oranges like the hors-d'œuvre to a meal; and the cost of feeding him, like that of his Atlantic crossings, was enormous, but it was all worth it for nobody had seen such a large gorilla in captivity and those who had seen one in the jungle had not lived to tell the tale. He was a great lad with the girls and whenever a good-looking and well turned out one appeared he watched her from the time she entered until she left. I am not sure how I should have reacted to this had I been a good-looking girl but to a male observer it looked as if he was a good picker and that his stare, even if rude, must be taken as a compliment.

He loved to have things to play with, but destroyed everything we gave him in seconds until he was given a giant motor lorry tyre; he could not destroy this quickly, although he crushed and twisted it as though it were tissue paper.

Eric, an embalmed whale which was housed in a seventy-foot American railroad freight car, did not prove the attraction we had hoped it would. The whale and wagon together weighed over seventy tons and to crane it out of a ship in the London docks cost £250. Then it had to be loaded on low-loading trailers and hauled by two steam traction engines and, as the load was 110 feet long, the journey to Olympia took thirteen hours. When we arrived we had to manœuvre the thing into

position without crossing a spot where there was a cellar—
and that was like a Chinese puzzle. We had to see that the
landlord's property was not damaged and to satisfy the inspectors of the London County Council whose job it is to safeguard
the public from accidents; in connection with these officials I
am reminded of an incident which took place many years ago.

Every year the tiered seating had to be certified as safe, and
one day a man who was new to the job and a bit too enthusiastic
told the Olympia superintendent of works that he wanted this,
that and the next thing done. The Olympia man told my father
at once and said he could not possibly get the work done in time
for the opening. This was serious, for we had to have the certificate before we could open and if we opened without it the
L.C.C. licence would be cancelled and we should be in breach
of our agreement with the landlords. My father asked the man
to arrange for the inspector to come to his office the following
morning and when he arrived it was suggested they should
go down to the seating to see what had to be done. As they
entered, Father pointed to the right where, on about the sixth
tier, there were four fully grown elephants; as he did so there
were flashes from three press cameras and it was quite evident
from their position that the photos they had taken would include the image of the inspector. The discussion had ended
before it began and then some more pictures were taken, showing only Father and the elephants, and when they appeared
in the papers the next day they had captions explaining how
Bertram Mills ensured his seating was safe. The inspector had
made a nuisance of himself and in doing so had produced a
publicity stunt which nobody had thought of before. No other
inspector ever asked for the modifications the new man had
wanted and they had not been carried out thirty years
later when the seating was scrapped.

Where the safety of the public was concerned Bernard and
I were brought up in a hard school as, for many years, Father
was chairman of the committee of the London County Council
which issued the licence to Olympia and other places of entertainment, and we should have looked pretty stupid if we had
done anything to produce an adverse report which had to be

dealt with by the committee. I must say, however, that in all my dealings with L.C.C. inspectors I found them both helpful and understanding whenever we had problems.

If I ever felt a bit squeamish about a side show it was that of Zaro Agha, a Turk, who claimed to be the oldest man in the world. When I first saw him my guess was that he might be a hundred or a little more, but by then we had signed a contract with some American promoters and had to allow our conscience to be soothed by the fact that we were able to exhibit a passport, on the basis of which we had signed the contract, which proved the man was entitled to celebrate his 156th birthday when he was with us on the 19th August 1931. Even so, I still wonder just what kind of records were kept in Turkey in 1775.

Many people think it wrong to allow human beings to be exhibited in a side show and where objects of pity are concerned this is undoubtedly true, but curiously enough exactly the opposite is the case where others are involved. A giant or a midget is inevitably stared at wherever he is during his whole lifetime. He does not even have to get used to it, for it has happened as long as he can remember anything; being used to it he becomes a natural exhibitionist and if people take no notice of him he is as upset as a film star who has reached the stage when there are no press cameras to greet her at London Airport. In addition, he is handicapped in getting a job in the ordinary walks of life and this can only create an inferiority complex which immediately disappears as soon as he can turn his disability to good account. In a side show he is stared at, which is normal, but he earns ten to fifteen times what he could earn anywhere else and two or three times what his brother may be earning in an ordinary job. His physical abnormality has become an asset, rather than something which he must fight to overcome. Having been a burden to his parents he is self-supporting and often earns enough to support them in their old age more easily than they were able to support him in his younger days. I must admit it must have been hard to be the 'Ugliest Woman on Earth' during the first few days, but even she was accustomed to being stared at; the only thing that was new was her title and even that had a flavour which was not entirely bad when it came to pay day and produced a pay packet about ten times as big as it had ever been before.

A few years ago a man took a space in the fun fair to exhibit a giant octopus and very soon Stanley Bird, the manager, had a call from an inspector of the R.S.P.C.A. who said they had had complaints and would like to see it. Bird was told that they had letters saying the creature was in dirty water, which included a cigarette butt, and that it looked emaciated. The inspector was taken towards the exhibit, but half way there Bird did not think it fair to leave him in the dark any longer, for he was a sincere and reasonable man, so he was asked whether he had been told that the octopus was embalmed and had been dead for years. What had fooled those who complained was the fact that the showman had rigged up some kind of gadget with a football bladder inside the body and this was connected by a concealed pipe to an air pump, which filled it, and then a valve released the air so that the creature appeared to breathe.

This is only one of dozens of incidents there have been to show how well-meaning people rush off to make complaints about things of which they know all too little. In this case the water was not as clean as it should have been and the showman was ticked off, so perhaps I should be thankful, but if the time of R.S.P.C.A. inspectors is wasted like this often their job must be a thankless one.

My father was as alive as anyone to the value of publicity in the press, but he had one rule which neither he nor we were ever to break. No newspaper was ever to be fooled and if something was to be produced or enacted for the sole purpose of making a story or pictures the editor had to be told the truth and it was then for him to decide whether we should or should not go ahead. Things like turning an animal loose and then pretending it had escaped were absolutely forbidden, even though some others did that sort of thing.

There was, however, one time when we fell down badly. At Olympia we had a bright and energetic young man as assistant to the P.R.O. but he was doing this kind of work for the first time and was so determined to hit the headlines that he forgot the rules—or else his boss had failed to brief him properly. One of the side shows contained a snake charmer, sword-swallower, giant and a charming little male midget; one day this little man was missing and none of us knew where he was. The Missing Midget became news in every national newspaper—except one. Reporters haunted Olympia day and night for stories, but the subject was never mentioned by one paper and we were convinced the editor thought it was a put-up job and believed that several people in Olympia knew the truth and therefore his reporters' job was to unearth it.

At board room level we also suspected something, but the P.R.O. denied knowing anything about it so his assistant was summoned and admitted he had smuggled the midget away and was caring for him. He was forbidden to tell a soul and sent home and told to stay there, so that he could not be interviewed and forced to lie.

The problem was, to get the midget back quickly without his being spotted by reporters, but by the fourth day the story had gone cold and it was generally assumed the midget had become fed up with England and gone back to Germany. As soon as the pressure was taken off the midget was put in a car at 4 a.m. and dumped on the doorstep of the goods entrance of Olympia, where he rang the bell and was admitted by the gateman who, being in the dark, telephoned us to say he had the man. He had been briefed perfectly and when interviewed by reporters explained, through an interpreter, that a lady had invited him to dine at her flat and he had remained there in the lap of luxury (and perhaps that of his hostess) until his conscience had pricked and he had remembered that pay-day was drawing near. What he did not reveal was that his hostess was the wife of our assistant P.R.O. and when asked where the flat was he said he was a stranger in London and having gone there and back by car he had no idea of the address. All the papers except one reported his return and we had far more publicity from the affair than we deserved; I do not think the whole truth has ever been told until now.

The thought of midgets in the fun fair always gives me a nasty turn, because two were involved in a serious accident one year. Gösta Kruse was presenting our elephants that winter and to reach the ring they had to walk through the fun fair and pass a side show in which there was an elderly midget and his midget wife. The elephants were adults; they had been everywhere and seen everything and were about as quiet and reliable as farmyard cows, but there is one thing no elephant will put up with—being attacked by a yapping dog—and there is an unwritten law in the circus that anybody who introduces a dog must keep it under control. The midgets had worked in at least one circus before and they and their associates knew, or should have known, the rule; however, one of them broke it and as the elephants ambled past a small barking dog started trying to bite their legs and then when attacked by an elephant retreated into the side show. The elephant followed, caught the dog with its trunk and killed it with one stamp of a foot, but in doing so it wrecked the side show and both midgets received injuries.

Our insurers made every effort to settle out of court, for in English law an elephant is a wild animal and its owner is responsible for all damage it does. There was no disputing the fact that damages were payable and the only question was, how much. The sum offered looked generous, but the midgets were advised to go to court, although I doubt whether they were any better off after they had done so. I have always been very sorry for them, for although they appeared to have recovered by the time they appeared in court they had spent some time in hospital and it is always far more serious when little people are victims of an accident.

One of the oddest vehicles we ever owned was a converted Land Rover, which we called the elephant jeep. We had decided that an elephant driving a jeep would be a valuable gimmick when the animals paraded from the station to the circus and when the work of conversion was finished the vehicle had to be driven from our workshops on one side of the road to that part of the winter quarters which was about two hundred yards down the road. On the way a policeman ordered the vehicle to stop, told the man at the steering wheel that he was not exercising due care and attention and asked to see his licence. At that there was unrestrained laughter from below the seat of the car where the real driver was concealed like the driver of an armoured car. The man whom the policeman assumed to be driving was a groom, who was just having a free ride from one part of the premises to the other.

Elephants seem to produce more questions than anything else. How much does an elephant eat? About a ton of hay a week with some root vegetables and at times, when they are not too expensive, some apples and pears are well received. Why are their skins darker at some times than at others? Assuming they are clean, the reason is that at regular intervals we greased them with boiled down animal fat to prevent the skin getting dry and cracking and their toe-nails need regular pedicure too. Why are they always female and Indian rather than African? A bull elephant, like an adult farmyard bull, can be very difficult to manage at certain times and Indian elephants either have bigger brains than African ones or know better how to use them. Most Indian elephants come from Burma, where great numbers have been used in the teak forests and have become domesticated; whereas, so far as I am aware, the African elephant is only found in the wild state.

I think the funniest question I was ever asked about elephants had nothing funny about it until its reason was explained. A man wrote to me asking whether it was possible that any of our elephants had been on the road from Ascot to Bagshot on a certain night at about half past eleven. He had arrived home from a stag party much later than his wife had expected him and had told her he had seen six elephants on the Bagshot road. They lived some distance away and did not know where our winter quarters were; the wife had assumed he had had too much to drink and was late because he had taken time off on the way home to sober up. In fact, the circus had returned to winter quarters on the night mentioned and he had seen the elephants and when I wrote to him giving details of their movements the family quarrel ended.

The elephant jeep was demonstrated to the press at one of the parties we gave at Ascot to provide a preview of what was being prepared for Olympia, but it was difficult to prevent annual parties of this kind becoming routine affairs and each year we had to try to dream up something that would make good pictures. Film stars, television personalities and even well-known professional boxers were invited and if any of them rode an elephant or got mixed up in some slapstick with the clowns it usually made a picture in a newspaper. One year I tried my hand at producing something with Henry Lewandowski. He was a Pole who joined us just after the war and was given the job of hanging the side walls of the big top, which can be done most conveniently on stilts, and during the next few years he became as good a stilt-walker as I have seen. He went into town every day to distribute handbills and at each performance sold programmes at the main entrance. Just another programme seller, one would think, but he always sold several times as many as anyone else and it was amazing to see how many people preferred to stand on tiptoe and reach for a programme in preference to buying it from somebody standing on the ground.

The press photographers used to travel to Ascot in a private bus and I thought that if Henry could stand across the gateway on stilts long enough to allow the bus to pass beneath it would make a good picture. Finding bamboo poles long and strong enough and making them into stilts needed all the skill of our workshops, but we could only get Henry on to the stilts by hoisting him up with a block and tackle—and a gust would bring him down—so we had to fake things a bit. Two long poles were erected at the gateway and a very thin wire stretched between them and this just gave Henry the little extra balance he needed. The photographers ate it up and their picture editors were very kind, for somehow the wire did not show in any of the pictures.

Getting plenty of publicity and getting it quickly is essential to a circus and P.R.O.s have to work very hard. Anyone who has done this kind of work for a detergent, where only whiteness counts, must think publicising a circus is a piece of cake. There are great possibilities, but they are not endless; so many people have been at it so long that it is now very difficult to think of anything new or original. In the provinces a few good stunts can be repeated from town to town with the local press and TV Stations, but no national newspaper will use anything that has been flogged in small town papers. It has to be something new and worth-while to satisfy a London editor or a B.B.C. or Independent television producer and if anyone earns his keep with a circus a good P.R.O. does.

Chapter Thirteen
The training of
circus animals

I expect to be criticised by a vociferous minority whether I mention the training of animals or not. If I skip the subject they will say I dared not write about it and if I say anything it will be said I have no qualification for doing so, as I have never trained an animal.

That is perfectly true and even if I had ever thought of doing so it would not have been possible, if only for the reason that it takes a very long time—far longer than my other activities would have enabled me to devote to it. On the other hand I have seen a great many animals at every stage of their training and probably know a little more of the subject than those who allege cruelty in one breath and boast they have never been to a circus in the next. There are probably two or three hundred such people in the country, but there are also many people who believe everything that gets into print must be true—well-meaning people who pay their subscriptions regularly, but without ever stopping to ask whether there is a shred of evidence to support the allegations made.

There are far more societies for the protection of animals

than for children in this country and, whilst I am sure the big well known ones are doing splendid work in many areas, there are others which I regard as little more than subscription gathering organisations—and in some cases one-man shows.

Stories have been concocted and allegations without any supporting evidence have been made. Some of these have been so fatuous that those who know anything about animals have treated them with contempt, but the underlying purpose is usually the same—to appeal to the heart and, through the heart, to the purse of well-meaning people. If proof of this is needed it is only necessary to look at the appeal for subscriptions at the bottom of the pamphlet. Allegations are usually directed against circuses as a whole and in such cases there is little any one circus owner can do, but if a circus or an individual is named and there is a clear case of libel or slander, it is of little use going to court unless there is a reasonable chance of being able to recover costs. What, for instance, would be the use of suing an undischarged bankrupt or one whose possessions had been tucked away beyond the reach of the court? Even if an injunction is granted in connection with one statement it does not prevent a different one being made later and we come back to the point where we feel it is of little avail suing a man of straw in the civil courts.

Some of those to whom the gathering of subscriptions seems to be all important are very careful about where they spend their money on posters and pamphlets. They gave us plenty of attention in London and in well-to-do residential towns in the provinces, but none in grubby industrial centres—perhaps they feel that what is wrong in one place is right in another, but perhaps they do as we do and spend their money where they think it will be most profitable to do so.

What some of these people try to hide is that since the Performing Animals Regulation Act was passed in 1925, with the support of circus owners and the animal protection societies, all animal trainers have had to be licensed by the Home Office and all places where animals are trained or where they perform must be open to inspection by qualified veterinary officers appointed by the local authorities, and by all police officers at all reasonable times. These last four words have been attacked on the flimsiest grounds, for it has been said that a circus owner could refuse admission to an inspector if he thought the time at which the visit took place was unreasonable. In my view if it is reasonable to train animals at three o'clock in the morning it is equally reasonable to inspect at that time, but the question does not arise, as nobody trains animals in the middle of the night. Circus people sleep then, just as others do, and never since the act was passed has any inspector or policeman been refused admission at any place where circus animals were trained.

The reports of the inspections which take place at frequent, but irregular, intervals and at nearly every place the circus visits are made available to the Home Office, so that if a question is asked about them the Government is always able to answer. Over the years we have done our utmost to let the truth be known; we have given passes to Olympia which were valid day and night to inspectors of the R.S.P.C.A., but we have always said we would appreciate it if they came in civilian clothes because we did not want to know, and did not want our employees to know, when they were present. We have thrown open our training quarters at Ascot at any hour of the day or night to any member of either House of Parliament and a great many members have gone there to watch training.

Just before the war a prominent member of the R.S.P.C.A. introduced a Bill to restrict the training of circus animals, but at that time we were about to begin the training of a group of young tigers and we invited him to watch it. Fortunately he was a man who, given a chance to see both sides of a picture, took it. During the next five or six months he spent an enormous amount of time at Ascot. He saw the training of the tigers and that of several other animals and, having satisfied his conscience, withdrew the Bill and sent us a copy of the letter he wrote saying why he had done so.

In more recent years the subject was debated in the House of Lords at a time when Lord Mancroft was Under Secretary for State for the Home Department and it fell to him to speak for the Government. He is recognised as one of the most brilliant speakers of our time and as such he makes very sure he knows his subject. Therefore, although he was completely unknown to me, I was not surprised when he wrote asking if he could come and see things for himself and perhaps have a word with some of the trainers.

At that time we had in the Olympia programme Rudi Lenz (Chimpanzees), Gösta Kruse (Elephants), Alex Kerr (Wild Animals) and Fredy Knie (Horses) and the proper course to take was obvious. Here were four highly experienced and reputable trainers and I introduced them to Lord Mancroft and told them to answer his questions and give him any demonstrations he wished to see.

I can already hear the screams of my opponents saying: 'What can anyone see of the training of animals if only shown those which have already reached the stage where they are appearing at Olympia?' At first glance a fair question, but in fact one which shows an abysmal ignorance of the subject, for the training of an animal continues during its whole life as a performer. New routines and tricks are always being taught at every rehearsal so that the same animals can appear three or four times at the same place in 'new' acts. Elephants may do a standard routine one year and play football or cricket or skittles the next. Almost the same troupe of Schumann horses appeared at Olympia for nine consecutive seasons and by varying routines, costumes and music the acts were always new in the eyes of the audience. Colonel Podhajsky, of the world famous Spanish Riding School in Vienna, once told me the normal lifetime of a horse is not long enough for the training to be completed— which is the same as saying an animal, like a man, is never too old to learn.

Gösta Kruse had seven elephants—three adults and four babies, whose training was just beginning. In fact they appeared in the act, but were only 'dressing', as they did no more than walk around as exhibits, but being so small they were attractive. During a rehearsal one morning Lord Mancroft, having seen the baby elephants do what they already had been taught, asked whether any of them had been trained to sit down. None had, so Gösta gave a demonstration by leading one of them until it was standing facing the centre of the ring with its hind legs touching the ring fence. He then put his hands on the upper part of one of its hind legs and pushed so the little animal was eased backwards and downwards towards a sitting position on the fence. Of course the elephant did not sit down, for that takes weeks or months to learn, but the method had been demonstrated and it is the method which counts.

In addition to Home Office records Lord Mancroft called for reports from the police in all areas where circus training quarters were and when he spoke in the House of Lords he took no sides. He just told the House what he had seen for himself and what the records showed and, among other things, said that our action in throwing open our training quarters to Members of the Houses of Parliament did not look like the action of guilty men.

Few people seem to realise that a place like our winter quarters is little less than a factory, employing up to 150 people, and that only a small percentage of them are concerned with animal training. We built practically everything the circus needed and our staff, in addition to four or five trainers and the grooms and keepers, included secretaries, telephone operators, mechanics, carpenters, painters, welders, electricians, seamstresses and a host of others and, as most of them lived there, local tradesmen called every day. The staff was recruited like that of any commercial undertaking and it is just too absurd to suggest that all these normal men and women would become perverted or subverted as soon as they were employed by us. Few of them had ever worked for another circus and they represented a normal cross-section of the community; they would be the first to open their mouths if they saw animals being treated badly. To suggest that harsh treatment could exist without their getting to know about it, and in fact seeing it, is sheer nonsense.

One peer was so badly briefed that he wrote a letter to a newspaper saying that our winter quarters were enclosed with barbed wire. Any resident of Ascot or any one of the millions of people who have passed along the Ascot to Bagshot road knows there was never an inch of barbed wire there except during our absence, when the place was an internment camp, and the first thing we did when we returned was remove it. Just imagine what could happen if a horse broke loose and got tangled up in barbed wire.

I can only be sorry for people who, with all the good will in the world, make such stupid statements; rather than lending their names and acting as parrots for the type of subscription gatherer who will say anything calculated to appeal to the potential subscriber they would serve their cause better if they took the trouble to check allegations before repeating them. I must be fair and say that the big and reputable animal protection societies, like the R.S.P.C.A., do not circulate false information; if they dislike circuses they have every right to say so. If there are black sheep among circus people the sooner they are exposed the better; there should be prosecution and neither I nor any other reputable circus man would lift a finger to defend anyone against whom charges, supported by proper evidence, were preferred. What I resent, and I resent it bitterly, is that because there may be a black sheep somewhere all circuses and all circus people should be branded. One might just as well say that because one company director is convicted of fraud all company directors are swindlers. Someone once said : 'Of all the indigestible myths served up to choke the functioning of reason the flap-doodle about this subject effortlessly takes the cake.' If the subject was the training of animals it was not far from the mark and perhaps I should leave it at that, but for the sake of those who have never seen the training of a circus animal I think I should give away a few of what some people may regard as secrets though from my point of view there is nothing to be secretive about. It should not spoil people's entertainment if they know something of how the tricks are taught; on the contrary, it may give them a greater appreciation of the difficulties involved.

Others with far better qualifications have dealt with the subject at length and to those who are interested enough to study it I recommend the books they have written : *No Bars Between* by Alex Kerr, *Trunk Call* by Gösta Kruse and, especially, *The Psychology of Animals in Zoos and Circuses* and *Wild Animals*

in Captivity by Dr. Hediger, Professor of Animal Psychology
at the University of Zürich and Director of the Zoological Gardens at Zürich and Basel.

Let us start with horses, for most people assume that being
so highly domesticated they are probably the easiest to train,
but in fact the horse is not the brainiest of animals—if by that
we mean the ability to comprehend our wishes. Brain is essential for learning and a good trainer will spot a stupid animal
quickly and will waste no time with it—to sell it and buy another is only common sense. What every trainer has to do when
he has a good animal is study it and decide for what tricks it
has a natural aptitude. A school-master has to do the same,
for it is common knowledge that it is useless to try to make a
classical scholar of a boy who is a born mathematician. It is
also necessary to study the animal's aptitudes and again the
human analogy applies, for although any boy can learn to play
football only his inborn ability will produce a Stanley Matthews.

So we start with a dozen untrained horses, three or four years
old, and want to produce a liberty act—the kind of act in which
the horses will weave elaborate patterns in the ring under the
guidance of the trainer standing in the centre. We need twelve
good grooms, one to ride each horse. The trainer explains the
routine and their job is to guide the horses to show them what
is the meaning of each cue given by him. Every horse must be
named and the curious names circus animals have is because
there must be no similarity between the predominant syllables
of any two names. There may be a Whiskey and a Brandy but
not a Whiskey and a Friskey.

Each horse must be named every time it is to do something
and its name must be accompanied by some movement of the
trainer indicating what is to be done. Movement cues may be
in the form of raising one hand or both or by taking a short pace
forward, backward or sideways and are almost unobserved by
the public. Why the whip? It is nothing more than the extension of the arm of the trainer and is used just as it is at public
performances. If the leading horse is running round the outside
of the ring and the trainer steps forward and holds the whip
in front of the horse the groom turns the horse in the direction

in which it should go and as time goes on the horses begin to understand the meanings of the cues and to obey them with little help from the grooms; as soon as a horse no longer needs guidance the reins are dropped and the rider becomes a dummy. Soon after the trainer will let that horse work without a rider and this process continues until all the grooms have been dispensed with. Henceforward, only practice is needed to make perfect, but if one horse starts making mistakes the groom will go back for a few days and it is at this stage that the trainer's original selection of animals counts for so much, for if there is a brainless animal in the team the presentation of the act in public must be delayed until that animal knows as much as the others and in the meantime they can be taught nothing new. The rate of progress of the whole team is that of the slowest member.

When all the horses know the routine there are still things to do. During the early stages all must be quiet so that nothing diverts the attention of the animals from the cues but now we must do everything possible to attract their attention. There must be music from loud-speakers and applause; people must stand round the ring and do the sort of things and make the kind of noises the public will make. Again all must be done by easy stages and there must be no fireworks or anything to cause fright; the long term effect must simply be to accustom the animals to the sort of atmosphere that will exist when seven thousand people are present.

One 'trick' which always meets with public approval is that in which a dozen horses all bearing numbers are mixed up in the ring and allowed to find their own places in 1-2-3 order. In fact it is the easiest trick of all for the very first thing the horses are taught is their positions in the line and as these never change the animals naturally take their correct places as a matter of routine.

Some will say the training of horses is simple, but what about wild animals? Just as simple if you know how. We start with cubs eight or nine months old which, in their life span, is about equivalent to the age when children begin school. By this time muscles and bones will have developed to a stage where they are capable of the amount of exertion of which a child of eight is capable and it will be some time before any big effort is asked for. During the first four or five months the trainer will do no more than sit in the ring cage and read, or smoke and drink occasional cups of coffee, for several hours each day as his only purpose is to let the animals get used to him to the point where they regard him as an essential element in their surroundings —and eventually as one of them. He will have given them names and when he thinks he has caught the eye of one he will say its name and every time one approaches nearer than the others it will be named. The animals learn their names just as pet dogs do and, as cupboard love is an essential element of the training, a little bell starts ringing in the animal's mind if a scrap of meat is thrown to it whenever its name is spoken.

When the animals know their names and will come for tit-bits the second stage of the training can begin and 'chairs' are put in the ring always in exactly the same places. Each animal must learn which is its chair and whenever it goes near it the trainer will put a scrap of meat on it. The next stage is to get the animal to climb on to the chair; for this the meat must be held on a long stick just out of reach above the chair. Naturally the animal puts its front paws on the chair to reach the meat and is rewarded at once; even though it may take weeks, the next step is just as easy, for the meat is held at a height which makes it necessary for the animal to climb on to the chair. Each animal must go through these very simple routines many times, but only the one which has been named and encouraged with a titbit gets a reward and this goes on and on until every animal knows its own chair and goes to it automatically whenever it enters the ring. Thereafter, it is not difficult to teach sitting up and begging for a titbit held just beyond reach when the animal is sitting or standing on the chair; what happens later, when all the animals take their positions on pedestals and form tableaux, is only doing one of the things learned on the chair, but in a different place. Any wild animal will jump from one pedestal to another to get a piece of meat and so long as the distance between pedestals is only increased gradually the animal learns easily to jump within the normal limit of its capacity and if later it is asked to jump through a hoop this presents no problem for we can begin with a very large one and reduce the size by slow stages. Every trick gets its reward in the form of a titbit and in the long run the wild animal, like the horse, gets to know what is wanted when each cue is given. The titbits become less and less important and instead of giving one for each part of a movement it is only necessary to do so when the final position in the trick is reached.

Tigers sitting on their haunches pawing the air with their front paws are only doing what pet dogs do, and for the same reason, and they have been trained in exactly the same way. If the training of a wild animal takes so much longer, it is because the trainer has to spend so long letting the animals get used to him, but in every case the training takes a very long time and must be done by people with endless patience, who are completely dedicated, and they in turn must be employed by those who are not in a hurry and can afford to foot the bills during the many months the training takes. No animal trainer will tell you how long it will take to train an animal or a group, any more than a school-master will say how long it will take a boy to master the differential calculus, for the answer in both cases is a function of the master's teaching ability and the pupil's capacity to learn. But whether a boy or an animal is involved the end product is the outcome of the expenditure of a great deal of effort and money and is in the form of a capital investment; it is therefore not surprising that circus owners look after their animals so well and that, among commercial users, they probably house, feed and care for them better than many others.

Those who say wild animals only perform because they are hungry are wide of the mark, for once taught a trick they will do it without reward—just as a pet dog will—and in any event the number of trainers who feed their animals before they go into the ring is about the same as those who feed after the act. If animals only performed at a matinée because they knew they would be fed after, what would persuade them to perform in the evening having had their food a couple of hours before? A few stupid people have suggested they are drugged, but that is sheer nonsense, for any doctor or veterinary surgeon will confirm that doped animals would soon become as unreliable and unpredictable as human drug addicts are.

There are those who feel it is cruel to keep wild animals in captivity anywhere; that may be, but it rather depends upon what is meant by cruel. Every wild animal that ends up in a circus has been born in captivity or taken as a cub and in the latter case very often was abandoned by its parents. No trainer is fool enough to try to train any adult animal, as it cannot be done—the army learned that during World War I, when it imported adult wild horses from the Argentine for the cavalry and gunners. It is, of course, necessary that all animals should be housed in places of adequate size, even though the amount of space wild animals demand is very small—for the one trait they have in common is laziness. They just do not like taking exercise and seem to have no ambition to do other than lie about until the next meal is due. Their needs are very simple and when you have said sex, supper and security you have said about everything.

Nothing could be more cruel than the jungle in which nearly every carnivorous animal dies of starvation because it can no longer move fast enough to win its next meal. And what of the poor little zebras? I have never heard a voice raised in their cause, although most of them are destined to end their days as a lion's dinner, having first been torn to pieces alive.

It is often said that it must involve cruelty if animals perform to a time-table, but that again shows a complete ignorance of what goes on in circuses. Every regular circus-goer knows that animals miss their tricks, just as jugglers and wire-walkers do, and when it happens the trick has to be repeated. A missed trick, whether animal or human, can be like a slice at golf— it is a good thing to correct it quickly otherwise it may become a habit and for this reason no circus programme ever runs to a rigid time-table.

Of course there is a difference between animals and humans inasmuch as the latter will sometimes 'throw' a trick the first time to make it look more difficult, but I have always frowned upon this sort of bluff for it usually proves the trick is an easy one and that the performer has no big trick in his book.

As I said earlier, animals are creatures of habit and once accustomed to a given set of circumstances changes must be made slowly and with care. All circus performers spend the greater part of their lives in circuses where they enter the ring by passing beneath the bandstand and in the case of wild animals their chairs are always set so they face the main entrance on the opposite side and they have their backs to the band but Olympia is almost unique, as there are two ring entrances and the band is not above either. It is at right angles to the tunnel through which the animals enter so that when the music begins it comes from an unexpected direction. At the first rehearsal the animals turn their heads and you can almost hear them saying, 'The fools have put it in the wrong place'. The trouble does not last long, but the rehearsal cannot begin until the last animal has ceased to be interested and is ready to give its attention to the trainer.

The fact that there are accidents proves nothing about training methods, for if a fight takes place in the ring when animals are in season the trainer has to stop it and at such a moment he takes grave risks. In fact, wild animals are so thick skinned that the injuries they inflict on each other are seldom more serious than those resulting from a brawl between two men, but a fight between two big animals looks bad and, being a noisy affair like a dog fight, can be frightening to onlookers and therefore has to be stopped.

Trainers collect a number of scratches, but they are often the result of play, like those a child can get when playing with a cat or dog. But there are two big differences; man is so thin skinned that the claws of a wild animal do grave damage and as they are filthy there is the danger of tetanus. Nothing is said if you are bitten by a dog—you have to bite the dog to make news—but if you collect a scratch from a wild animal you have been MAULED by the time you read about it in the papers. We must, however, face the fact that wild animals can inflict terrible injuries—for the kind of thing that would leave another animal unscathed can kill a man. Trainers MUST be careful and this was brought home in a forceful way some years ago when the circus was in the North. Priscilla Kayes, our lion trainer, was visited by a girl friend she had not seen for years and took her to see the lions. The friend stayed behind the safety barrier, but Priscilla went to the wagon and put her hand through the bars and stroked the lions, as she had done count-less times. This sort of thing is safe enough if you know your animals and keep an eye on what you are doing, but Priscilla was too busy talking to notice one lion had put a front paw through the bars and before she knew what was happening had taken a playful swipe at her. The equivalent from a do-mestic cat would have produced a scratch an inch long, but this all but removed one of her breasts and was why she went to hospital and we had no lion act for a short time. Familiarity breeds contempt and in this context contempt spells danger.

There is one other big lie I must nail to the floor. Animal cranks are for ever saying that circus animals are trained abroad and brought here as ready-made acts. In this case it is pre-supposed that all foreigners are less humane than we are and having seen as many foreign circuses as almost anyone alive I utterly reject such a suggestion; it comes very badly from people who live in a country where the number of convictions for cruelty to children is positively shocking. The truth of the matter is that every animal that has appeared in every British tenting circus since the war has been trained *ab initio* in this country. (I except horses used in bareback riding acts which are only trained to run round the ring.) People then ask about Olympia and other big static circuses where slogans like 'First time in England' are often used. The answer is simple; there are not enough home-trained acts to supply all these circuses if they are to meet the demand of the public for new programmes each year. We therefore have to import foreign animal acts just as we import foreign acrobats and jugglers and for the same reason.

Many years ago one of the acts at Olympia consisted of a tiger riding a horse; the two had been together since the tiger was a cub, but even so the horse was completely protected by a thick leather cover. For some reason this was thought to be cruel and a subscription-gatherer organised a protest. About two hundred well-meaning people were persuaded to buy seats for the circus and were to walk out in silent protest as the tiger entered the ring. The horse went into the cage and as it did so two flunkies marched round the ring fence carrying huge notices reading: 'Members of the Birmingham party are reminded that their train leaves in 12 minutes.' The tiger entered and two hundred people walked out, but there was nothing silent about their protests to the organiser a few minutes later. We had benefited to the tune of about a hundred guineas and other members of the audience were unaware there had been anything in the nature of a protest and had been able to enjoy the performance without interruptions.

Having said my piece I will leave the subject with one suggestion. If someone who professes to know it all says that circus animals can only be trained by cruelty will you please ask for a description of the kind of cruelty involved in the training of pigeons. I should very much like to know the answer for, as far as I am aware, even the most fertile brain among those who write propaganda material against performing animals has been unable to dream up anything on this subject.

Chapter Fourteen
Circuses here and there

Some people have thought that a long trip in search of talent is second best to a round-the-world tour with all expenses paid, until they have had to do it themselves and have then taken the first opportunity to pass the job to someone else. It may not be too bad for anyone who is employed simply as a booking manager, but it is a very different matter for anyone who has to take care of the day to day running of a fairly large business for, while he is away, even though urgent matters are dealt with by those who are holding the fort, things accumulate and produce a heavy back-log of work which has to be dealt with as soon as he returns.

Even the tour itself is not as easy as it looks, for finding one's way around has its own difficulties. You cannot look up the address of a touring circus in a book and a telegram to its winter quarters is often unanswered—at times because the place is closed and at others, because the owners of some of the smaller circuses do not want anyone to know where they are. Either they do not want their routes leaked to competitors or they may have found some good new acts and do not want big circuses to bid for them. To establish confidence with some of these people takes a long time, but once done it is a very personal affair and cannot be handed down to a successor.

When I visited the Adolf Althoff Circus in Germany, in 1948, Adolf did not want to know me and was quite frank in saying he wished I had stayed at home. We had won the war and they had lost it and an engagement outside Germany and away from the shortages was a prize for any artiste. I told Adolf there was nothing in his show I wanted and that if there had been my first approach would have been to him, to ask when he would need the act no longer. He and I became and remained friends, but there are people who try to pinch acts; some are circus owners who do not know better and others are agents, some of whom are not worried about the interests of those for whom they do not book.

I found it difficult to work with many agents, for they considered that anyone who did business with them should give them the right to book the whole programme. No agent controls enough top acts to be able to produce whole programmes of the quality we wanted, so if we gave one an exclusivity he had to book some acts through other agents and split the commission with them, and they could not be expected to part with their best acts which they could book elsewhere and receive the whole commission. The result is that a manager who only books through one agent cannot have all the acts he wants and sometimes finds himself landed with one or two that have been left on the shelf by others.

When travelling from one country to another a great deal of time can be wasted if you do not know the ropes, since conditions vary so much. All continental circuses play a seven day week, but in Germany there is never a matinée on the first day in town so, if two shows are to be seen in one day, the first must be that which has already been in town at least one day. Some of them skip the evening performance on the last day because some of the less reputable shows are in such a hurry to move that they cut their programmes and the public has become wise to this piece of mischief. Nothing is more frustrating after a three hundred mile dash in a car than to find the circus already on the move and to have to follow it to the next town and wait twenty-four hours to see it.

In Denmark the circuses are easy to find, as they play nearly the same routes each year, but in Norway there is one which travels by boat up the fjords and if it gets too far north it is a job to catch up with it. In Sweden there is only one big circus now; it was started by the Bronett family and since the deaths of the four brothers has been run by the widow of one of them, Käthe Bronett, one of the most hospitable people in the circus world. It is called Circus Scott and how a Swedish circus came by such a name is said to be accounted for in the following way. The Bronetts, who did such very funny water *entrées* for us at Olympia in the early years, were German and Jewish; by the time they decided to start their own circus in 1935 Hitler was in the saddle and they wisely decided to go to Sweden. In their first programme they featured the Dagenham Girl Pipers and it seems that the thought of bagpipes and kilts produced the name.

Scandinavian circuses cannot begin their seasons until April, when the snow has melted, but anyone wanting to see Circus Scott should go fairly early, unless willing to journey north of the Arctic Circle and see it in the Land of the Midnight Sun.

In Germany the rules enforced by the authorities are the strictest in the world where public safety is concerned. It is a thousand pities there are so few regulations here, where tenting circuses are concerned, and the consequence is that the big, reputable circuses here spend huge sums voluntarily complying with regulations which they make themselves, and which only common sense dictate, while one or two of the smallest shows, having no regulations, can pocket the money that ought to be spent on fire precautions and safety measures generally and are therefore able to compete unfairly.

If Germany emerged from the era of naphtha flares in the 1920's the leader was probably Hans Stosch Sarrasani. He started his circus life as an animal keeper earning about ten shillings a week with the Ciniselli Circus. Later he bought a few animals and, dressed as a clown, worked them in small circuses and music halls. By 1926 he owned one of the biggest circuses in Europe, with some four hundred animals including twenty-two elephants and about sixty wild animals. His big top was as big as any and to move the show by road he had about a hundred new Mercedes Benz lorries and as many trailers. Most German circuses were well organised, but the organisation of Sarrasani was superb; if anything was wrong it was that the man was a megalomaniac, for as he walked round the show every male employee was expected to raise his hat and every female to curtsey. Time off for the staff barely existed and the chauffeurs who drove his lorries had to stand at attention beside them as the public entered and then line the gangways during the performance. Male artistes had to line the ring entrance standing at attention during the whole show except when they were performing and every female had to act as an usherette and that meant being on duty from the time the doors opened until the end of every performance. When Sarrasani entered the ring to present his elephants it was already dressed by almost every member of the circus in oriental costume and his entrance reminded one of that of a Maharajah at a Durbar. The show was always good and a source of acts for Olympia and when I was studying what equipment we should use for our own tenting show I learned more by spending a few days with Sarrasani than anywhere else. We copied much of his equipment, but none of his personal idiosyncrasies, I hope.

Until 1965 there were three very large circuses in Germany, run by members of the Althoff family, and the other big one was that of Krone—which I now consider to be the best organised circus in that country and certainly the one with the most spit and polish. It is also by far the biggest circus in the world, outside the States, and even if others have claimed to be bigger to impress the public their doing so has only served to take advantage of people's ignorance of the subject. Krone has more artistes, more animals, a bigger staff and a larger fleet of vehicles than any circus here or in Europe. If any other circus has anything bigger than Krone's it would be splitting hairs to boast about it, for it is quite certain that Krone's capital investment is by far the largest. I have never understood why some circus owners are so anxious to have people believe their circus is the largest; ours at Olympia seated seven thousand and that is considerably more than any other since Barnum and Bailey were here nearly seventy years ago, so I suppose we could have made a genuine claim about our size; but it seemed to be a pointless exercise and we always felt that if the quality was good we had done more to promote business than any amount of bragging would do and we tried never to forget that *The Times* had once said, 'Bertram Mills combines dignity with showmanship'.

The Krones had one superstition which I think was unique. The founder, Karl, had died and the circus belonged to his widow and although it was run by Frieda, the daughter, and her husband Carl Sembach, the old lady travelled with the show until just before she died. In the spring each year a suck-ing pig was given to Frau Krone and it was believed the circus would have good luck as long as it lived. Everything possible was done to safeguard the little pig, for it was guarded like the Crown Jewels and whenever Carl passed he gave it some dainty morsel, for in his eyes it was the most important animal in a menagerie containing about 250 valuable animals. I never dared ask what happened to the pig at the end of each season.

Before the war Krone had an old circus building at his winter quarters near the centre of Munich, but it was destroyed by bombs and replaced for a few years by a temporary one; a new building was put up five or six years ago and is without doubt the best suited to its purpose of any in the world, for it was de-signed to meet the needs of the present-day circus and has just about every facility a circus owner could desire; during each winter it operates for about three and a half months and is usually packed.

The Sarrasani Circus was reborn some fifteen years ago and is now run by Fritz Mey who worked with Sarrasani as a young man. For the rest there are half a dozen medium sized, but well run, shows in most of which I could find acts from time to time. On the other hand I was always surprised that so many German circus owners engaged acts which had been seen every-where in other circuses in previous years. That this is so may follow from the fact that nearly all of them appear in the ring;

they have a 'thing' about doing so and believe the public will
feel slighted if they do not put in an appearance. Being tied to
their own shows they are unable to see all the others, as I did,
but I believe the public is more interested in a good new act
than in seeing the same horses or elephants presented by the
same individual ten or fifteen years in succession. With one or
two exceptions British circuses have been far more progressive
and only on rare occasions have the major ones booked acts
which their competitors have shown already.

Holland usually had two tenting circuses, but Belgium no
longer has an important one and for the most part the Low
Countries rely upon the invasions of German circuses. Perhaps
that sort of thing will happen here if we enter the Common
Market. France had four big circuses until recently and there
are several small ones which are to be found travelling with
fairs. Pinder is the best of the big shows and undoubtedly the
best organised one and they, like the others in France, travel by
road using a huge fleet of modern lorries and trailers the size
of which is so great that they would be illegal on our roads.
They usually open their seasons at the *Portes de Paris* or on the
Riviera and never stay more than one day except in places like
Lyons and Marseille and the way they plaster the countryside
with posters is disgraceful; anything to which a bill will stick
gets one and nobody seems to mind. Business has been difficult
in recent years and some have resorted to gimmicks in the form
of highly paid pop singers, some of whom have done well
whilst others have been ghastly flops. The one thing that seems
to ensure success is sponsorship by a radio organisation, which
means that the circus and its whereabouts are plugged several
times a day by radio and the second half of the programme
becomes a silly quiz with give-aways and an overdose of commercial advertising. It looks as if the commercials have gone to
the circus and made it pay, but I cannot think this is the sort of
thing a British audience would tolerate. Forty years ago there
were four permanent circus buildings in Paris, but only the
Cirque d'Hiver and the *Cirque Medrano*[1] now remain. Both

1. Known in recent years as the *Cirque de Montmartre*, it was being
run as a German beer garden under the name *Brasserie de Munich* early
in 1967 and there is a suggestion that the *Cirque d'Hiver* may suffer the
same fate.

are owned by the Bougliones, but the seasons are short and at many times there are only performances on three days each week.

In Italy the circus picture is like a broken-up jig-saw puzzle and nothing is more difficult than planning a tour there. Even those circus owners who know will not tell a soul where they are going and the performers seldom know today where they will be tomorrow, so that their relatives have little chance of communicating with them. In some cases the owners work on such a hand-to-mouth basis that even they do not know where they will be in a week's time.

Experience taught me that by the middle of May there would be a circus somewhere between Tarvisio, Belluno and Trieste, so if I arrived in Italy by way of Vienna and Klagenfurt I only had about four hundred square miles to search and by the time I had spotted two old posters I had an idea in which direction the circus was heading. But on one occasion, having discovered where it was yesterday, I lost it for twenty-four hours; I searched every likely place until 9.30 p.m. without result, for although I was within twenty miles of it I had not guessed it would leave the main road and go to a tiny village up in the hills for one day.

Once I found the first circus things were a little easier, for nearly everybody had relatives working in other circuses and by means of the grape-vine they tried to keep track of each other, or at least to keep themselves informed of the areas in which other circuses were. I had to piece together any scraps of information I could glean and if all else failed I made for Milan, knowing there would be at least one circus within a thirty mile radius—but even that left about sixty towns as possibilities. Once, when I did this, I hit the jackpot for there were five circuses within a twenty mile radius and by the time I had seen them all I had a very good idea of where all the major Italian circuses were.

I could take little interest in the dozens of small circuses there are, for each one is run by a large family whose members, between them, do the whole show. There were good acts in many of these shows, but I could never book them because each person worked in several acts and if one act was taken away four or five others were broken up. There are also many shows called arenas, which is a polite way of saying the performers are buskers; they set up their show in the open air and go round with plenty of hats afterwards, but it would be a mistake to dismiss either the small circuses or arenas as worthless, for they are spawning grounds and some of the greatest circus artistes have spent their kindergarten days in them.

It is nearly impossible to establish one's *bona fides* with some Italian circus owners and one, in particular, used to assume I was about to take his best acts away by offering big salaries and he knew it would be very easy for me to do so. He had a rooted objection to signing anything that committed him and all his artistes were engaged on verbal contracts which he could terminate whenever he found a better or cheaper act.

When I visited this man's circus in 1959 he had a bareback act which, if it was as good as it was reputed to be, would have interested me and I should have approached him to find out when he would finish with it. However, I was not trusted and when the act appeared there were three men, instead of four, and none of the big tricks were attempted. During the interval a man standing behind me whispered, 'I am sorry, Mr. Mills, the director told me I had a broken leg as soon as you arrived.' I glanced over my shoulder casually and saw him walking away pretending to limp with the aid of a stick. A few minutes later another artiste, whom I knew well, confirmed the man had nothing wrong with his leg. I almost decided to wear a false beard the next time.

It is quite normal for two or three Italian circuses to use the same name, because their owners are brothers or relatives, and if they add their first names on posters some do so in very small type to confuse the public. The one with the small circus tries to persuade people it is the big show of a relative that is coming; but they do not stick at this only, for there was one occasion when Big Brother, having plastered the town with posters, arrived on the appointed day to find that Small Brother had pulled in twenty-four hours earlier and was playing on the ground he had booked and was doing good business on his advertising. Apparently Small Brother had gone to the official who controlled the ground and agreed to pay more for it. In Italy all is fair in love and circuses.

The performances usually start late in Italy, but where lateness is concerned Spain easily takes first place and there it is nearly as difficult to locate circuses as in Italy. The routes are supposed to follow some kind of plan, according to the time of year and the dates of the big fairs; but if there is a plan it takes a good deal of understanding, for it is disregarded as often as not. Fortunately I had two very good sources of information—printers who supplied posters—and these coupled with the fact that the circuses advertise on local radio stations made it fairly easy to pinpoint a circus once I reached the area covered by the radio.

For the circus artiste engagements in Italy and Spain have the attraction that they last a full year, but salaries are low by our standards and artistes have told me they are not as 'comfortable' there as they are with us. That could mean anything, but I have observed that comparatively little attention is given to things like sanitation and I am quite sure there are few circuses where artistes had mail and newspapers delivered to them, where tradesmen called daily and their laundry was sent forward to the next town so that it was ready when they arrived, as it was at our show. The other problem with circuses that operate all the year round is that there is no period when the show can be re-equipped and repainted and things are usually unkempt, if not tatty.

The country in which things are most unusual to our way of thinking is the U.S.A. There, a circus must be big if it is to attract and that means three rings and often as many stages; to try to watch three performances at the same time is hopeless, so I had to see each show three times. Thirty years ago it was the practice to have three similar acts, one in each ring, and the best was always in the centre, but standards have not been maintained and in these days it is not unusual to see a wirewalker in one ring, a juggler in another and a couple of acrobats in the third and this seems little better than a cinema with three different films at the same time.

Until about ten years ago the Ringling, Barnum and Bailey Circus was by far the biggest tenting show in the world; it had some eight hundred workers who moved the show at night and did most of their sleeping by day in any quiet or shady spot they could find. It moved by rail and hops of a hundred miles were normal; loading the special trains was an enormous task, made worse by the fact that they had to build their own loading ramps up which the trailers could be hauled. In comparatively recent times elephants were used to haul wagons from muddy lots and draught horses, which walked between the tracks, pulled the wagons down the trains once they were up the ramps. Some would say this is old fashioned compared with our use of tractors which moved on the trucks to push the wagons into position, but in fact it was quicker as several wagons could move down the train at the same time.

Labour and other problems eventually forced the 'BIG ONE', as it was always called, off the road to the extent that, having played Madison Square Garden in the spring as they always did, they now operate in large arenas of which there are enough to keep them going most of the year. Most of the other shows have continued tenting and they, too, do one-day stands most of the time; it is therefore not surprising that most of them lack the spit and polish we expect of good circuses here and on the Continent.

The other big difference between American circuses and ours is their method of giving admission, for everyone has to buy a general admission ticket and this only admits to that part of the seating known as the 'bleachers'. These seats are at the ends of the oblong tent and only command a good view of one ring and they are primitive in structure—just benches, on which people sit on the feet of those behind them as they did in British circuses forty years ago. Around the three rings is a hippodrome track on which 'spectacles' (what we would call parades) are presented and at the time when the public is entering there are on this track a number of little boxes from which grandstand tickets (numbered and reserved) are sold by men working competitively on a commission basis.

The thing that annoys me in an American circus is the 'Candy

Butchers' who press through the rows of seating shouting their wares throughout the performance. At one big show I visited there were eighty of these men and I was told the concessionaire who employed them paid a thousand dollars a day for the right. The turnover must have been colossal to bear such overheads, but whereas we in Britain are expected to sell ice cream and drinks at shop or cinema prices, the American public is quite happy to pay fifteen cents for a drink that may be bought for five anywhere else. Candy butchers usually have to wear caps showing the prices of what they are selling and the words 'PAY NO MORE' are often added, because some of the men tell customers the advertised price applies outside the tent only and that they are allowed to charge more inside. It also seems that anyone who refuses to pay the asked price is a marked man and likely to have his feet trodden on by candy butchers who follow.

There has been price-cutting in one form or another in almost every country. On the Continent it usually takes the form of vouchers giving the right to two seats for the price of one; if these were only distributed in large factories or to members of recognised organisations it would be reasonable, but when they are distributed like hand-bills and can be picked up in cafés it is too bad. No worse, however, than what happened here when the owner of a big circus which was doing bad business issued complimentary tickets by the thousand, rather than have empty seats, for in that instance the next circus that came to the town had no chance at all.

Some American circuses have adopted methods which are very near the bone and, in some cases, wholly unethical. First, there is the 'sponsored' circus which sells itself to a charitable organisation in every town and it is then for the charity to sell the tickets and try to make a profit. Now nobody wants to prevent charities making money and to sell a performance is perfectly legitimate, provided it is established that there is an organisation capable of selling the tickets and making profit a certainty. The whole operation takes a very different complexion when it is undertaken by promoters, who use the techniques of door to door salesmen of the worst type. In this case the only object is to sell and whether the charity makes a profit or a loss does not matter to the promoter—little wonder is it that 'promotion' has become a dirty word.

Some charities that have been caught up in this sort of thing have had to adopt methods which were almost as bad, for they have shared the tickets out among their supporters who, in turn, have passed them on to tradesmen with whom they dealt and who were expected to pay for them, even if they were unable to sell them. It is clear that anything of this kind lends itself to serious forms of abuse, as any tradesman who did not pay could so easily be black-listed among members of the sponsoring organisation; one of my informants even hinted that this sort of thing was not unknown.

One night, when travelling with a small sponsored circus, I was told twenty thousand tickets had been sold by the sponsoring charity in the next town. This being far more than the circus could seat I asked what would happen if there were more people than seats. The answer was, there would not be, as that had happened before and people regarded what they paid for tickets as donations. When it had happened people were told a mistake had been made, but as it was all done in the name of charity nobody complained. I hate to think what would be the result if one of our charities did anything of this kind. Perhaps the thing which shocks me most as a circus man is the thought that a circus operated in this way need not worry whether its programme is strong enough to appeal to the public; all it needs is a promoter smart enough to sell it every day to charities by persuading them to believe they will make big profits.

Nothing of this kind is done by the big reputable American circuses and happily we have been spared it in this country, but this is not to say the British circus world is entirely clean, for there is one disreputable little show which is the bane of all others. It changes its name as a chameleon changes its colour; it is assumed it does so to prevent debt collectors catching up and to persuade the public it is not the show at which they were short-changed the year before.

Some thirty years ago John Ringling told me about some of the rackets he found in less reputable American circuses during his early days in the business. At one show ticket sellers paid fifty dollars a week for their jobs and got the fifty dollars back and their living by short-changing the public. At another, where the side show attracted large crowds in front of the main entrance, there was a man who addressed the public every ten minutes. What he said amounted to a warning that as the show drew such large crowds there was a danger pick-pockets would be attracted. Eight or ten men had each picked what looked like a wealthy man as he left his carriage and when the announcement was made it was only natural for men to make sure their wallets were safe. Immediately the position of every wallet was known and in the crowded conditions prevailing it was child's play to lift them during the next few minutes. Of course there were pick-pockets, for they paid the owner of the show for the right to operate and it was part of the deal that the warnings should be given and the man who gave them was one of the gang.

Even if none of the big American shows allow anything of this kind now I have seen a couple of things which were pretty shocking during the last forty years. At one tatty little show a team of men played craps with the coloured workers between the tracks while waiting for the trains to leave and having seen their winnings I had not the slightest doubt that the dice were loaded. At another show I asked the owner how he could afford such a very expensive programme and he let me into the secret. One seventy foot railroad coach had a tiny bar where sandwiches and drinks could be bought, but only artistes were permitted to enter and the rest of the coach was just a plain gambling hell; the owner told me he could afford high priced artistes so long as they were gamblers, for he could count safely on getting seventy per cent of the salaries back each week. Whether the dice or roulette wheel were loaded in this case is beside the point, for the results were what counted.

It would not be fair to leave the impression there has never been gambling in British circuses, for lots of artistes like to while away spare time playing cards, but stakes are usually low and the management never takes part unless it is to stop something that is getting out of hand and that happened once in the very early days of our tenting show. One highly paid artiste liked to play poker, as did the head of a troupe of Chinese acrobats, and whenever they played the Chinaman seemed to win. The game took place in the male artistes' dressing tent and among the spectators were always several members of the Chinese troupe who stood around making jokes, in Chinese, and laughing. Nobody else understood what they were talking about and as it was just possible they were passing information and laughing because others were so stupid to let them get away with it we thought it better to have the game stopped in a place over which we had control but if it continued in one of the artiste's caravans it was no business of ours.

In order to put the record straight, and to clear up some misunderstandings there have been, there is a show called Mills Circus in the States but it is not, and never has been, connected in any way with Bertram Mills Circus.

If there is one man I have met in my travels who is unique it is Father Schönig, a Roman Catholic priest. As the great majority of Continental circus artistes are Roman Catholics he has been appointed by the Pope to an incumbency which embraces all the circuses and fair grounds in Europe and he spends his time travelling between members of his flock. Our circus had its honorary chaplain, but Father Schönig's position is exceptional and his knowledge of circuses and circus people is limitless. I met him almost every year and we were able to exchange information about people we both knew, but I had to be tactful about questions I asked him. If I wanted to know the location of a circus in Italy it is certain he would know it, even if he was in some other country, but his information was due to holding a position of privilege. On the other hand, if I was going to Italy there was no reason why he should not tell me the whereabouts of Italian artistes we both knew and if I knew which circuses they were with it gave me an indication of their whereabouts.

Chapter Fifteen
Television and the circus

By the autumn of 1937 B.B.C. television was an established
fact, although the only one of its kind in the world, but the
cameras needed an enormous amount of light and the only
things we saw were produced with the aid of studio lighting or
sunlight. Nothing had ever been broadcast from the stage of a
theatre or the ring of a circus, but B.B.C. engineers said our
lighting was good enough to make proper pictures possible and
I agreed with my old friend de Lotbinière to let them broadcast the circus 'live' for half an hour on each of five consecutive
days during public performances at Olympia—and they were
not to pay a penny for the privilege. Philip Dorté produced
and directed and Freddie Grisewood was the commentator,
except on the day when he was taken ill at the last moment and,
there being nobody else, I deputised for him. In present times
to make any arrangement of this kind with the B.B.C. would
be suicide, but the number of viewers then was tiny and the
broadcasts gave us publicity of a kind we had never had. The
newspapers made a big feature of what was a new thing in
television broadcasting and those who owned receivers spent a

great deal of time telling their friends and fellow workers about what they had seen. There were probably more eyes on each goggle-box that week than ever before, but most people only saw about a fifth of the show and thousands flocked to see what they had missed or what friends had told them about.

Our broadcasts had been the first in the world made from a public entertainment and we had become a small part of history. I cannot forget the one anxiety I had. The broadcasts were to take place in the presence of ordinary paying audiences and I wondered what our position would be if some woman at home spotted her husband in the audience with a girl friend, when he was supposed to be working late at the office. Apparently nobody had thought of this and I insisted there should be notices warning people that the cameras would be present and saying that, if anyone had reason for not wishing to appear, he should apply to the house manager who would provide seats out of shot.

Under the conditions which prevailed then, and when the B.B.C. restarted after the war, we were able to use television for the benefit of the circus, but with the coming of the commercials and the competition for T.A.M. ratings which ensued, things changed rapidly. After three or four years, during which attendances at Olympia decreased, we had plenty of reasons for thinking that television broadcasts were damaging and that the modest fees we received for them provided totally inadequate compensation. If we had had any doubts they were resolved by the number of telephone calls we had at the box office every day from patrons, or people who should have been patrons, asking the date on which the circus would be broadcast, 'because they wanted to give a big children's party that day'.

Some years later we were able to re-enter the television field on a limited scale, for video tape had arrived and by this means we had already sold two programmes to American television and been paid very large sums for them. Tape meant we could record a part of the programme and let it be aired when our season had ended and we made it a condition that there should be no announcement of a forthcoming broadcast until we were well away from Olympia. We also tried to protect the interest of others by stipulating that the broadcast should take place on a date when no other circus in Britain was operating. We knew that any broadcast of ours would get a very high viewers' rating and hurt any circus operating at the time and hoped that protective measures of this kind would be taken by others when they made tapes, but these pious hopes were stillborn. In fact some people made tapes out of season so that viewers could be flooded with circus during the Christmas season when we were trying to sell live circus.

Competition between the two channels had the effect of increasing the fees the broadcasters were willing to pay and there were those with comparativly cheap programmes to whom the larger fees were so attractive that little less than a free-for-all began. Some circuses produced two, and others three, programmes a year and few people took any heed of what the long term effect would be on the whole business, so long as they were paid fees which they thought were good ones. The joke was still on them, for many accepted fees which belonged in the pea-nut class; they were either too lazy or too naïve to study commercial television advertising rates which would have shown them that a one hour programme networked in peak viewing hours could be worth from forty to fifty thousand pounds in advertising revenue. Some programmes were sold so cheaply to a commercial television company that it had them for virtually nothing and was able to resell them at a huge profit.

We tried to have output limited by negotiations, but if British circuses held back it was only too easy to send the cameras to the Continent, where some circus owners, by insisting the recording should not be shown in their own country, were able to feather their own nests without regard for what happened to us—and the fees they accepted were even lower.

The limit was reached when, in a period of twelve months, there were seventeen long circus shows on television, which meant there was the better part of an hour of circus every three weeks.

Over exposure has only been part of the problem for we, like theatres and even football, have suffered from there being too much entertainment on television and all of it free. People are being encouraged to be too lazy to leave their homes and children are being brought up in the belief that canned entertainment is as good as the live version; one might as well say the same thing about canned and fresh peaches.

A clever television director can use cameras and lighting in a way that enables him to get by with acts which would have little chance of an engagement in a first class circus. A badly costumed woman of dreadful appearance will not be noticed because she is only seen in long shots and all the close-ups will be of the animals she is showing. On the other hand, television can never capture or transmit the atmosphere which is the essence of live entertainment, for it is created neither by the producer nor the performers, but by the thousands of live people in the audience. Invited studio audiences are never the same and in any event people at home are not part of that audience and do not know how it really feels. Too many people know about the activities of 'warmers-up', and all the false applause they produce, and producers who use dubbed applause and laughter from records have not woken up to the fact that they fool themselves about as much as their audience.

A large percentage of television sets are hired, or bought on the never-never, and their owners feel they must get their money's worth each week and parents whose children want to go to the circus have a pretty good excuse if they do not want to go themselves. Although it is quite untrue, they pretend they bought the television to please the children and, as there was a circus on television two weeks ago and there will be another next week, why on earth should anyone want to see another, especially if it means leaving a warm room on a winter's afternoon?

Two things were noticeable as television gathered strength. Whereas the best seats were still sold easily, selling the cheaper ones became increasingly difficult and there was a marked falling off in evening attendances and an increase in those at matinées. These symptoms seem to correspond with the belief that the soap opera type of programme is designed to appeal to the lowest common denominator, for high ratings must be main-

o

tained and the flow of advertising revenue ensured. I am not alone in thinking that the B.B.C., with an assured income, would have been well advised to stand aloof from the battle for viewers which many people regard as a rat race.

I think live entertainment in this country has suffered more than on the Continent as, from what I have seen there, our programmes are better than theirs; this is in part due to the fact that we speak the same language as the Americans. In the States there are more than three times as many potential viewers as in Britain and fantastic sums are spent by the commercials on programmes, but once a show has been networked it becomes a practically worthless piece of tape and can only be sold or rented at a knockout price because there are, in most cases, only two bidders and both are British. All that is best in America should, therefore, be available to us at low prices, but having locked themselves in a desperate and unending battle for viewers the two channels spend their money where they think it will produce good ratings and in a sense, therefore, they are both engaged in the detergent war.

But we must face the truth, which is that television has been more successful at persuading people to stay at home than other forms of entertainment have been in encouraging them to go out. Many of us hoped—and even believed—that the television 'honeymoon' would only last four or five years, but we were very wrong and there are still few indications that the appeal of the goggle-box is weakening. Tomorrow we shall have circus in glorious technicolour by Telstar, but from the few examples I have seen, it looks as if colour television has a long way to go before it achieves the degree of perfection of the cinema and it will never produce the sense of urgency which is so vital a part of a live performance. A man is about to attempt a triple somersault on the flying trapeze and on television you can bet your life he will do it, for it is almost certain that the show will have been pre-recorded and if he missed the first time there will have been a retake. At the circus you are only one of thousands who will hold their breath or cross their fingers for him; you know that if he fails he will have to try again—we don't have to finish the programme to make way for a commercial or a weather forecast.

If I have painted a gloomy picture of the future of the circus in Britain it was not my intention to suggest that it is doomed. At the moment it is a virile and popular form of entertainment and there is still a good market, especially for the smaller shows where large family contributions enable expenses to be kept down, but we cannot overlook the fact that history may be repeating itself. It may be that we are now at the top of a slippery slope and that economic factors may force circuses to become smaller and smaller until the point is reached when all that has been done in the last forty years to enhance the prestige of the circus will be lost and we shall be back where we were at the time when the whole business was said to have reached its nadir.

In the present economic climate the future of the big circus hangs in the balance. Few people realise that the cost of running a big tenting show is more than £1,000 a day and that putting on a six weeks show at Olympia involves an expenditure of about £150,000. Even fewer have ever thought that if Christmas Day falls on a Saturday it can be the cause of a five or six per cent drop in the season's takings. Bad fogs or a freeze are, with epidemics, among the hazards that have to be faced, but the extent of the damage they do depends upon whether they occur during the school holidays or not. But whenever we had them they produced headaches and much extra work. It is not customary in show business to exchange tickets, but when people were unable to attend on account of weather conditions or illness we always tried to do so—only those who wanted to transfer from one Saturday to another were unlucky as the seats had usually been sold.

Chapter Sixteen
Royal performances

In the summer of 1952 those few of us who knew the secret were tingling with excitement and hoping with everything we had that it would happen. In the past year admissions, both at Olympia and the tenting circus, had been disappointing; even the fun fair had taken a knock, for whereas it had formerly enjoyed something of a monopoly in London, there was now one in Battersea Park. Our takings were still enormous, even if not as great as in the boom years, but profit margins were getting narrower and we had little control over the increase in costs. Newspaper advertising, railway charges and the price of everything we had to buy rose month by month and if at the beginning of a tour we had added sixpence to the price of each seat, by the time the tour ended we were still sixpence or more behind the times.

We knew that Tom Arnold's Circus would still be at Harringay during the 1952–3 winter and that Jack Hylton was starting one on our doorstep at Earls Court and that this was likely to draw its audience from those parts of London upon which we relied. In fact Jack Hylton ran only two circuses and neither of them hurt us in the least, for paid admissions to Olympia were higher in both those winters than they had been in 1951–2, but the fact that there were to be three big circuses in London the following winter did not look good. The reason why we were tingling with excitement was that it seemed very probable that Her Majesty the Queen and His Royal Highness the Duke of Edinburgh would attend a gala charity performance at Olympia.

In 1798 Philip Astley was calling his establishment the Royal Amphitheatre because the Duke of York, in whose army he had served, and the then Prince of Wales had honoured him with their patronage, and in March 1887 Queen Victoria had visited the first circus ever held at Olympia—but that had been a private visit which took place one morning and Her Majesty and some children of the Royal Family were the only members of the audience.

Our first connection with the Royal Family was in 1926, when His Royal Highness, Edward, Prince of Wales, made it known to my father that he and a party of friends would like to see the circus, but it was to be a hush-hush affair. I met the Prince, whose arrival was timed carefully to take place a few minutes after the performance began, at a small door which gave access to a stairway leading through unused passages to the balcony. Thence there was a bridge leading to a totally enclosed box at the back of the seating and by the time the party was seated not a soul had spotted the Prince; as there was no light in the box (the bulb had been removed) it was impossible for people on the opposite side to recognise the occupants.

Ten minutes before the end of the show I conducted the Prince and his friends back to the cars by the same route and they departed unnoticed. There had not been a single reporter or photographer and there was never a press reference to the visit. It would have meant a great deal of prestige for us if there had been an announcement, but we had managed to do just as the Prince had wished and were rewarded when he made other visits later and when, during the time he was living at Fort Belvedere, he often went to Ascot to watch the training of animals. His visits and those of his week-end guests prompted us to build and furnish a box and I think ours was the only training establishment to have one; it was certainly the only place to have a box of which the chief occupant was always the heir apparent.

The Princess Royal visited the tenting circus in Leeds in 1931. Prince and Princess Arthur of Connaught attended the opening luncheon the same year and the Duke of Kent, the father of the present Duke, came to it in 1933. King George of Greece visited the tenting circus in Scotland and the following year was followed by the Emperor of Abyssinia, during his exile, but in 1935 there took place at Olympia an event which was to mean far more than any of us realised at the time. The Duke and Duchess of York made a private visit with their two small daughters the Princesses Elizabeth and Margaret. It was their first visit to a circus and never for one moment did it cross our minds that the elder sister would be the monarch one day.

Although the visit was a private one there was no secrecy of the kind for which the Prince of Wales had wished. At this and all other private visits we were informed well in advance, but were expected to keep our knowledge to ourselves until our guests arrived. From then on any member of the public could give the press the tip and by the end of the performance reporters and photographers would be swarming round the building. Pictures presented no problem, but I was always embarrassed when asked what members of the Royal Family had said about the circus. In fact they were always very kind, but I never considered what had been said was for publication and gave evasive replies or just said: 'I think they liked it.'

I have always believed that it may have been during their first visit that the Princesses developed a liking for the circus, but it was not until they came to the tenting circus at Reading in 1946 that we were to see them again. That visit, and the one the next day by the Duchess of Kent and her children, began something which was to gather momentum for the rest of our days, for between 1946 and 1966 we were honoured by royal visits on nearly fifty occasions. Queen Mary came to Olympia once and the two Princesses four times each. There were six visits by the Duke and Duchess of Gloucester, Prince William

and Prince Richard, including three to the tenting circus; the
Duchess of Kent came at least seven times and I have lost count
of how many visits we received from Prince Edward (now the
Duke of Kent), Princess Alexandra and Prince Michael although I have photos proving at least fourteen visits by one or
more of them.

As time went on Prince Charles and Princess Anne were
allowed to come to the circus and during one of their visits we
were all caught napping. The performance had been on for
about forty minutes when Joan Kruse, the wife of our elephant
trainer, asked me whether I realised that Princess Anne was
sitting in Block 6. I certainly did not, and although the boy
sitting near her looked very like Prince Charles I could not
believe my eyes. I asked Bernard to have a discreet look, but the
lighting in the ring seats was, by design, anything but bright
and even he was not sure at first.

In fact Prince Charles and the Princess Anne were among
a number of their school friends, one of whose parents had
bought the tickets, and a similar thing happened during my
last season at Olympia. The Duke and Duchess of Kent brought
their little son, Prince George, who was only three and a half
years of age and while I was talking to them I said I thought he
was still too young to sit through anything that lasted two and
a half hours. As I have said, I do not like repeating anything
said by a member of the Royal Family, but this time I must
break my rule for the reply of the Duchess was so charming and
so kind I shall never forget it. She just said: 'Yes, he really is
too young, but this is your last circus and we did not want him
to grow up without having seen it.'

As we returned to the circus after seeing the animals during
the interval I saw a flash, which meant a camera was at work,
and it was too far away to be photographing those I was escort-
ing. There had been two press photographers at the beginning
of the interval, but now there was only one, so as soon as the
Duke and Duchess were in their seats I returned to the fun fair
to see who else was about and soon spotted a royal nannie and
a detective, but the photographer had gone. The Queen had
allowed Prince Andrew to make his first and only visit to the

circus and I think it had been hoped that by keeping the visit secret he would be able to enjoy himself without being surrounded by a battery of cameras. But for the fact that the Duke and Duchess of Kent were there and that one of the photographers had sharp eyes, we would never have known about Prince Andrew's visit; but the fact that he came gave us great pleasure, for it meant that every living member of the royal family old enough to do so had seen our circus.

All the early visits of the Royal Family were, however, preludes to what was to take place in 1952, for it was then that we were able to announce that Her Majesty the Queen and His Royal Highness the Duke of Edinburgh would attend a charity performance at Olympia. I am quite unable to express what this meant to us, for never before had a reigning monarch made a public visit to any British circus. If anything made all the hard work done since 1920 rewarding, this did, and when the wonderful news came I could not help thinking back to the days when my father had started the ball rolling; when circus had sunk as low as it could; when it was considered low class entertainment and to visit it was just not done. Nor did I forget, at a time when it would only have been human to think in terms of triumph, that it was from the foundations which Bertram Mills had laid so well that we had been able to reach the point at which we were. Bernard and I had carried on the business which he started; we had our ups and downs, but we tried to maintain the standards and traditions of the past, knowing that if we were able to do so we should succeed more than we dared to hope.

In the words of the Variety Club the performance was 'sponsored' by them, but I always took a poor view of the use of that word for the Oxford Dictionary says a sponsor is : 'One who pays for a broadcast programme into which advertisements of his wares are introduced.' Members of the Variety Club did splendid work by selling tickets, producing the printed programme, obtaining free advertising and in other ways, but it was Bertram Mills Circus that paid all the expenses of the performance.

To have had the royal performance a few days after the

opening when the programme had settled down would have been onerous enough, but the only day on which it could be arranged was that on which the circus was due to open, so the opening had to be postponed one day. Upon reflection I must have been mad to agree to any such arrangement, for any show being presented for the first time is likely to over-run and the presence of Royalty only adds to the risk as performers are tempted to spin out their acts. However, it had to be December 18th, or no royal performance, so I had no choice and things were only made worse when I found myself landed with two additions to the programme. Dame Ninette de Valois and the directors of the Sadler's Wells Ballet gave permission for Nadia Nerina and members of the company to appear in 'Clowns and the Dancer', a ballet specially produced for the occasion by Alan Carter—a thing that had never happened in a circus in this country. Sir Adrian Boult agreed to conduct the circus band for the ballet and by way of contrast Eddie Calvert was to play his golden trumpet, although I felt this had little to do with circus and was to some extent out of place. However, it was all in aid of charity and all the extra people were giving their talent without payment.

With all this on my hands the scissors, for which I was well known when cutting acts, looked impotent and I let it be known that this time I had a big knife—a knife-switch on the ring lighting and even if I made it look like a power failure for a brief moment I should use it if an act over-ran more than a few seconds. I was under an obligation to end the performance by a certain hour and was determined to do so.

In the event all went well and the artistes timed their acts perfectly, but when I looked for Calvert ten minutes before he was due to appear he was not to be found. Whoever had arranged for his appearance had failed to tell him when he was to make it, but there was time to warn other acts to be ready to go on early; I was able to make time for him after the interval and the audience knew nothing of what had been a period of anxiety.

Before we reached the stage of giving the performance there were a great many extra and special things to do. Every yard of carpet in the seating had to be new and laid after the dress rehearsal the previous day and there had to be red carpet from the entrance to the circus. A royal box had to be built and suitable chairs found for it; one of the stands in the fun fair could not be built, as the area it occupied was needed for the building of a royal retiring room. There had to be a reception area clothed in flowers where we should present members of the organising committee to Her Majesty and Prince Philip; B.B.C. television was to cover everything, including the first twenty minutes of the performance, and that meant special lighting and all the complicated arrangements that go with a 'live' broadcast.

Bernard and I were to meet the royal party and conduct it to the reception area where a bouquet was to be presented to the Queen and it was in connection with this that we had one of our biggest headaches. Anyone could have produced a pretty little girl to make the presentation, but that would not have been circus—it could have happened anywhere. On the other hand, what was more symbolical of circus than a white faced clown in a magnificent sequined costume, but at the same time what would people have thought in 1920 if anyone had suggested that a bouquet should be presented to the Queen by a circus clown? But times had changed, and circus had changed, and there was no longer any reason for not doing such a thing, provided it was done in a dignified way.

After what seemed like years of anxious preparation and the overcoming of innumerable obstacles the great day arrived and we were assured of a full house. When the royal cars arrived precisely at the appointed time we walked up the red carpeted stairway to the entrance of the Grand Hall where Percy Huxter, the most immaculate of all clowns, stepped forward quietly, bowed and presented the flowers to the Queen. Never had there been such a moment for any clown—his costume, made specially for the occasion in Paris, was the most magnificent I have ever seen and Percy played his part as if he had done it a thousand times. The presentations over, we made our way to the circus where the audience was already seated; Charles Hotham, the musical director, gave the cue to four State Trumpeters to sound a fanfare announcing the arrival of Her Majesty and Prince Philip. The audience rose and when the royal party had reached the box the band played the National Anthem and then the parade began. All the preliminaries seemed to have gone perfectly and it was now up to me to see that what was to follow was equally perfect.

Little did I expect there would be trouble within seconds. Among the ring boys was one able to make beautiful sawdust patterns in the ring and on this occasion he had produced a masterpiece in colour, but as the first two horses entered the ring led by a groom they jibbed. Neither had seen coloured sawdust before and neither was prepared to tread on it. The wretched groom was in despair, for his arms were not long enough to allow one horse to pass on either side of the design, so he did the only thing he could and let one horse loose, hoping it would rejoin him on the far side of the ring. Fortunately it did, but for a few seconds seven thousand people probably wondered what sort of a muddle there would be. Tony Yelding, the ringmaster, always spotted anything wrong instantly, and he rushed some boys into the ring to kill the design with rakes; the rest of the parade and indeed the whole performance went without a hitch.

The Queen, of course, had seen what a mess I had made of the parade and during the interval she made a joke about it, but with her understanding of animals she knew why we had run into trouble and I soon forgot the episode. But, believe it or not, when we had the second royal performance, in 1955, Her Majesty's first remark to me when we met in the interval was, 'Mr. Mills, you have done it again', and indeed we had. Both Tony and I had completely forgotten what happened in 1952 and again there was a huge coloured design in the ring; neither of us had heard a bell ringing until the first pair of horses entered and what we heard then was like a thousand fire engines. To make the same mistake in identical circumstances is unforgivable, but it had provided a joke at my expense and when one is tense, as is inevitably the case on such important occasions, nobody is more able to put people at ease than the Queen.

It was in 1959 that the Queen and Prince Philip brought Prince Charles and Princess Anne to the circus for the first time, but it was a private visit and not a soul knew about it until they arrived. However, a former P.R.O. of ours happened to visit us that day and, seeing Bernard and me waiting at the main entrance just before the matinée, guessed there was something important in the air. He hung around until he had seen the Royal Family arrive and I have a shrewd suspicion he then tipped the press off and made a scoop, or several; if he did not, he was asleep at the switch, for someone else did and by the time the performance ended there were more photographers in Olympia than I have ever seen—for the first visit of the Prince and Princess was big news.

The next royal performance was in 1959, in the presence of the Princess Margaret, and that was followed by one in 1960, attended by the Queen and the Duke of Edinburgh, in aid of the Imperial Cancer Research Fund and the Central Council of Physical Recreation. In 1963 there was another, like the one in 1959, in aid of the Olympic Games Equestrian Fund and this was to have been attended by the Princess Margaret but she was indisposed and her place was taken by Princess Alice. All these performances involved every bit as much planning as the first and there were often additions to the programme which added to the complexities of my job, but the fact that these performances took place gave the circus a kind of prestige which nothing else could give it. As they all took place after the opening I had fewer worries, since I was dealing with programmes which had had a day or two in which to settle down and with artistes about whom I knew more than I knew of those who took part in 1952.

If the circus basked in the sunshine of royal visits the fun fair was not neglected and at one time or another I think every younger member of the Royal Family spent some hours there; of course the popular things were the big rides like the dodgems, which those splendid showmen the Botton brothers, Albert and James, brought to us each year and which did so much to make the fun fair attractive. Year after year, when they were younger, I received messages from Iver or Kensington Palace saying that

Prince Edward and Prince Michael would like to spend an afternoon in the fun fair and we tried to arrange the visits to take place during matinées, when there were few people in the fair, so they could have a little fun without being stared at or bothered by too many photographers.

On one occasion, however, we had a ride which consisted of a circular rotating wall to which riders were 'glued' by centrifugal force and utterly helpless until the thing slowed down. Now there is no danger in a properly run fun fair, but I always felt I should accompany the Princes when they went on rides which took them above ground level; they were young and if they had been scared by height there should be someone there to reassure them. In another sense, what was good enough for them should be good enough for me, and it was in these circumstances that I found myself glued to that ghastly wall with Prince Edward on one side and Prince Michael on the other. We all hated it, but what I did not know was that a press photographer had arrived and was having a field day.

The pictures in the papers the next day were horrors. We all looked unwell and terrified and to say the whole thing was undignified would be a gross understatement. I felt I had blotted my copy book and sent a letter by special messenger to Sir Philip Hay asking him to offer my apologies to the Duchess of Kent. His reply was typical of the kindness one always receives from members of the Royal Family. The Duchess had seen the pictures and had been much amused by them; she understood that the avoidance of photographers in such circumstances was impossible and I was not to worry. And as if that were not enough I received charming hand-written letters from the two Princes the next day saying how much they had enjoyed the afternoon.

Some things go less well than others and in 1949 I was taking a Very Important Youngster round the fair and he—being very young—could take just about everything, but I—a bad sailor—was feeling green by the time we had done the rounds for an hour and a half. Among the rides was one which would turn the stomach of a cat and although my guest liked it I did my utmost to divert his attention every time we went near it. After the last ride on this machine I was searching desperately for something that would give my stomach a rest when he said : 'Mr. Mills, I'm going to be sick.'

Some members of the public were about and the obvious answer could not be given in this case, so all I could do was tell him to do his best to hold out until we could reach somewhere private. I took him to my office and gave him an easy chair, but he was thirsty and the only thing I had was the ersatz orange squash with which we had to be content in those days. I thought if anything would complete the upset that would, but it had to be risked; he drank two large tumblers of it and then, after fifteen minutes' rest, rose, patted his tummy and said : 'Now I feel fine—let's go and do it all again.' We did, but gave that machine a miss and at the end of the afternoon he ate a good tea—but I have always been thankful that the cream in the cakes was also ersatz.

Chapter Seventeen
Borra joins the circus
Circuses clash at Salisbury

It was in the spring of 1952 that Borra, the pick-pocket, joined the tenting circus when the tour opened in a snow-covered tent at Cardiff and we discovered we had with us not only an extremely accomplished performer with a charming and talented wife, but a man with a highly developed sense of humour. In this he was in good company, for neither Maurice, the comedy cyclist, Pepe Cavallini, the man with the crazy 'T' model Ford, nor Eddie Raspini, the juggler, ever missed a chance for a practical joke and some of the pranks they got up to would have done credit to a cart-load of monkeys.

Practical jokes in a circus can be too much of a good thing and the one which involved covering a juggler's hoops and clubs with treacle which was done on a continental circus would not have gone with a swing with us. Generally speaking anything involving the performance is out, although there have been one or two exceptions to the rule, usually on the last nights of a season. Fredy Knie, the head of the Knie Circus in Switzerland, is well known for practical jokes and one year, when he was at Olympia with his horses, we had an Australian who did a sharp-shooting act. One day this man took a pot at a balloon held by a girl on the far side of the ring and a dead duck, purchased at a poulterers, fell at his feet. The public took it for the good laugh it was, but the Australian was not amused.

We got back at Fredy later when he was showing an act in which half a dozen zebras ended their performance by leaving the ring one by one behind him. Fredy is an artiste of the highest standing and when he does something it always receives applause and he was, therefore, embarrassed when he received none at the end of the act. When people began to laugh he turned to see what was the cause and found there was still one zebra in the ring—two of the other artistes in a prop zebra skin sitting on the ring fence in a somewhat uncomplimentary attitude.

Fredy's duck reminded me of a shock I had a few years before when a man walked into the office and put a kitchen knife on the desk saying : 'That fell and touched my sleeve and that of my small daughter, but no damage was done—I thought you ought to know about it.' The knife was smeared with dried paint the colour of that which outside contractors had used when painting the roof of Olympia six months before. It had presumably been used to stir paint and left on a ledge by a careless man and vibration over the months had dislodged it; we were lucky that the patron involved was not the type who claims for shock at the slightest chance.

Borra was a big draw and by the second day in town everybody was talking about the 'pick-pocket', for opening performances were always attended by the Mayor, members of the Council and senior officials, including the Chief Constable, who were our guests, and I am afraid we gave Borra the seat numbers of all likely clients. This list never contained the name of anyone we had ever met, for if such a person became one of Borra's 'patients', as he called them, somebody would say, 'He knows the Mills Brothers and is stooging for Borra.'

The Mayor, wearing his chain of office, was inviolate, but anyone else who looked as if he could take a joke was fair game and the number of Chief Constables who lost their wallets, watches and even braces is legion, but we never received a complaint until Borra was at Olympia when there was one. An indignant woman wrote to say her husband had been held up to ridicule by having his braces removed in front of seven thousand people and that she would never visit the circus again as she feared Borra might remove her knickers. It has always been my belief that complaints should be treated with respect and if we made a mistake the easiest way was to admit it and say we would try to do better in future, but in this case I thought the complaint frivolous and having thanked the woman for her letter said that, knowing Borra as well as I did, I could assure her that nothing would interest him less than her underwear.

In many of the larger towns we gave parties of a semi-official kind to introduce Borra to the press and important personalities and at one of these both the Mayor and the Chief Constable were present and when Borra had been introduced to them he asked the Mayor the time. He fumbled in his waistcoat pocket, pulled out a watch and said, 'Good God, it's been dehydrated.' The C.C. laughed, for he knew the Mayor had a large Hunter watch, but he only saw the other half of the joke when Borra asked him the time and he found the Mayor's watch in his pocket. Unfortunately for us none of the press reporters were very bright, for the episode screamed for a story under the headline 'Chief Constable turns pick-pocket'.

We all watched Borra's act whenever we could, because of the very different reactions of those who became his 'patients'. I probably saw it as often as anyone especially during his first few months with us as I was naturally anxious lest anybody should be too smart for him, but he was always at least two thoughts ahead of everyone although he nearly met his match on the second Friday of a two-week stay in Aberdeen. He had reached the stage with three men seated in the ring when we all knew the next one was due to have his tie taken. As Borra approached him he said: 'You can't do it. I saw your act last week and you are going to try to take my tie but it is sewn in.'

It was about three thousand to one against this man being picked from the audience for this trick, but Borra had reached the point of no return and professed disbelief and asked to be shown how it had been done. The collar was raised first on one side and then the other and in each case there was stitching and to make quite sure the man showed some stitches at the back near the stud.

Borra engaged him in conversation and pretended to be interested in his watch, wallet and cigarettes, but he took none of them. Finally, he patted the man on the shoulder and said : 'Never mind, you are too much for me, but if you come back tomorrow I will take something from you.' The man returned to his seat . . . minus his tie, and the audience, who had heard the conversation over the loud-speakers and had seen the tie taken, roared with laughter.

While Mr. Cleverstick was pointing out the stitching he failed to see Borra running a tiny pair of embroidery scissors through it and while pretending to be interested in other things Borra had taken the tie without any difficulty. That was the secret of Borra's tricks; while he riveted your attention on what he was only pretending to do, the other hand was doing the pinching and the joy of the whole thing was that everyone except the 'patient' saw all that happened.

A few days later our P.R.O. returned to the circus and, pretending he knew nothing of this incident, challenged Borra to remove his tie, thinking that as he was not in the ring he would not be prepared for trickery. Borra accepted the challenge and, while putting one hand in the P.R.O.'s wallet pocket, cut the two long tails of the tie off just below the knot. He still had the scissors, but was not having his leg pulled by a member of the staff.

On one occasion he and Ilse, his wife, were among a dozen of us who went to a country hotel to dine one Sunday evening. When the waiter served cocktails Borra whispered something to him. He knew I had a passion for pea-nuts and when the waiter returned with them he was asked the time, but his wrist-watch had disappeared when the nuts were ordered. When I took a handful of nuts and took the first bite I had to splutter the lot over the floor, for Borra had substituted some of his own. The business with the waiter's watch had not been to amuse him only; its real purpose was to take my eye off the pea-nuts for a second or two. He had spent the whole afternoon drilling holes through pea-nuts, filling them with cayenne pepper and sealing the ends with butter.

One Sunday afternoon, while the circus was being built up on Southsea Common, John Gindl found that two new tyres he had just bought were missing from the boot of his car. Borra confided to Pepe Cavallini that he had them and was going to put them in the car of Maurice; he then suggested that the police be fetched and asked Pepe to go into town and find a friendly cop and explain the situation. In due course Pepe returned, but could hardly keep a straight face for the thought of what Maurice would do when the tyres were found. The policeman searched a number of cars before reaching that of Maurice and when he arrived there the tyres were not to be found. So the search continued until the policeman came to Cavallini's car, which was gone over in spite of the owner's protests, and of course that was where Borra had put the tyres while Cavallini was fetching the cop.

Pepe had been the fall guy again, just as he had a few weeks earlier when he had found a strange animal of a kind he had never seen. It was a common hedgehog and he turned it loose, but found it in his bed when he retired that night. His shock, however, was no greater than that of a friend of ours who came to spend a few nights at the circus and occupied Bernard's caravan. Entering the bedroom, from which the electric lamps had been removed, he saw by the light reflected from the sitting room what looked like a dark skinned naked girl in his bed. We were rehearsing a new liberty act in which the horses were ridden by dummy Arab tribesmen and had used one of the dummies and a long haired black wig borrowed from the wardrobe department.

Borra's most successful practical joke was the one he played on the Yugo-Slavs, his countrymen at the time. During the later stages of the war he was employed to entertain the troops, but the time soon came when he was told he would have to revert to being an ordinary soldier. He told his C.O. he had been an illusionist before the war and had done a two-hour show and that if he could have his two assistants and a few days to collect his props he could do the big show for the troops.

The C.O. thought it a good idea and gave him one permit to go to Belgrade where the props were stored and another to go to a small town near Trieste where the senior assistant lived.

Armed with the necessary papers he made straight for Trieste where he hung around the station in the hope of being able to conceal himself in a goods truck bound for Italy. He had thought out alibis in case of failure; the props had been destroyed by bombs or the assistants had disappeared. His chance came on the second day when a Russian officer who was the worse for wear arrived and Borra carried his baggage to the train and when it left he was still aboard. He was able to ingratiate himself still further by serving drinks, but when they reached the frontier controls he, with no papers authorising a crossing, was in trouble. However, he had already promised to carry the Russian's baggage; when he was challenged the Russian said he was his servant and he was allowed to pass. Such is Borra's ability to take one's eye off the ball and the Russian had been like putty in his hands.

The following day he sent a telegram to his C.O. saying the name of his biggest illusion was 'The great disappearing trick' and that he had already performed it. One would think a Yugo-Slav wandering about in Italy in time of war would very soon land in the hands of the police, but again he was too smart, for within hours he contacted the British and a few days later was working for ENSA which later sent him to Austria, where he and his wife were reunited, and after the war they both became Austrian citizens.

I have often been asked what circus artistes are like and whether, with their good salaries and the spare time they have on their hands, they drink too heavily. The answer is they do not, for no heavy drinker can maintain the physical and mental condition circus work demands and in all my forty-five years I can only remember one case of drunkenness. The interval had just begun at the tenting circus when I heard a pail being rattled and saw a clown running down a gangway and into the ring, where he threw the pail up and allowed it to fall on his head. If it had been plastic, or even an ordinary tin pail, I should not have worried, but it was a heavy gauge steel fire bucket and could have split the man's skull. The audience laughed and thought it a good piece of clowning, but it took two of the ring boys to remove the body back to the dressing room and I gave instructions that the man was to be sent to me at the end of the show. As he entered the office I said, 'You were drunk during the matinée'. He replied: 'Yes, I was in very bad shape during the first half but a bucket fell on my head during the interval and that sobered me up very quickly.' It was a first offence and there was nothing more to say except that it was not to happen again.

Stanley Franklin when he was box office manager at Olympia told the story of a man who had obviously had too much to drink and was told by the cashier there were no seats available. Seeing other people buying at adjoining windows he demanded to see the manager and as no method of persuasion was successful he eventually had to be told that he could not have a ticket because he was drunk. 'Of course I'm drunk,' he replied, 'do you think I'd want to see your ruddy show if I were sober?'

It was during Borra's first season with us that we had one of the biggest scares of our lives. The circus was in Cheshire when Jock Morrison, the new master of horse, announced that two of the horses had strangles, a disease which spreads like fire among kindling and is often fatal. When a local vet confirmed his diagnosis we were threatened with having a circus with no horses for weeks and perhaps being left with only the remnants of three or four acts. Penicillin was rushed to us by passenger train in gallon lots and Jock spent nearly all his time going round with a hypodermic needle and every horse was saved, but it had been a narrow escape. We heard there had been strangles in a racing stable near a town we had visited recently and if a groom from that stable visited ours and touched a horse it could have started the trouble.

At the Oktoberfest in Munich that year I saw enormous balloons in the shapes of animals and men flying over the city advertising various products and it was obvious that something of this sort would be valuable to the circus, so I asked the makers whether they could make one in the shape of an elephant twenty feet high. They could, and we placed an order, but when we were ready to use it the following season our troubles began. The Air Ministry said it must not fly at a greater height than three hundred feet; the gas needed to raise it was nitrogen and it was difficult to get permission to buy and use it and it cost about £40 in each town. In a gale the thing was an unmanageable monster even when anchored on to the ground, but in fair weather it could be seen for miles and of course the name MILLS was painted on both sides in huge letters.

One morning in Cambridge the elephant was found lying deflated on the ground with several rents in it. The police had to be called, though with reluctance, for we suspected undergraduates might have been responsible and did not want a silly prank to be the cause of anyone getting into the kind of trouble which a charge of malicious damage merits. Having been at the university I knew my way around fairly well and by the end of the day we knew to which college the culprits belonged—and even the names of some of them—so I went to see the tutor and asked him to be good enough to let it be known that we were well informed, but did not intend to take any action. On the other hand, it must be clearly understood that it was not to happen again for if anyone had been smoking when the nitrogen was released there would have been an explosion which could have wiped the circus out.

We all make mistakes and I have probably made as many as anyone, but few have been worse than the one I made in a British Railways station. I had seen the circus trains loaded in one town and motored over to the next to take care of unloading, which was due to begin at 5 a.m. The man in charge of shunting had typed instructions explaining everything that had to be done and the quick and easy way of doing it, but he preferred his own ways and there was one muddle after another. We were due to open that afternoon and instead of having the trains unloaded by 7 a.m. it was after nine when we finished. I had tried to explain how the muddle with the first train could be avoided with the second, but my efforts were of no avail and as the precious hours passed I became less and less patient and, as everybody in the circus knows, I can be very impatient with people who are persistently stupid and reject the help of those who have done the job hundreds of times. My impatience was almost matched by that of members of our train unloading team, as they had worked all night and would only get some sleep when the job was finished. In the end I gave the man a piece of my mind and almost usurped the office of Superintendent of the Line. At the ground we made up all the wasted time and at four fifteen I was at the entrance of the circus awaiting the arrival of the Mayor, who was to open the show. The car arrived and out stepped His Worship wearing his chain of office . . . my friend of the early hours. If ever anyone had good reason for wanting to get lost I had, but the Mayor was a sensible man; he realised I had been up all night and probably remembered that during our argument I had said something to the effect that it would be a nice do if we were not ready in time for the opening by the Mayor.

Since then I have kept a very civil tongue in my head when dealing with employees of British Railways.

In 1955 the circus was in Swansea when the railway strike began. We had not enough tractors to move all our trailers by road and had ahead of us half a dozen three-day towns—and that meant three mid-week moves. We enlisted the help of travelling showmen and they, with their huge tractors, were able to haul three trailers at a time, but the speed at which they did it was too much for vehicles intended to move slowly to the station and then travel by rail. More than seventy tyres were burst on the journey to Haverfordwest and, as they were smaller than those used on lorries, the makers only had a few in stock and had to borrow back from customers to keep us moving. Unable to do mid-week moves we had to stay a week in each of four three-day towns and business was bad, but to close would have been worse and as we were insured it was up to us to minimise the loss by all possible means.

We expected difficulties with the elephants, for there were three large ones which had never been separated and as no motor vehicle was large enough, two would travel together and the third alone. Even a female adult would be difficult to manage if frightened, but Gösta Kruse travelled with the one which was alone and again it was a case of what was good enough for him was good enough for her. By the time the strike ended we had moved four times by road and done 160 miles; the moves had been among the most difficult we ever made and everyone had had enough by the time we were back on rail.

I suppose the next thing we all remember best was our 'clash' with Chipperfields in 1957. We had planned our route months ahead and were due in Salisbury towards the end of July, but for some reason they changed theirs and announced they would be there a week ahead of us on another site. We were nearer and calculated they could not arrive before July 8th; to do this they would have to miss one town in which their tickets were already on sale at local agents. We therefore decided to open in Salisbury on July 8th, which meant they must either abandon the town or go there on the same day. Having thrown down the gauntlet they could hardly reject the challenge to play day and date with us and when their advertisements appeared alongside ours the 'circus war' was on.

The fortunate thing was that John Hinde, who at one time had done all Chipperfield's publicity, had left them and soon after he was free we had offered him the same job with us. His assistant at Chipperfield's had been Bill Dredge, who had taken over. They had been intimate friends for years and now were to do battle on behalf of their respective employers. Both are extremely able and they each put up a magnificent fight, although I do not think any two circuses had ever been engaged in this kind of battle before. There had been countless clashes between others over the years, but they were rough and tumble affairs with few holds barred, whereas this was to be a battle of brains between two gentlemen and neither allowed a single poster belonging to the other side to be covered.

Bill Dredge fired the first shot with a clever move by booking the only unloading dock at the main railway station in the centre of the city for the one train which carried Chipperfield's animals so that we, with four trains, had to unload at an out-of-the-way goods yard on the outskirts. But this did not worry us as we always had our trains unloaded and everything up at the ground before people were about on Sunday morning. We therefore lost no publicity, but what hurt was that following

Circus on the move

A 65 ft. king pole weighing nearly two tons goes up

The big top canvas is spread

Each stake is fitted with a cap to prevent people barking their shins

Electricians install spotlights

Ready to open

OVERLEAF *The Circus at Windsor, with the Castle in the background*

Ascot Winter Quarters

A section of the stables
Elephant pedicure
Chefs in the staff mess
Feeding time in the wild animal house
The blacksmith's shop

the unloading of their train in the afternoon Chipperfields planned a big parade from the centre of the city with all their artistes and animals. Chipperfields were equipped to do this, as they moved by road and had suitable vehicles, whereas we had never done more than parade our animals from the station to the circus on foot as we did not think it good publicity to cause big traffic jams in the centres of towns, or that it was right to ask highly paid performers to exhibit themselves in the streets. It had been done in the old days, but that was a long time ago and for men like Borra and Rudi Horn, who were at the top of their profession, to walk through the streets in costume was undignified and could give nobody the remotest idea of the outstanding performances of which they were capable; for parade purposes a third rate troupe of Arab tumblers in national costume would be a better bet.

Every evening, when one of the P.R.O.s had placed his order for the following day's advertisements, the other would go and order twice as much space; then the first would return and double up again and very soon the advertising manager knew that whatever the size of the space taken by one would have to be available to the other. National newspapers took up the story on an editorial basis and for days there were round by round accounts of the 'Circus War' with each P.R.O. trying to out-do the other in the production of news items. Both circuses received fantastic amounts of free publicity. I spent the week before the opening with John Hinde and Jimmy Chipperfield was with Bill Dredge; of course we all met frequently and with but one thought in our minds—what will the others do next and what can we do to catch them unawares? I think I was the only one whose leg was well pulled, for having left my car outside a hotel while I dined I returned to find a sticker advertising Chipperfield's Circus on the rear window. I have not the slightest doubt that the credit for it is due to Jimmy.

Both circuses did fantastic business, but I am sure neither made money during the three days for we had both spent far too much on publicity, but if they took more money than we did they should have been delighted. Their normal expenses were lower than ours, but we with over 17,000 seats to sell filled all but about a hundred. In a way it had been a battle to the death, but fought the way it was nobody was hurt and those with whom we spent money on advertising had a field day. The Chipperfields and we were, and still are, friends, but there was nothing phoney about the clash and although many people thought we had ganged up to hit the headlines there was nothing of that sort. If either of the P.R.O.s had thought up such a scheme and we had put it into operation the thought would have been a stroke of genius, for we could have achieved the same ends with only a comparatively small advertising expenditure. That, however, is hindsight and before the event there was nothing to suggest that a place the size of Salisbury could fill two big circuses for three days; we had every reason to assume one show would get the business and the other would not and each of us had to make sure we were not the also ran.

Floods were part of our bread and butter and when grounds became inundated the only thing to do was dig trenches and deep pits and then pump the water away with the fire engine. Usually the most difficult part of the operation is to find a place to which the water can be pumped. When we were flooded in Glasgow, in 1938, the only place was the road alongside the circus and there it went, with four or five tons of mud, and although paying for the mud to be scraped off the road and carted away was expensive, it was cheaper than losing a performance.

One of the most anxious weeks we had was at Reading, where the circus site adjoined the river. Every day the water rose in the river until it began to spread across the circus ground. A few years before I had seen a Danish circus in similar trouble and by the time the big top was in three feet of water the only way the show could get back on to the road was by loading it piece by piece in dinghies. The thought that we might have to do the same with a much bigger and heavier show caused us to consider pulling down, but losing Friday and Saturday is no joke, so we decided to take a chance. The flood water came to within feet of the stables and big top and then receded; there was a lock a short distance downstream and perhaps some kind person opened it.

The flood in Elgin was even worse, for on the day we opened the only road leading to the circus was under two feet of water and we had to organise a public ferry service using trailers and tractors. Worse was to come, for on the day we moved to Inverness a river burst its banks, washed away a section of the railway line and made part of the main road impassable. The journey for the circus trains was increased from thirty-nine to about 120 miles, which appeared to be more than we could do between an evening performance and the matinée the next day; but everybody made a supreme effort and although the train with the big top did not arrive until 11 a.m. the circus was built up in record time. When the doors opened the only people who could collect tickets were girls from the office and the wives of artistes, for all the men were getting washed and dressed, but the show began at the advertised time.

For the 1959–60 winter programme I booked the Carolis, who are unquestionably the best clowns at the present time, but there were doubting Thomases when I let it be known that one of their acts would be the so called 'riding machine'. This consists of one person giving a demonstration of how to ride a bareback horse with the assistance of a safety belt, to which is attached a rope that goes through an overhead pulley, and the end of this is held by a man standing in the ring so that when people fall, as they always do, no damage is done. Members of the public are then invited to have a go. It is an act that has been done by little circuses for longer than anyone can remember and it suited them as it cost nothing. People, therefore, had reason to be surprised when they learned I was to use the highest paid clowns there are for this sort of thing and when I announced the 'riding machine' would be the last act in the programme some of the old-timers were saying: 'Now we know he is round the bend.' Nobody believed that the sophisticated London public would have anything to do with it; it was the sort of thing people on the village greens would like because most of them could ride, but Londoners, 'Oh no!' Where I had the advantage over others was that I had seen the Carolis' way of presenting the act and others had not.

I took the precaution of having plenty of stooges ready in

case there were no volunteers, but as soon as people saw it was safe and good fun they came forward in far greater numbers than we were able to cope with and the act produced as much laughter as any we ever had and I repeated it during the two following winters and for three seasons with the tenting circus. It had not been done by others in recent years, but within months almost every circus was trying to copy it, though none of them produced anything really worth while. Young Caroli who took the end of the rope had a dozen tricks up his sleeve and once the belt was around the waist he could do anything he liked with the rider; the only worry we ever had was that there were so many girl volunteers, for there was always the chance that when a girl fell she might land upside down and give the audience a bigger eyeful than it had paid for, but Caroli was very careful to keep girl riders the right way up and, although there were a few near misses, nothing shocking ever took place.

Of course it was one of the Carolis whose trousers came off at the end of the act, but for the rest we relied upon the public to provide the laughs. Except one. I was watching the act at Olympia one night when it became the turn of a girl member of the audience. Although it was years before the mini-skirt was thought of hers was above the knee and she wore a tight fitting jumper, a flower-pot hat and a pair of long mauve cotton gloves. The skirt was so tight that when she tried to run across the ring she fell over; she had either seen the show before, or had been told about it, and had taken great pains to wear the right underwear—which was a good thing, for by the time she was sitting astride the horse the skirt was where the belt belonged. Her appearance was funny enough, but her actions were a scream and I don't think I have ever laughed so much at anything. As soon as she left the ring I said to my personal assistant : 'Grab that girl and see if you can talk her into doing that at every performance. Pay her well and we will keep her as long as she does it like that, but the day she begins to look like a stooge we shall not need her any longer.' The girl accepted the offer and later did a whole season with the tenting circus without losing her amateur appearance, for she had the sense to vary her antics and even we never knew what to expect next.

Chapter Eighteen
The Irish tours

Although there were ups and downs during the years 1950 to 1960 it looked as if the tenting circus was working at an ever increasingly low profit margin, but it was not possible to produce separate accounts which would reflect the relative profitability of Olympia and tenting, as the two things were complementary. Directors and executives served both shows as did the London Office, which had a fairly large staff all the year, as it did the accounts for the tenting circus, party booking for Olympia and several other chores. The cost of running the winter quarters was enormous, and was one which clearly had to be borne by the tenting show, but that show produced acts for Olympia and all the Olympia equipment was stored and overhauled there. Things done for Olympia by Ascot would have to be charged back, but this could only be done on a basis of approximation and to decide how the cost of feeding animals and paying trainers and grooms during non-operating periods should be apportioned would require the wisdom of Solomon.

One thing only was quite clear. The closing down of either show would throw an additional burden on the other and there would be long periods when there would be nothing for large numbers of people to do. We were already doing all we could to keep expenses down in the face of ever rising costs and had to concentrate all fresh effort on increasing receipts. Chipperfields had taken their circus to Ireland five years before and had done enormous business and I had always assumed that Smart, who also moved by road, would follow and could never understand why he did not, unless he was frightened by the cost of crossing and recrossing the Irish Sea. Chipperfields returned to Ireland two years later, but said they were disappointed with the result compared with that of the first visit. Perhaps Ireland only wanted a big circus every eight or ten years and perhaps Smart had realised that, but we observed that Chipperfield's programme during the second visit had not changed very much from that of the first and this could have been the reason for less satisfactory results.

We had been relieved of the payment of entertainment duty, but had not done well in the Midlands in 1958 and, as we were due to return there in 1961, during the early months of 1960 we were thinking seriously of going to Ireland the following year. I had been to Ireland to explore the possibilities during my father's lifetime, but we had abandoned the idea when I was unable to find enough suitable railway trucks in the whole country. Bernard went in 1960 and, with the co-operation of the railways of the two countries, managed to scrape together enough trucks to transport all the essentials so that by leaving a number of caravans and all the trailers containing equipment without which we could manage in England we should be able to get the show from town to town.

As soon as our intentions became public property we were flooded with advice. One man said that before we could go to any town in the Republic we should have to have the agreement of the Fathers of the local church, but this was sheer nonsense and if it was ever necessary for anyone to open doors for us it was done when Bernard and I were received by the President of the Republic at his official residence, during our stay in Dublin.

We told Dicky Chipperfield of our plans and he said he had

no intention of going to Ireland again in the near future and asked Bill Dredge to make available to us everything they had learned. The information was of the greatest possible value and saved us going up blind alleys which they had discovered. One piece of advice he gave us was that at a town near the border we must appoint two ticket agents and he gave us the names of those he recommended. One was a Roman Catholic and the other a Protestant and as there were people of both faiths in the town he was sure they would prefer to shop on their own sides of the street.

We knew the cost of getting to and from Stranraer and that the cost of crossing the sea twice would be enormous; rail travel was to be only a little more expensive per mile, but allowance had to be made for the fact that the length of the average journey from town to town was a good deal greater than it is here. There was, however, one big plum which, although its value was unknown, could be set off against all the extras and unforeseen contingencies—we could play a seven day week in the Republic and expected every Sunday would produce three full houses. Even this might not be an unmixed blessing if it meant that people spent all their money at week-ends and had nothing left during the other five days, as so often happens when we have a bank holiday here.

We first ran into trouble during the crossing to Larne. The sea was rather rough and when I went to the car deck to see how the vehicles were travelling several, which had been loaded hurriedly and not roped properly, were rolling backwards and forwards; if it became rougher serious damage would be done when they collided, so members of the crew had to be fetched quickly, as any moving cargo is a great danger to the ship as well as to itself.

On arrival my job was to load the circus vehicles on to the Irish railway trucks and when I saw them my heart sank. They were of half a dozen different lengths so, instead of loading our trailers as they came off the ferry, I had to pick out one suitable for each truck. In some cases our trailers were longer than the trucks so we had to put an empty truck in front of and behind each laden one to take care of the overhang. The floorboards of the trucks were, in some cases, in the last stages of disintegration and when I loaded the first really heavy trailer its wheels dropped through and it rested on its axles. There was no crane and it took three hours with jacks to get the vehicle back where it belonged and we had to lay timbers beneath the wheels to prevent it happening again. I had had a similar problem once in England, when someone gave instructions for one of our trains to be pulled out when the front wheels of a trailer were on the last truck and the back ones on the dock. The twelve-ton trailer dropped on to the tracks, but it was one of my lucky days, for alongside there stood a mobile hand-operated crane and I don't think anyone blamed me when I insisted that three bowler-hatted railway executives should turn the handle while our men guided the trailer back on to the truck.

We explained to the railway people in Belfast that we could not risk any more accidents like the one in Larne and they agreed to cover the floors of all the trucks with steel plates. Even so, loading in Ireland was slower and more difficult than here, for several towns had no end-loading docks; temporary ones had to be built and these were usually so steep that our trailers had to be winched up them—and winching is a very slow process.

After doing capacity business in Belfast we moved to Londonderry, a dry city on a Sunday, so like most owners of cars we motored over the border to dine. Returning after midnight we had to pay late night fines at the Customs of the Republic but the Ulster customs house was closed and this looked like an open invitation to smuggle cigarettes and liquor, which were so much cheaper on the other side. A couple of miles further on we felt thankful we had not been tempted when red lights were waved in the middle of the road. Having stopped we realised we were surrounded by policemen with sten guns who, when told who we were, allowed us to pass with an explanation that a bridge had been blown up five miles away that night. Anyone who might have been foolish enough to disregard the red lights would have received a warm welcome into the Six Counties, for a couple of hundred yards further on there was an even bigger battery of sub-machine guns. I saw nothing in the papers the next day about the blowing of the bridge—it was just part of the Irish way of life and not worth a mention.

Going into the Republic was plain sailing, but leaving Ulster in a way that would enable us to return there or to England was another matter. We had to prepare an inventory of every-thing we took and this, running into hundreds of pages, had to be certified before our departure so that it could be pro-duced when we returned.

Not daring to add a long journey to the time we expected to lose crossing the frontier we played three days in Dundalk before going to Dublin. In the meantime the advance depart-ment and the billing unit were making things ready for us in the capital. They wanted a really good site for the down town booking office, a huge streamliner type trailer built specially for this work, and decided an ideal spot would be alongside the Nelson pillar in O'Connell Street. That was rather like want-ing to put it in Trafalgar Square and obviously permission had to be granted. Application was made to one high authority after another, but we were always referred to someone else and in the end the circle was completed and we were back where we started. Nobody could give permission, but nobody would refuse it, and in the end it was suggested we should occupy the site and wait for somebody to ask us to move. Nobody did and there was a queue for seats there all day and every day.

I can think of no words to describe the business we did in Dublin, but even if we had taken £10,000 less in the three weeks I should have felt assured that the tour of the Republic would be a huge success. After the first two or three performances we did capacity business and turned people away in hundreds and often in thousands. It was reminiscent of the post-war boom years and, as business had not been good before we crossed the sea, the change was very marked. The ground, however, left a great deal to be desired; it belonged to a man who bought old wine casks and rebuilt them and before we could move in we had to employ a bull-dozer to clear space for the tents and caravans. Worse still, it was infested with rats and fleas.

Only the man in charge of forage worried about the rats, but the fleas were altogether too much and by the time everyone and all the costumes were alive everything was sent to be fumigated. It would be hard to think of a more useless exercise, for within hours the fleas, or new ones, were with us again and we soon realised they were something we had to live with—perhaps the price we must pay for the fantastic business we were doing. I imagine local shops did equally well, selling huge quantities of every known kind of insecticide to everyone belonging to the circus.

We only spent August and September in Eire, but in those two months we crossed the country to Galway and then turned south and visited Limerick, Tralee and Killarney before going to Cork, so we saw all the most beautiful parts of the country at the best time of the year. After Cork we made our way through Clonmel and Waterford to Wexford, where we turned north and made the long jump back to Ulster.

It was then we made the one big mistake that summer. We had played ten and a half days in Belfast and when we left it looked as if there were as many people to come to the circus as had already been, so we decided to stop there again for five days on our way to Larne. It was the first time we had ever played a town twice in one season and it taught us a sharp lesson. For some reason few people were interested; the circus fever had gone cold and we did most disappointing business. Even so, the whole Irish tour could only be described as a triumph; more than three-quarters of a million people saw the circus that summer and the receipts had never been greater except just after the war. From the point of view of profitability, however, there was no comparison, for all our normal operating costs had increased during the intervening years and to these there had to be added the heavy extra expense which going to Ireland involved.

We had a fairly good season at Olympia that winter and by the end of the financial year had kept our heads well above water, although a year before it had looked as if we should be in the red unless we went to Ireland and did well there.

The seven day week in the Republic meant more and harder

work, but everybody seemed to enjoy the visit; it was remarkable to see how even the lowest paid working man gives everything he has when he sees the circus of which he is part packed at every show. The Irish are wonderful people and their hospitality is unmatched—and they have not forgotten how to enjoy themselves. On the other hand, their inability to be punctual for anything was trying, as the time between performances was the minimum necessary, so if the first one began late everything that followed that day was late. When we told our friends what time the show began they usually asked whether we meant English or Irish time, as the latter is about half an hour later. A thing that puzzled me was that even those who had tickets and arrived in good time made no attempt to enter when the show was due to begin; they all seemed to have something to talk to friends about. Perhaps it was because the circus drew people from such very great distances and provided them with an opportunity to meet people whom they had not seen for some time. At first we assumed it to be our duty to get everybody seated before starting the show, as late-comers are so disturbing to others, but nobody cared how many late-comers there were. When the music started they did not believe it signalled the beginning of the performance and assumed it was being used as a come-on, as it had been by some other circuses, and that the circus itself would only commence after ten or fifteen minutes of music. They did not know anything of the rules of the Musicians Union, or perhaps it was another aspect of the Irish way of life, as were the directions given me when I asked the way to a post office. The man pointed and said : 'You go to the bottom of that hill and there you will see a sign which says "Turn Left Only" and it's just there you turn to the right.' And that, so far as I could see, was the only way of getting there without going via Brighton.

Some years before we had made a wild animal ring cage of net, but had never been able to use it as it had to be raised and lowered on a strong metal ring forty-three feet in diameter and we could find no safe way of doing it in a tent with only two king poles; but by the time we were in Ireland we were using a four-poler and I decided to try again. I sent to Ascot for the net, but was told that as it had lain about for ages without being used it had been thrown away as junk and we had to make a new one. Getting it to work properly took a long time and produced some anxious moments when we first turned a mixed group of wild animals loose in it. A puma ran round it like a motor cycle on a wall of death; a tiger had a go at it with its claws and a lion tried to eat its way out; but everything held. It was a mistake, however, to put netting over the door of the tunnel through which the animals entered and left the ring, for they could not see whether it was open or closed and one huge tiger, seeing what he thought was the open door, took it as his cue to leave. He went across the ring at full canter, hit the almost invisible netting and bounced back as if shot from a catapult. We thought he might have broken his neck but he was unharmed and thereafter the door was marked with broad white tapes. The 'Mills type' cage as it was called gave the public an almost uninterrupted view, saved time and spared the ring boys having to carry a ton and a half of ironmongery twice at every performance. It also had the advantage that it was unclimbable and so it was not necessary to put a net over the top. London saw it for the first time the following winter when Yvonne, a glamorous Dutch girl, presented a group of lions and the newspapers published photos in which she and the animals appeared to be uncaged in the middle of the audience.

When we returned from Scotland at the end of 1962 I had a winter programme in which I had a great deal of confidence, for it contained Schumann's horses and the Peters, an aerial act which was to cash in on the outer space business by entering the ring in a sputnik enveloped in a white cloud. Their act, which ended with some sensational mid-air tricks done on a rocket with fireworks belching from the tail, was to be the last in the programme. We had a magnificent group of lions, tigers, pumas and panthers and also chimpanzee, sealion and elephant acts and then there was Lilly Yokoi.

She had been no 'find' for she was about the highest paid circus artiste in the world and having had to do battle with all the great circuses I still had to wait two years until she was free.

She had played all the top places in the States and the *Lido* in Paris and, although I was paying her an enormous salary, I felt sure I was getting my money's worth as she had never appeared in the West End and before coming to London she had the whole of her bicycle plated with gold. When some of my co-directors knew what I was going to pay one girl to ride one bicycle they probably thought I needed to have my head attended to, but Lilly Yokoi began where all other trick cyclists left off and although I am loth to prefer one artiste at the expense of others I think she was one of the greatest performers I ever engaged. She was an artiste down to her fingertips, her costumes were magnificent and she had a smile which was so infectious that her audience was with her in the first minute—and this in spite of her being of Japanese parentage which, to European eyes at least, so often produces an expressionless face.

With all these acts and a strong supporting bill it was to be hoped that business would be good, but the slow downward trend continued and as our tenancy of Olympia still had three years to run, it was beginning to look as much like a liability as an asset—and this was not our only worry. During the 1962 summer receipts had been running at a high percentage of capacity and, as there seemed to be little likelihood of increasing them substantially, the possibility of reducing costs had to be examined again. We were determined not to lower the standard of the show, but if we could run a three or four month static season in a seaside resort during part of each summer there would be enormous savings in advertising, transport and staff. Blackpool and Yarmouth both had long seasons, but they also had permanent circuses; Torquay would have been ideal, but the only site was much too far from the centre of the town and the sea. Paignton was considered, but again the ground was too far from the centre of things. We were due to be in the south in 1963, but when it was suggested we should make a long stay at Newquay I could not make sensible arithmetic of it. The resident population was about 11,000 and if this became fifty thousand in the high season and most people stayed two weeks, there would only be about twenty thousand new people who would be potential patrons each week; and that was about the number we needed just to pay expenses. No entertainment which needs ninety or one hundred per cent of all the potential patrons is viable and there could therefore be no question of a long stay, but we decided to go for three weeks instead of three days as on previous occasions.

Sometimes gambles have to be taken in show business and we knew that no great damage could be done in three weeks. In the event the experiment only proved what had been expected and we then had to consider the whole future of the tenting circus. If we followed our normal route in 1964 we should be back in the Midlands and that would include Lancashire so we started thinking about Ireland again, as it would be three years since we had gone there and we should have a new and very strong programme.

We assumed takings would be about ten per cent less than during the first visit and that expenses would be ten or fifteen per cent higher and if these figures were realistic, and we stayed there a little longer, the show should just about wash its own hands. So we decided it was to be Ireland in 1964, but no decision was taken about 1965.

The next thing to deal with was Olympia. I had a nasty shock ten days before the opening when I received a cable saying that because the head man, upon whose work that of several others depended, was in hospital that act would not arrive and it was an important act. Two days later the situation was confirmed by letter and a medical certificate which was badly written in a foreign language; the only thing I understood was that it referred to a boy of twelve who was not even in the act.

I telephoned a friend who lived a few miles from where the act should have been playing in a circus in Italy and that night he confirmed that everyone in the act was working, but the son of the head man was in hospital with appendicitis. The mother was not in the act and could have remained with the child, but the truth of the matter was the father had secured a six months contract which, even if the salary was lower, would produce more money than the short engagement in London and had thought I should not notice that the medical certificate referred to a twelve year old boy whose three names were the same.

Threats would have produced nothing, but after telephoning all over the world for a replacement I found an excellent one. However, I was only able to get it to London in time because of all the help I had from the Home Office, Foreign Office and the Ministry of Labour and even so had to pay air fares over a thousand miles on a very large troupe and an enormous quantity of excess baggage. When all is told the breach of contract, only the second I ever had, cost us about £1,000, but we kept faith with the public and that was what really mattered.

For the 1964 visit to Ireland the programme was presented in a rather different way, as we wanted nothing to resemble anything we had done there in 1961. It was put together rather in the form of a 'spectacular' and a troupe of girls was added and we were fortunate to the extent that the Republic had not yet been saturated with television spectaculars. Business everywhere was as good as we had expected and our estimate of expenses was reasonably accurate.

I was unable to travel with the circus that year as we had taken a financial interest in a new company which was to present Cinerama under canvas. We believed a suitable tent was under construction in France but when, after waiting months for it, we had not even seen drawings we decided to produce one ourselves. I went to our tentmakers in Konstanz to see if a modified version of a tent I had seen a year earlier could be made with walls forty feet high. No such tent had ever been built but, as our screen was to be a hundred feet long and thirty-seven feet six inches high, nothing lower would do.

The resulting tent was a steel frame structure clothed in canvas and was probably the most expensive one ever built, but it serves its purpose although it naturally takes much longer to move than a circus tent. We had been invited to take part in the new company because we had had experience with mobile units; it was therefore only natural that we should have to design the seating and generally do all the donkey work in the production and launching of what was virtually a new form of mobile entertainment.

All this meant an almost unbearably heavy load fell on Ber

nard's shoulders as he was the only director with the tenting circus in Ireland. In the past we had shared the day to day running of the circus, but when either of us was away the other did everything. That worked well for short periods, but to have the lot for a whole season is heavy going, especially as Cinerama work had kept me away from the tenting circus for long periods during 1963. The fact that the circus went to Ireland in 1964 meant that all the extra things done in 1961 had to be repeated and things were made worse by a decision we had taken to economise by using less rail traffic and moving a considerable part of the show by road.

Everybody had to work even longer and harder. A circus is like a ship at sea; it is at work twenty-four-hours each day and this means the boss, like a captain, is on call all the time. Bernard must have had a harder season than any since 1929 or 1930 but, even if nobody else realised it, he and I knew that the future of the tenting circus was at stake and it was far from certain that it would exist in 1965.

By August the Cinerama Mobile Theatre had settled down for a long run in Paignton and I took a short holiday; in fact it was hardly a holiday, for I took the records of the tenting circus with me and a note of the receipts in Ireland was sent to me every day. Graphs and the trend they showed drove me irresistibly in one direction, although every bit of me wanted to go in the opposite one. If, between August and November, there was no improvement and no worsening in receipts we should just about clear expenses on the season, but if we tented in Britain in 1965 we should probably make very big losses. It meant that the tenting circus must close at the end of the 1964 season.

During the years 1962–3 and 1963–4 we had made losses which together totalled a little over £60,000, but although there had been a downward trend in London it was less marked and in any event we were committed at Olympia at least until 1965–6. Another serious problem was that our contract with British Railways was running out and if it was to be renewed it could be done by agreeing to a 15% increase.

I told Bernard and my other co-directors what my conclusions were and in a very short time we were all agreed that the tenting circus must close for ever and that the permanent staff and artistes must be told by Bernard and me.

Only Connie Yelding, my private secretary, was told the sad news and it was she who had typed all the letters I carried when I arrived in Clonmel on the 5th October. Bernard and I signed them, but before they were delivered we had all senior members of the staff and the permanent trainers together and I had the painful task of breaking the news. It was the worst job I have ever had to do and the fact that bad news had to be given when we were doing good business only heightened the shock. Good business had built up a sense of security, but they all knew what things had been like in 1962 and 1963 and could guess what they might be like in 1965—and nobody could overlook the fact that Chipperfields had announced they were packing up and going to South Africa.

As we left the meeting there were tears in many eyes; for it meant the end of a circus which in many ways had been quite unlike any other—a sort of Mills way of life. Perhaps those who had most to fear were the trainers, for they saw the possibility of being separated from their animals—even those animals which belonged to us were always referred to as 'theirs'—but we assured them that we should do everything possible to ensure that those who bought animals would engage the trainers and in the course of time we were remarkably successful in doing so.

By the time I visited the circus again it was in Liverpool, having had to fight its way home on account of strikes. As usual the billers had finished their season's work by sticking the last poster upside down, but in doing so on this occasion it had meant very much more than just the end of a season. News of the closing of the show spread like wildfire and by the time we reached Liverpool we were entertaining buyers from all over the world; by the end of the week we had sold one big top and all the horses and the elephants but, as these were going to be used at Olympia, they were to be delivered in February.

The last performance at Liverpool was a sad affair; some others were unable to watch it, but I did and although I was upset I could not forget that perhaps an even sadder day lay ahead. We had two more Olympia seasons ahead of us and although we had had preliminary discussions with our landlords about a new tenancy I had a feeling that the results of the 1964–5 season would determine whether a new agreement would ever be signed.

Again the show was to be presented in the new format, but I was not happy about this sort of thing for London. With its programme sub-titles like Russian Roundabout, Edwardian Era, Extravaganza and Brazilia and a bunch of girls thrown in it was beginning to look like something which can be done much better in a film spectacular. Any programme of this kind tends to bunch acts together according to the costumes worn without regard for the work the artistes do and therefore produces a badly balanced result. However, it had been done in Ireland with success so it was worth trying. But worse was to come. Somebody said the circus was not 'with it' and that we ought to have a pop group. If ever there were mixed feelings and opinions about anything concerning Bertram Mills Circus this produced them. For my part I could not believe the proposal was anything but a joke, but I was in a minority of one.

In the past I had booked all the acts for years, but my programmes had not produced big enough audiences even if well over a quarter of a million people still saw the circus at Olympia each winter. My position therefore was a simple one. If we had no pop group and the downward trend continued I alone should be to blame because I was not 'with it'. On the other hand, if we had a group we should at least feel we had tried even if attendances were not increased.

So a pop group, and a good one, was booked but my worst fears were realised. I was flooded with letters of complaint the general tone of which was that a circus is no place for this sort of thing; there was more than enough of it on television, but at least in that form it could be switched off by those who did not like it. I answered every letter and spent more time doing that than anything else during the season, but I could do no more than admit we had made mistakes and say we would try to do better next time as the situation had been aggravated by the fact that there were two long acts in the programme (Borra was the other) which had little appeal for the younger children and the pop group occupied the spot in which people expected to see wild animals, of which there were none.

Attendances at Olympia that winter were down again and neither the pop group nor the new format had reversed or even checked the downward trend. We had tried to be 'with it' but had only proved that those over fifty years of age who try to do so usually finish by being 'without it'.

Only one course remained open to us. We had to tell Olympia that we did not wish to renew the tenancy and that the 1965–6 season would be the last.

Chapter Nineteen
My last year and
the 'take-over'

With the tenting circus closed and only one more Olympia season ahead of us there had to be drastic reductions in the length of the pay-roll. Two directors resigned their executive positions with effect from the 5th April 1965 and, as one department was closed after another, those employed in it became redundant. We could afford no passengers or part-timers and only those who could be employed fully could remain. Fortunately, most people had come to us from other walks of life and although it was sad to say good-bye to those who had been so loyal there was little difficulty in finding them employment elsewhere.

Early in 1965 it looked as if Bernard and I would be back where we had been before the war and until the company became a public one—just the two of us running the business with four or five key people, but in February Bernard was taken ill. I assumed he would be back in a couple of months and that by the autumn, when the heat would be on, we should have him with us and things would be no more onerous than in our early days together.

It is not always that brothers working together form an ideal partnership, but Bernard is a wonderful man to work with and whatever one of us did was always good enough for the other. That this was the case was undoubtedly due to the fact that we had worked together with Father and had the same objectives. His illness, however, lasted a very long time and he was only able to return to the office in October and, even then, had been warned by his doctors that he must get back into harness by slow stages. For me this was the real crunch, for during the summer I had had to keep an eye on the box office, accounts, advertising and the bank balance, as well as getting a programme; now, when we were getting really busy making arrangements for the build-up in Olympia and the arrival of artistes, I was still the only fully active executive director.

Nobody could have been more fortunate than I was in the team which was working with me. Harry Coles and Tich Howe were in the box office where they had always been; Trevor Woodward, whose last job had been manager of the tenting circus, and Margaret Griffiths were doing accounts and several other jobs and Vicky Pankhurst was taking care of the general office, manning the telephones and doing other things for which nobody else had time. Connie Yelding, my private secretary, having been with me a few years before the war and a great many since, knew as much about Bertram Mills Circus as anyone and could always help anyone else who was doing something for the first time. Lastly there was my step-son, Frederick Meredith, who had been my personal assistant for several years and was a tower of strength. In the ordinary course of events the possibility of any member of such a small team falling out through illness would be a worry, but I had none, for Trevor Woodward had had plenty of box office experience both at Olympia and on the road and could hold the fort easily if there was illness in the box office and Frederick knew a great deal of what went on in every other department. There was, however, a great deal to do and there can be few occasions when members of a small team have been called upon to deal with so many widely diverse jobs in addition to those which they did normally. Nobody wasted a minute and if anybody

was missing from his office it was certain he was helping someone else out. There was never a letdown and I knew that if
the season for which we were working was a success it would
be entirely due to the efforts of my little team. To an outsider
the London Office must have looked more like a forced labour
camp than a holiday one, but nobody had to be forced unless
it was to go home when more than a hard day's work had been
done.

Even if things were going well there was one big gap in the
organisation. David Monk had been the circus P.R.O., but he
had taken over the management of the Cinerama unit; Harry
Nutkins, the doyen of circus fans, had been his assistant for
many years and was returning, but it would have been unreasonable to ask him to carry the whole of what is a heavy
load. I could think of only one man whom I knew would do a
splendid job—Bill Dredge, who had represented Chipperfield
at Salisbury, but who was now in business in Eire with John
Hinde. They produce quite the best coloured postcards I have
ever seen and I thought it just possible that they might not be
too busy in winter.

Two days after I wrote to John he telephoned me to say he
and Bill were coming to London to see me. We met at my
home and John said he was releasing Bill temporarily so that
he could do the job, but having discussed it they had to make
one condition—neither was to receive a penny. I was delighted
by the first half of the news but the second covered me with
embarrassment and I said I thought it wholly wrong that we,
an ordinary commercial undertaking, should agree to such an
arrangement. They were both adamant and I agreed, for I
needed Bill very badly, and looking at it from the proper angle
I realised they were paying us as big a compliment as we had
ever received. They are both circus lovers and, knowing it was
to be the last Bertram Mills Circus, were as keen as I was for it
to be a success. In the past Bill had only worked for one other
circus and had probably regarded us as his biggest competitor,
yet here he was insisting on doing for nothing what any circus
would willingly pay him a very big fee for. Nothing like this can
ever have happened before.

I had one stroke of luck after another. David Chorley was able to return to his old job in ticket audit; Roger Cawley, Charles Hotham, the musical director, and Gordon Stumcke, the fun fair manager, all of whom had been with us many years, were coming back as was Charlie DeWachter, the chief electrician, who had been on loan to Cinerama. Norman Barrett, the ringmaster, had spent the summer with Circus Scott in Sweden and was returning and without him I should have felt that one hand was tied behind my back when running the show. I therefore had all the key people who were needed and they were ones with whom I had worked for years.

For the programme I had booked all the things which I believe a circus should contain. There were trampolin and flying trapeze acts; a sway-pole thriller and wonderful cyclists; lions, tigers, pumas, panthers, chimpanzees, dogs, sealions, elephants and pigeons; clowns and two other comedy acts and the Schumann horses including twelve grey Arabs which were to enter the ring alone without harness in an artificial cloud. This caused problems for the horses had never done it when they arrived five days before the opening. They did not mind the cloud, but it prevented them from seeing the ring fence and at rehearsals it had to be lined with ring boys to prevent them stumbling over it.

From the middle of November advance booking indicated that the season would be a good one, but the picture of the future, unpleasant though it was, had to be faced squarely. Stock-holders had invested money in a company whose business it was to produce circuses and profits which were a fair return on the sums invested and there would not be a Bertram Mills Circus in three months' time. It was a logical conclusion that the company would go into voluntary liquidation and that was the unpleasant job which would be ours early in 1966, but certain people had expressed an interest in the company and among these was Maxwell Joseph, from whom we received an offer for all the shares held by members of the Mills family and an undertaking to make a similar offer to other stockholders.

Bernard and I, being confident that we should make a profit

during the last winter, were inclined to hold on, but the interests of minority stock-holders and the views of those who might prefer the bird in the hand had to be taken into consideration. Agreement was reached in a very short time; the offer was accepted and in doing so we relieved ourselves of the possibility of having to wind up the company.

Knowing Olympia was already let for what would have been a part of our 1966–7 tenancy I assumed Maxwell Joseph was buying the company for reasons which did not include the running of circuses. It therefore came as a surprise when he asked us to negotiate a short tenancy and announced the company would produce a circus the following winter.

Had I realised there was the remotest possibility that the circus bearing my father's name would ever be controlled, if only in part, during my lifetime by anyone other than Bernard and me, or one of us, nothing would have persuaded me to sell a single share to anyone or at any price.

However, the deed was done and Maxwell Joseph asked me to carry on 'as if nothing had happened' at least until the end of the Olympia season.

The thing which was uppermost in my mind when preparing my last circus was the need for economy of a kind which would not affect the show or the comfort of the public. On the other hand I had made up my mind that the programme would be the best of which I was capable, regardless of cost. One of the things which would not be missed by the public was the opening lunch and most of those who would have attended knew we had been in the red and could hardly be surprised when they learned it was to be replaced by a First Night Cocktail Party. But there still had to be a small lunch, for the Lord Mayor had promised to open the show and there were a number of peers to whom we wanted to show a small expression of gratitude for the way they had defended circuses when they had been attacked earlier in the year. To these there had to be added seven or eight ambassadors who were friends of long standing, two directors of Olympia and half a dozen of our oldest friends.

The lunch was held in the Pillar Hall which had been the best restaurant in the old days, but which by now had become

an exhibition hall. Sir Norman Joseph took things in hand in
the way only he can; the hall was literally clothed in flowers
and special lighting was installed with the result that it became
a room with an atmosphere of intimacy and charm. The table-
ware was gilt and the china similar to that used at royal garden
parties—never let it be thought it was the same. The kitchens,
unlike those which had been strained to their limits in previous
years, were adequate for the preparation of a really excellent
meal at which there were only seventy guests. As usual, when
coffee and liqueurs had been served and we had had the loyal
toast, each man received a Havana cigar with the special band
of Bertram Mills Circus, cigarettes and book matches, but we
had yet to come round to the fact that many ladies smoke and
they still had boxes of chocolates; on this occasion each box contained a glass circus horse which stood on its hind legs and was
made specially in Italy.

The toast-master then announced our honorary president,
the Marquess of Exeter, who rose to make what must have been
one of the most difficult speeches anyone has ever had to de-
liver. He was presiding for the twentieth and last time and nobody could help feeling this was anything but a prelude to the
demise of the Bertram Mills Circus. Having dealt with this
unhappy state of affairs he paid a tribute to the Mills family,
including our wives, without whose patience and encouragement our work would have been impossible. It was a tribute so
touching and kind that everyone was deeply moved. Then he
gave us a few minutes of the amusing kind of which he is such
a master.

It was then my turn and I had prepared nothing to say, for
things had never been like this before and what I should say
would depend on what had gone before. I have always found
it comparatively easy to say a few words to a large gathering,
as a microphone makes things less personal, but on this occasion
everyone was so close, everything was so intimate and I knew
everyone present so well. I made a very bad job of thanking
David Exeter for the kind things he had said and all the help and
friendship he and the other guests had given us over the years.
While I was trying to do so I realised something which I had

R

to tell them even though it hurt. I was standing within a few inches of where my father had stood when he made the first speech of his life to his guests before the opening of his first circus in 1920. I was turning the last page of the book he had opened forty-six years before and it was December 17th, the very date on which Bertram Mills Circus was born.

That evening before the cocktail party for five hundred guests Bernard and I were asked to arrive early on the pretext that somebody wanted to take a picture. Peter Cadbury, the 'King' of theatre ticket agents, presented each of us with an inscribed silver salver which had been subscribed for by all the agents who, during the forty-six years, had sold about £2,000,000 worth of tickets for us. We had often joked with them that the circus provided their Christmas dinners, but their gifts were tokens of friendship and no greater honour could have been conferred within the realms of show business.

In the autumn I had realised that the 1965–6 winter season would present us with the last chance we might ever have of doing anything worth while for charity. I mentioned this to Sir Edward Ford who kindly spoke to Her Majesty, whose assistant private secretary he was. The Queen graciously said she would attend a charity performance which was to be given in aid of the National Society for the Prevention of Cruelty to Children, the London Federation of Boys Clubs and the Children's Country Holiday Fund.

The performance took place four days after the circus opened and when it was known who was coming one press man said that it looked like a royal straight flush, and that was hardly an exaggeration, for the royal party consisted of the Queen, Prince Philip, the Prince of Wales, the Princess Anne, the Princess Margaret, Princess Alexandra, the Earl of Snowdon and Mr. Angus Ogilvy.

There was a time when I feared that cars coming from Buckingham Palace, Kensington Palace and Richmond Park would arrive at different times and in the wrong order, but the Princess Margaret resolved my worries by inviting all those who were coming to Olympia to Kensington Palace before the performance.

There was no coloured saw-dust in the ring this time and everything went according to plan. Making the arrangements was not difficult, but carrying them out with a staff of whom about ninety per cent were temporary employees was not easy and meant that those who knew the drill had to do what two or three people had done in the past. We had no permanent white-faced clown by this time, so Coco, who in the meantime had been decorated by the Queen for his Road Safety work, was chosen to present the bouquet to Her Majesty when she arrived. At the interval Bernard and I, and our wives, joined the royal party in the retiring room where refreshments were being served and it was then that things took an unexpected turn.

I had said that if Prince Charles and Princess Anne would like to go through the stables and menagerie there was somebody ready to escort them and when she knew they were going Princess Margaret expressed a wish to go too. And then everyone wanted to go. Going to the royal retiring room we had had red carpets lined with men in uniform; there had been six of us to act as escorts and now there was nothing and it was my job to lead the procession through the crowds which were rushing towards the bars. Had we been expected everybody would have made way for us, but we were not and I had to do what I could to make a way and doing so without walking in front of the Queen was impossible.

By the time we had been in the stables a few minutes things were out of control for it was not possible for Bernard and me to escort such a large party properly and I soon noticed that Prince Charles and Princess Anne were missing and, while the Queen and Prince Philip were looking at horses at opposite ends of the stables, they had gone into the menagerie where one was looking at the elephants and the other at a baby lion.

Time was marching on and we were a little worried about how to collect the scattered members of the party together and take them back to the royal box in an orderly fashion. What had begun as a formal occasion had developed into something in which formality seemed to have no part and had given place to what I can only think of in terms of kindness and friendliness. If the Queen noticed I was worried about Prince Charles and

259

Princess Anne wandering about unescorted in a place where there were many animals I saw no anxiety on her part and eventually the baby lion became a focal point and it was not difficult to organise the journey back to the circus.

The second half of the programme had gone well and the last act, the flying trapeze act of the Gaonas, was on. This was the one act about which I was worried, for Victor Gaona was doing the triple somersault to the hands of the catcher, a trick that had not been seen in London since Alfredo Codona did it at Olympia in 1925–6, and I really did not want this to be one of the very few occasions when he would fail. If he missed the first time it was no more than was to be feared on such an important occasion; if he missed twice both he and we had had it. He was only the second man in the world who had done the trick consistently for months on end, so if he succeeded the Royal Family would see something they had not seen before and might never see again.

As the time for the big trick approached my hands became clammy and I held my breath; the crucial split fraction of a second arrived and he missed and crashed into the net. My heart sank and as he climbed the rigging for the second attempt I almost felt like praying for him.

When he began the first of the two huge swings I think seven thousand people were batting for him as hard as I was and then—he made it. One of the most perfectly executed triple somersaults I have ever seen and the audience gave him the thunderous applause he had earned. We all knew that up there was a young man who had not deliberately 'thrown' an easy trick to make it look difficult, but one who had failed at the most important performance of his life. If he had failed a second time he would have been spoken of for the rest of his life as 'the man who missed it in front of the Queen'. Having done it at the second try he had been able to overcome all the tensions which the occasion produced . . . but how very wrong we all were.

I had not the slightest suspicion when he missed, for his timing was bad and the third somersault had ended at a point at which his father could not possibly catch him, and therefore it was a normal miss. What I did not know was that as he entered the ring he whispered to Norman Barrett, the ringmaster, that he was going to 'throw' the triple the first time and there was nothing poor Norman could do to prevent him doing so. It was a very naughty thing to do, for he knew that if he really missed the second time he would have to give up. He knew he was allowed just two attempts for I take the view that if a man fails twice the public is entitled to assume that he cannot do the trick or that it is a fluke when he does and I never paid artistes big salaries for important tricks unless I was satisfied they could do them eight times out of ten.

That Victor should have done what he did shows what perfect control he has over his body, and especially his nerves, and to those to whom I lied after the performance I now apologise, for I did not know the truth and only learned it the next day by accident as most people thought it better that I should not know.

After the performance all the artistes in costume lined the red carpet to form a sort of guard of honour between the circus and the main entrance. On previous occasions members of the royal party had left quite quickly in order to be away before the audience filled the fun fair, but this time things were very different and so much less formal. During the evening I think every member of the Royal Family had said how sad it was that this was to be our last circus. On their way across the building both the Queen and Prince Philip stopped to speak to several of the artistes about their acts and I suspected that they might be sharing my feeling that there would never be another occasion quite like this. Those last few minutes were very precious and when I bowed as the royal cars moved away that night I knew that one of the things I cherished most in my business life was going for good—it was indeed the beginning of the end of the road.

To go on from a point like this and see the circus attracting so many more people than in the preceding years was a great relief, even though I knew my days were numbered, as were those of Bertram Mills Circus as we had all known it. The three performances on the last day were sold out; circus fans from all over Britain, old and dear friends and hundreds of others who had seen the show already, came to the last performance, but even so it was one of the saddest evenings of my life. Many people said we were going out in a blaze of glory but even that did not help very much—we were still going out.

My wife and I watched the last performance from start to finish and I kept saying to myself 'I shall never see that again' and I knew there was still one ordeal to be faced. At the end of the show I should go into the ring surrounded by all the artistes and make a short speech, as I had done on so many other last nights. When the time came I tried to express my thanks and those of Bernard to the artistes, the staff, but for whose magnificent efforts the season could only have been a shadow of what it was, and the public who had supported us over all the years. For the rest I did what I hope was my duty by Maxwell Joseph by confirming what had appeared in the press and saying there *would* be a circus at Olympia next winter.

When I came to the end the band played *Auld Lang Syne* and the National Anthem and then, as the audience left, we did something which had never been done in Bertram Mills Circus before. At my request the band played the audience out and the tune I had chosen was *Que sera, sera*. I had felt there should be a little something to relieve the tension, but I think it went over most people's heads.

A few days later I tendered my resignation as chairman and joint managing director of the company, but it was not until August that I was able to know the result of my last season. The company made a profit of just over £25,000 and that was the biggest profit since 1960–1. That the result was so satisfactory was due almost entirely to two things. Compared with the previous year about fifty thousand more people saw the show— many of them because they believed it would be their last chance to do so. Secondly, there was a big saving, as the balance sheet showed, in top executive salaries. All the administrative work was done by a very small team of people; they made the economies while I spent the money, for I had made up my mind that if I could find the talent the show would be one which would be remembered and that people would say that Bertram Mills Circus went down with the flag flying.

That I was not disposed to stay with the circus under its new owner was, to a large extent, due to lack of faith in the future. Rising costs, and our inability over recent years to increase prices and attendances enough to meet them, had convinced me that there was little prospect of making a profit which would bear a proper relation to the capital employed and the risks involved. Accountants had come to the same conclusion a couple of years before and the Board had agreed with it when it was decided not to renew the tenancy of Olympia. Even the fact that we did so much better during my last season did nothing to change my view, for even if the programme was a good one we had pounded home in all our advertisements that it was to be the last season and I think we were believed, in spite of the turn which events took.

Only the accounts for the 1966–7 season will show whether I was right or wrong.

We could have carried on producing circuses at Olympia and we could have reduced some of our expenses very much but the public would have suffered; the circuses would have been shoddy by comparison and very soon the name of Bertram Mills would have been tarnished and his circus would have died, as so many others have done, perhaps even as a bankrupt concern.

That I am sure will never happen, for Maxwell Joseph is not a man who would want to be associated with anything shoddy or that is a permanent flop and Bernard is still managing director of the company. The 1966–7 circus was his to the extent that he booked the acts and produced an excellent show even though he was largely in the hands of temporary staff. He needed plenty of *Hals und Beinbruch* and nobody wished him more than I did.

Even so, the 1966–7 circus was the last that any of us are likely to see at Olympia for the building is let for years to come for exhibitions in winter and I am told that those parts of the seating which could not be sold have gone for scrap, so it seems unlikely that Olympia will ever see another big show with a seated audience.

A new winter home is being sought for the circus, but finding one will not be easy. A Bill which would have enabled a tented version to appear in a royal park failed to get a second reading. Even if it ever became a reality I do not imagine a London season could last more than three months and to get a good programme for such a short period will be nearly impossible, as any first class act can secure a thirty-week engagement with a tenting circus. If no suitable winter building can be found the only alternative might be a tent something like the Cinerama one, but it will be difficult to persuade Londoners to go to a tented show in mid-winter.

It has been a cause of satisfaction that the circus never had, or needed, a censor and we have always tried to remember what *The Times* said about dignity and showmanship. From the very early days we called Bertram Mills Circus the 'Quality Show' and on one occasion we had the impudence to say it was the show that put the 'O' in Olympia but I expect there were those who may have said it was the one which put the 'cuss' in circus. Whichever it was, it is dead as I knew it, if only because I have always felt so much a part of it and the people that belonged with it.

If the results of my last season have shown that the hunch to hold on when Maxwell Joseph made his offer was right I have no regrets and certainly no hard feelings and I said so when I asked Charles Hotham to play *Que sera, sera* at the end of the last circus performance I was ever to produce.

Chapter Twenty
Tailpiece

Several people have asked me how it feels to have nothing to do with the circus after having spent nearly the whole of my working life with it. The answer, like my feelings, is mixed.

Between 1920 and 1938 I saw one man build what had begun almost as a bet into a prosperous business which some people were kind enough to call a national institution. Then came the struggle through a period of great loneliness, followed by the war, which in its turn was succeeded by an era during which the circus arose from its own wreckage and prospered on a scale hitherto unthought of.

I was chairman and joint managing director during an epoch when it made over a million and a quarter in profits and also during two years when it lost £60,000. If the first ten years after the war were a piece of cake, some of those which followed contained indigestible crusts, but these may be forgotten for there were so many things which were rewarding and memorable and ups and downs are every circus man's bread and butter.

No longer need I worry about the plight of the circus or its people and animals when there is flood or a gale that would tear the big top to shreds; no longer need I spend the greater part of my life away from my wife and children, but if the circus gave me plenty of worries there were many big rewards to compensate for them.

I had the honour of meeting every member of the Royal Family, the leaders of the nation in commerce, industry and the arts and I was able to make friends from one end of the country to the other—these are things which few business careers offer.

I have been able to see the greater part of the world, to watch huge audiences enjoying themselves and to hear the screams of delight of the hundreds of thousands of under-privileged children who came to the dress rehearsals. These are pleasures few have known and of course I miss them.

Having spent so much of my life among people than whom none are more loyal or dedicated is far more than any man is entitled to expect and to be away from this must cause a big gap. On the other hand, not having been born in a caravan it was never my wish to die in one and I realised many years ago that if Bertram Mills Circus continued to prosper, even if my health remained good, there would come a time when it would be right for me to step aside in favour of those who were younger and more able to carry on. Even if the circus were flourishing today I should have felt that on reaching the age of sixty-five, or soon thereafter, would have been the proper time to take things a little more easily and, as I have now reached that age, circumstances have not changed my position very much. On the other hand, if I had continued to be a controlling stock-holder I should still have been keenly interested—perhaps too interested—and I might have become an interfering old man and that would not have been good for the business or those running it.

If I had my life to live again I would do the same thing, but would hope to avoid the mistakes I have made. Some people will ask: 'Why, when there must be so many easier ways to earn a living?' To that I can only think of one answer and it is a saying we had at the circus: 'You don't have to be mad to be a member of the Mills organisation but it helps a lot if you are.'

Perhaps that explains everything.

Glossary of Circus Terms

Antipodist As the derivation indicates an upside down man; a man who juggles with his feet while lying in a trinka (q.v.).

Auguste The man with a red nose and baggy suit who is always at the receiving end when water or custard pies are flying.

Balloon Paper hoop through which a bareback rider, usually a girl, jumps.

Bender A contortionist.

Bounding Rope Act The performer works on a thick slack rope to which is attached a spring which enables him to bounce the rope up and down.

Butcher's Shop Act My own way of referring to anything in the nature of a strong-man act.

Cats Wild animals (tigers, lions, pumas, etc).

Clown The white-faced man in the spangled costume.

Construction A metal or wooden-framed 'tent' used by a few small continental circuses; in fact a portable building which takes about four days to erect and two to dismantle. Seldom seen now.

Cushion Small sloping ramp used by some bareback riders to assist them when jumping up on to horses.

Flying Trapeze Act Aerial act in which people (flyers) fly from one swinging trapeze bar to another or to the hands of a catcher.

High Wire Act A wire-walking act done at a great height with or without a net. The phrase is often used incorrectly by journalists and others to describe any aerial act.

Josser Anyone outside circus business.

Lunge A safety device used to prevent performers falling and injuring themselves when learning or practising difficult tricks. Often referred to as a mechanic.

Perch Act One in which the under-man or bearer supports a long pole on his shoulder or forehead while a partner does tricks at the top.

Rosin-back Horse used in a bare-back riding act.

Run-in Clown One who appears only between acts while props are being set or removed. Also referred to as a carpet clown.

Trick Any feat performed by a circus artiste or animal, there being no suggestion that trickery, as commonly understood, is involved.

Trinka Upholstered cradle in which a performer lies when juggling with the feet.

Voltige A rider or riders vaulting on to and off a horse.

Index

Index

271

Index